ADVANCE ACCLAIM FOR *SNAPSHOT*

"A pitch-perfect plot that tackles some tough issues with a lot of heart. *Snapshot* brings our world into pristine focus. It's fast-paced, edgy, and loaded with plenty of menace. Lis Wiehl knows what readers crave and she delivers it. Make room on your bookshelves for this one—it's a keeper."

—STEVE BERRY, *NEW YORK TIMES* BEST-SELLING AUTHOR

"*Snapshot* is fiction. But it takes us along the twisted path of race in America in a way that is closer to the human experience than most history books."

—JUAN WILLIAMS, BEST-SELLING AUTHOR OF *EYES ON THE PRIZE: AMERICA'S CIVIL RIGHTS YEARS*

"Once again Lis combines her keen legal mind with her generous heart to bring us a gripping human story of justice too long delayed."

—KATHIE LEE GIFFORD

"Inspired by actual historical events and informed by Lis Wiehl's formidable personal and professional background, *Snapshot* captivates and enthralls."

—JEANINE PIRRO, BEST-SELLING AUTHOR OF *SLY FOX*

"Riveting from the first page . . ."

—PAM VEASEY, SCREENWRITER AND EXECTIVE PRODUCER

ACCLAIM FOR *A MATTER OF TRUST*

"This suspenseful first in a new series from Wiehl and Henry opens with a bang."

—*PUBLISHERS WEEKLY*

"Wiehl begins an exciting new series with prosecutor Mia at the center. The side storyline about bullying is timely and will hit close to home for many."

—*RT Book Reviews*, 4 stars

"Dramatic, moving, intense. *A Matter of Trust* gives us an amazing insight into the life of a prosecutor—and mom. Mia Quinn reminds me of Lis."

—Maxine Paetro, *New York Times* best-selling author

"*A Matter of Trust* is a stunning crime series debut from one of my favorite authors, Lis Wiehl. Smart, suspenseful, and full of twists that only an insider like Wiehl could pull off. I want prosecutor Mia Quinn in my corner when murder's on the docket—she's a compelling new character and I look forward to seeing her again soon."

—Linda Fairstein, *New York Times* best-selling author

ACCLAIM FOR THE TRIPLE THREAT SERIES

"Only a brilliant lawyer, prosecutor, and journalist like Lis Wiehl could put together a mystery this thrilling! The incredible characters and nonstop twists will leave you mesmerized. Open [*Face of Betrayal*] and find a comfortable seat because you won't want to put it down!"

—E. D. Hill, FOX News anchor

"Who killed loudmouth radio guy Jim Fate? The game is afoot! *Hand of Fate* is a fun thriller, taking you inside the media world and the justice system—scary places to be!"

—Bill O'Reilly, FOX TV and radio anchor

"Beautiful, successful and charismatic on the outside but underneath a twisted killer. She's brilliant and crazy and comes racing at the reader with knives and a smile. The most chilling villain you'll meet . . . because she could live next door to you."

—Dr. Dale Archer, Clinical Psychiatrist, regarding *Heart of Ice*

SNAPSHOT

DISCARD

ALSO BY LIS WIEHL

The Mia Quinn Mysteries (with April Henry)
A Matter of Trust

The Triple Threat series (with April Henry)
Face of Betrayal
Hand of Fate
Heart of Ice
Eyes of Justice

The East Salem Trilogy (with Pete Nelson)
Waking Hours
Darkness Rising
Fatal Tide

SNAPSHOT

LIS WIEHL

THOMAS NELSON
Since 1798

NASHVILLE   DALLAS   MEXICO CITY   RIO DE JANEIRO

Published in Nashville, Tennessee, by Thomas Nelson. Thomas Nelson is a registered trademark of Thomas Nelson, Inc.

Thomas Nelson, Inc., titles may be purchased in bulk for educational, business, fundraising, or sales promotional use. For information, please e-mail SpecialMarkets@ThomasNelson.com.

Publisher's Note: This novel is a work of fiction. Names, characters, places, and incidents are either products of the author's imagination or used fictitiously.

ISBN 978-1-4016-9072-4 (ITPE)

Library of Congress Cataloging-in-Publication Data

Wiehl, Lis W.
  Snapshot / Lis Wiehl.
      pages cm
  ISBN 978-1-4016-8952-0 (hardback)
1. Government investigators—Fiction. 2. Cold cases (Criminal investigation) 3. Civil rights—United States—Fiction. 4. Photographs—Fiction. I. Title.
  PS3623.I382S63 2014
  813'.6—dc23

                                    2013029522

Printed in the United States of America
14 15 16 17 18 19 RRD 6 5 4 3 2 1

For retired FBI Special Agent Richard Wiehl, the man who took the snapshot in 1965 and began this story. But most of all, for just being my dad.

PROLOGUE

Special Agent James Waldren reached around his jacket and felt the Smith & Wesson .38 Special concealed at the small of his back. He scanned the pedestrians up and down the street before responding to the tugs at his sleeve.

"Daddy, look. Daddy, I'm skipping." Lisa took off in an awkward hop and skip up the sidewalk.

"Wait for me," James said, picking up his pace. The camera hanging around his neck slapped his chest as he reached out for her arm. "Hold my hand now."

"And look both ways," Lisa said as they reached an intersection. The light turned green, and they crossed the street with a growing crowd hurrying forward.

James was keenly aware of the glances, and of how people moved ever so slightly away—some even crossed to the other sidewalk—when they saw him. This wasn't a neighborhood where a white man and his

1

blond-haired daughter would normally be seen. Lisa skipped along, oblivious.

The sounds of cheering and shouts echoing through a bullhorn increased as they closed in on the throng of people. As a tall man raced by, the placard he carried clattered to the sidewalk. Lisa released James's hand to run a few steps ahead, reaching the sign as the man bent to pick it up.

"Here you go, sir," Lisa chirped. She picked up the edge of the sign that had FREEDOM NOW painted in bold red against the white.

The man glanced from Lisa to James, then back to the child. She pushed the end of the wooden pole as high as she could with two hands.

"Thank you, li'l miss," the man said.

"You're welcome, sir," Lisa said, smiling back as he picked up the placard.

He gave James a tentative nod before racing up the street, sign in hand.

As the sidewalk congestion grew, James scooped Lisa into his arms, eliciting a joyful squeal. She rested in the crook of his elbow, and her soft hand reached around his neck, curling her fingers into his hair.

At the corner, the streets lined with tall brick buildings opened to a small park and public square. The air was electric with the energy of the growing crowd.

James surveyed the plaza where at least a hundred people lined the adjacent street, waiting for the approaching marchers: women in Sunday dresses, many with hats and white gloves, pantyhose, and dress shoes; men in crisp button-down shirts and slacks, some with ties and jackets even on this warm spring morning.

"Where is the important man, Daddy?" Lisa craned her neck.

"We'll see him very soon," James said, moving closer toward the parade route. His eight years with the Bureau had altered training into instinct, but in the eighteen months since President Kennedy's assassination in Dallas, every important event held the threat of danger, no matter how peaceful it was planned to be.

James had spent countless hours and overtime investigating the JFK assassination. He was assigned to the killer, the deceased Lee Harvey Oswald—his activities, friends, coworkers, family, and especially his Russian wife, Marina Oswald. Good ole cowboy country hid numerous underground connections and secret groups throughout Dallas, Fort Worth, and outward from the South and across the nation. There were Russian expats with connections in the USSR, hidden KKK members in political positions, and a growing group of black freedom fighters.

But today James tried to blend in. Just another bystander, a normal guy who'd brought his daughter to witness a historical event. Just any white dad who happened to have a revolver and FBI credentials in his wallet. The truth was, James couldn't be just a bystander. A special agent with the Federal Bureau of Investigation was never off duty, and an event like this had layers of possible intrigue. His wife would be furious if she knew he'd brought Lisa with him. She thought they were going to the park.

"Here he comes." James lifted Lisa onto his shoulders. She patted the top of his head, bouncing up and down with the cheers erupting around them. "See that man, the one in the middle?"

"The man with the big hat?" Lisa leaned down toward his ear. The girl was hat obsessed. She'd wanted to break out her Easter bonnet today, but his wife wanted it saved for Easter Sunday.

"Not that one. The shorter man with the red necktie." He lifted his camera with one hand and snapped a picture, then advanced the film and snapped another.

"I see him," she said, bouncing again.

"He's an important man, a very good writer and speaker."

James took pictures as they watched the progression down the street. Benjamin Gray was surrounded by marchers holding signs, the cry for freedom and equality on their lips. The crowd took up singing "We Shall Overcome." Benjamin Gray carried a Bible under his arm and slapped his hands together as he joined in the singing.

Lisa wiggled on James's shoulders, trying to slide down just as he spotted his partner, Agent Peter Hughes, up a block and across the street.

"Want down, Daddy," Lisa said.

The marchers made a sharp turn and moved into the square where Gray and other leaders would speak to the crowd.

James set Lisa on the ground, holding on to her arm, but she tugged away from him.

"Wait!" he called, weaving through the crowd after the blond head.

James watched as Lisa stopped a few feet from a little black girl close to her age who sat on a cylindrical concrete seat. The girl stared back at Lisa, then smiled when his daughter waved. Lisa clambered up the seat, pushing higher with her toes. It seemed that thoughts of parades and important men were pushed aside by the more interesting distraction of a potential playmate.

"I'm four," Lisa said as she held up three fingers, then the fourth.

James didn't hear the other girl but saw her show Lisa four fingers back. A nearby woman in a large white hat kept a watchful eye from an adjacent, slightly taller bench.

"Can I take a picture?" he asked her.

She leaned back, studying him and then the two girls before winking and breaking into a smile.

"Go right ahead," she said, and returned to watching the progression of marchers as they looped from behind them to curve around James toward the central square at his back.

He clicked several photos, struck by the poignancy of the images. These two little girls, one white and one black, sitting side by side, were the symbol of today's event.

James snapped another picture as the two girls leaned close, smiling and talking as if already friends.

A gunshot pierced the air. Then another.

James jumped to shield Lisa as he grabbed his gun. He moved the two girls directly behind him. His eyes jumped around the crowded plaza behind him, where the shots had come from.

The rally turned into instant chaos, with people running in all directions.

The black girl's mother screamed at James, hitting him with her purse as she reached for her child.

"It's okay, I'm FBI." He flipped out his wallet with the large letters clearly visible, but the woman continued to cry out, gloved hands at her mouth. James passed the child to her, and they were immediately enveloped into the crowd and out of sight.

"They shot him! Help, please help!" someone screamed.

Through the commotion James glimpsed a man on the ground. Beside the body, a Bible lay covered in blood.

James pushed forward with Lisa held against his chest. "Close your eyes," he demanded.

The faces around him reflected terror and confusion.

As he turned toward the man on the ground, James was certain that Benjamin Gray was already dead.

NOVEMBER 1971

Queens, New York

Former Special Agent Peter Hughes sat with the gun on the desk beside him as he looked out the second-story window at bare trees reaching like hands toward a gray sky.

Outside, Peter knew, people were preparing for the holidays. Thanksgiving was a week away, and Christmas carols already played in the stores. Peter wondered if Lisa was performing at her elementary school. He wished he could be there and see her wave to "Uncle Peter" as she'd done last year from the stage. He hoped she knew that he didn't want to go away.

Peter reached beneath the desk to the very far corner. He pulled back the wood and removed the object he'd hidden there.

He held up an old brass key and set it beside his revolver. He recalled watching as Robert Kennedy used the key to unlock a drawer. Together they'd admired the craftsmanship of the massive cabinet.

"Every drawer has a unique key. Isn't that remarkable?" Bobby had said.

"Sounds like a lot of work to me. And a lot to keep track of," was Peter's response.

"Brilliant, really." Bobby told Peter how the queen of England had given the cabinet to his brother John when he was elected to the presidency. Originally it had been given to the royal family three hundred years earlier.

Peter and Bobby believed they were doing the right thing that day, locking away the proof of a crime. It was for the greater good, and for only a short time. Bobby would be president, probably within the next few years. He'd pick up his brother's mantle and bring some right back to all that was going wrong. They'd wait just a little while longer, till Bobby was in office, then set everything right.

Bobby had turned the key, locking the secrets away.

And then he was shot dead, just when change seemed within grasp.

Peter wanted to fix things, but every attempt seemed to dig him in deeper. First he couldn't find the key. Then the cabinet was moved, along with the secrets it held.

Now he had the key. Right here in his hands. But he was hated and reviled by those he loved most. Peter knew his old friend James Waldren could right the wrongs.

A car turned around in front of the house and parked on the street.

He peered down and saw a young man rise from behind the driver's seat. The kid took a worn briefcase from the backseat, adjusted his tie, and moved up the walkway.

Peter recognized the look on the young man's face. He'd once had such dreams, and a belief in a world that could be better than it turned out to be.

The doorbell rang, and Peter heard his sister's footsteps moving toward the door.

He thought of little Lisa Waldren again. How many times he'd wished he had a child like her of his own. But that, too, could never be.

Peter placed the key and letter into a large envelope and sealed the top as he heard his sister talking to the visitor at the door. He set the envelope in the top compartment of the desk.

"There's someone here to see you, Peter!" his sister shouted from downstairs.

Peter looked again at the empty trees. Then he picked up the gun, placed it beneath his chin, and pulled the trigger.

CHAPTER ONE

PRESENT TIME

Boston, Massachusetts

Moakley Federal Courthouse

She needed air.

Lisa Waldren's quick footsteps were lost in the noise filling the marble corridor as she slung her satchel over her shoulder and wove through huddled groups of jurors, family members, and legal teams. She didn't turn toward the elevators that led to her office, but instead focused her steps toward the fresh ocean air waiting outside the building.

"Lisa, wait," someone called behind her as the glass rotunda entrance came into view.

She didn't slow until she'd pushed out the glass doors into the curved courtyard of Moakley Federal Courthouse. The scent of the sea filled her lungs and cooled her face, a welcome relief from the recycled air of the courtroom. But in her hurry to escape, Lisa had forgotten that the press would be waiting. They recognized her as the lead federal prosecutor and hurried toward her.

LIS WIEHL

"Ms. Waldren, are you pleased with the sentencing?"

"What did Radcliffe say to you? Did he show any remorse?"

The faces, cameras, and microphones pressed around her.

"We have an official press conference at two o'clock." Lisa pushed through the net that circled and squeezed in. Someone grabbed her arm, but as she protested, Lisa recognized a familiar face pushing around and leading her through the mob.

"That's all for now. Sorry, folks, more in a few hours," Drew Harman said with a commanding tone that brought a smile to the edge of Lisa's lips.

"Hey, Drew, you got an exclusive with her or what?" The reporter gave him a sly expression as a few others broke into laughter.

"You'd like to know," Drew said. As they moved beyond the gathering, he shook his head as if disgusted. "Sharks."

Lisa couldn't help but laugh, given that Drew was a former newsman himself.

"I'd say thank you, but that wasn't necessary. I have plenty of experience shoving past the press."

"Don't I know," Drew said with a wicked grin.

Lisa ignored the remark. "Do you have time for lunch? I'm starving."

"Sentencing bad guys to thirty years in prison works up an appetite, I'm sure."

The breeze wafting through the landscaped courtyard carried the scent from a Sicilian restaurant, teasing her grumbling stomach with visions of homemade linguini and fresh seafood.

"Today was good news," Drew said, and Lisa realized he'd been studying her expression.

He was right. A bad guy was going to prison, and that should make her feel good. But for the past three years, Lisa had spent countless hours with the victims of the multistate extortion case. A hundred and forty-three victims had been taken by a swindler—that's what it came down to. They were humiliated and disillusioned, but even worse, most had lost nearly everything they had. Lisa could see the faces and hear their stories: the Huffs had to move in with their

10

married children after losing the home they'd had for forty years; elderly Maryann Brown was scouring the job market after losing her entire life savings; Blaze Hampton survived being a POW in Vietnam but had lost his finances to a man claiming to be another veteran . . . the stories went on and on.

Sending Gerald Radcliffe to prison for thirty years didn't help the victims.

"Yes, good news. At least it's over." Lisa tried to muster up some acceptable enthusiasm.

They walked toward the blue waters of Boston Harbor that gleamed beneath the noonday sun. A large catamaran cut through the choppy waves, reminding Lisa of days when her husband was alive and he'd coax her and their young son out for a day at sea. The memory no longer stung but served to soften her mood and remind her of how time passed and healed. And tonight was one of her two regular weekly video chats with her now college-aged son from his dorm in London.

"It is actually over. That is a relief." Lisa glanced at Drew as the weight finally began to lift.

"You need to take that vacation now. Celebrate this and don't just hop on the next case. It's a huge victory. I know one thing—Radcliffe thought he was getting away with this, but he didn't expect Federal Prosecutor Lisa Waldren. You did good, so be proud of yourself." Drew's white smile beamed against the darkness of his skin.

Lisa nearly brushed away his words by saying that she'd been part of a great team and all the usual things people were supposed to say. But Drew knew the hours she'd put in and how determined she was to get the last nail hammered into Radcliffe's coffin. She'd followed a paper trail after it virtually disappeared, found family members that Radcliffe had thought he'd left behind and a partner in exile he wanted dead. Without her determination fueled by the victims' stories, Radcliffe would have never gone to trial, let alone been found guilty.

"I guess I did do all right," she said, breaking into a smile of her own.

As they stepped onto the harbor walkway, Lisa's phone rang. The name on the screen stopped her.

"My father?" She held up the phone as if to confirm that her eyes weren't tricking her.

"You should answer it."

Lisa hesitated a moment longer.

"Dad?"

"There you are. I didn't know if you'd be in court." The voice struck her as so familiar that the time since she had last seen her father disappeared in a moment. They spoke in short greetings on holidays and birthdays, though Dad had forgotten most of Lisa's. They were family, yet neither of them knew the details of the other's life.

"I just left a sentencing and am going to lunch. How are you? Is everything okay?"

"I want to talk to you about something. Time is critical with this."

"What's it about?" Lisa braced herself for the news she was about to receive.

"There's too much to go over right now. But do you remember when you were little, really little, I took you to a civil rights rally?"

Lisa frowned, trying to gauge where this was going.

"It was in Fort Worth. There was a shooting?"

"Do you mean the rally where that civil rights leader was killed?" Years ago, after her mother had brought up how upset she'd been that a man was killed so close to her daughter, Lisa had researched the event.

"Yes, exactly. His name was Benjamin Gray."

Lisa caught the rise of excitement in Dad's tone. She shifted from one leg to the next as Drew took the heavy satchel from her shoulder and motioned toward a bench near the water's edge. Lisa followed him and leaned on the thick chain railing.

"Didn't the shooter get the death penalty?" she asked.

"Yes, but he didn't do the crime. The wrong man has spent more than four decades in prison for the Gray killing."

"And?" A headache was growing in her temples, and she wanted to ask what this had to do with her, with them, with his abrupt phone call out of the blue.

"I want to right that wrong."

"That's admirable of you."

This was not like her father at all. Special Agent James Waldren had retired with accolades from the FBI over a decade earlier. He fit the G-man role naturally. He didn't share his feelings with anyone, he'd never go to therapy, and he wouldn't see the point of losing sleep questioning life decisions. Yet now Lisa detected the tone of someone impassioned by a cause.

Had he become obsessed with this case? Was he losing his mind? Words like *dementia* and *Alzheimer's* made her pulse race.

"It's not admirable; it's what should have been done long ago. And I need your help."

"Me? What can I do?"

"I don't know what you remember from that day, but the real killer couldn't have been in the spot where they arrested Leonard Dubois— the man convicted of the shooting.

"There were many inconsistencies and reports that never sat well with me. I have several files for you to look through, and much more here in Dallas. I know I'm dumping a lot on you at once, but we're running out of time. In seven weeks, the wrong man is going to be executed. We have to work quickly."

We? Lisa didn't know what to say. Her father obviously believed she should care. After all this time he popped into her life, not to know her better, but because of some old case from the sixties.

She hadn't spoken to him since she'd called him at Christmas. There were no inquiries about her son, his grandson. No sharing of pictures or telling stories of John going off to England, or how she'd slept in his room the first week or how empty the house felt without him. Nothing about her, nothing about them, nothing a father and daughter might usually share. No opportunity to mention that she'd just won one of the biggest cases in recent Boston history.

She closed her eyes against the throbbing headache, then she remembered the time.

"Dad, I have to hold a press conference in an hour. Can I call you when I'm home?" She couldn't give a flat-out no to her father, even if he'd turned his back on her more times than she could count.

"Oh yes, I heard something about your big case. Congratulations."

"Thank you." Lisa was surprised that he knew anything about it at all.

"Will you have some time off now? I wondered if you might come down here."

"Go to Texas? You're still in Dallas, right?" It was a question for a casual acquaintance, not a father.

"Of course. If you could see all this evidence and these pictures, and the letter Leonard Dubois wrote me from prison."

"I have a vacation sort of in the process."

Drew raised his eyebrows at her semi-lie.

"Well, I'm sure you deserve it. I can try mailing you copies of the snapshots I took at the parade. Maybe you'll remember something. But it'd be best if you came here."

"Why don't you e-mail or text them to me."

"I can't do all that stuff. Just call me back as soon as you can. There's a lot at stake here."

"Okay, Dad." Lisa would hear him out; she'd give him that at least.

She hung up the phone and stared across the water. The catamaran had sailed beyond view.

"He wants me to go to Dallas."

"You should consider it." Drew motioned for them to walk. He kept her satchel on his shoulder as he led the way toward the quaint cafés and shops across the bridge. A historic fishing vessel knocked against the dock and strained its mooring lines.

Lisa couldn't enjoy the walk as she normally would. She might have known Drew would side with any chance of her reconnecting with her father. In their eight years as friends, Drew had never met him. He'd met her mother and stepfather on numerous occasions, and Lisa knew Drew's family well. But Dad had never visited her in Boston, not once, while Lisa's career and single parenting had kept her from returning to

Texas. When her son was young, she'd tried developing a relationship between her father and her fatherless son. But Dad had never particularly enjoyed children, and she eventually gave up.

Now Dad called, acting as if he regularly phoned for a friendly father-daughter chat and that it wasn't outside of normal to request her help on an old case.

Why was this case so important to him?

"There is absolutely no way I'm going to Dallas."

Drew didn't look toward her as they walked.

"I think that you will."

CHAPTERTWO

Jefferson City, Missouri

Stanley Blackstone had the sudden urge for a cigar and a stiff drink, a desire that surprised him considering it was 10:00 a.m. and he rarely imbibed anymore.

A crowd of a hundred had gathered before a small stage at the outside entrance of the Jefferson City Mall. Stanley stood on the fringe with his arms crossed at his chest, carefully studying each person and scanning the surroundings, including the roof and the bushes along the entrance to the mall.

Above the platform a banner flapped in the morning breeze, surrounded by red, white, and blue balloons that bobbed and twisted against the clear May sky. The banner read:

HOPE IN ACTION!
HUBERT FOR SENATE

A podium and microphone awaited the keynote guest, Gwendolyn Hubert, though Stanley hadn't seen her arrive yet. She was probably in some private office or closed-off area inside the mall. He needed to leave before she appeared. Gwen had made it clear that the distance between them should remain, but Stanley needed to know she was safe. The world was darker than Gwen understood, with her idealistic views. She believed she could make a difference by running for political office, that the world was still worth fighting for.

Someone bumped into him from behind, and he whipped around to confront the offender. A thirtysomething man turned in unison, a baby attached to his chest.

"Excuse me," the man said lightheartedly until he saw Stanley's size and fierce expression. Stanley knew his glare and burly stature were an imposing combination. He'd learned to use them to his advantage.

"Sorry, man," the guy muttered and quickly herded his wife and children away. Not the best way to win supporters for Gwen's campaign, Stanley mused with only slight remorse.

He read the banner again. Gwen had changed her name to her stepfather's before she even entered high school. He deserved that, he supposed. But it didn't mean he had to like it.

Stanley saw a bearded man in a black trench coat move in close to the stage with his hands in his pockets. He seemed to be staring at the empty podium. Before Stanley could move forward, he saw Lancaster, his hired bodyguard, thread his way through the crowd toward the man without appearing at all suspicious—unlike Stanley, who had scared off a man carrying a baby.

At that moment a businessman-type guy raced up the stairs to the podium and tapped the microphone. Stanley knew he should be leaving now, but he moved through the crowd to watch Lancaster and the man by the podium.

"Is this on? Oh, it is, great," the guy said into the microphone.

Lancaster intercepted the bearded man as the announcer welcomed the crowd and explained who he was—some local city councilman or something. Stanley mostly tuned him out as he watched Lancaster escort the bearded man away from the stage and through the crowd. The man protested until Lancaster leaned in closer. Whatever he said or did was enough for a sudden exit without further objection.

Stanley smiled. He'd hired the right man.

"Today I'm pleased to introduce you to a woman I greatly admire. Gwendolyn Hubert is the quintessential . . ."

At the sound of her name, Stanley felt his hands begin to sweat. He had faced many imposing foes in his day. He'd killed men with his bare hands. But only this five-foot-seven, 115-pound woman could make his palms sweat like this.

She walked from the closest building near the stage and toward the back of the podium with several people beside her, probably her campaign manager and assistant. He didn't know the others, but Lancaster would report back to him.

A last glance at the bodyguard assured him that everything was fine here. His daughter was safe even if she didn't want his help.

"Gwendolyn's Missouri roots run deep," the announcer said.

Blackstone scoffed. She'd been born in Louisiana on the plantation that had been in the Blackstone family for generations. Her mother and stepfather may have raised Gwen in Missouri, but her roots were Deep South.

"Gwendolyn attended the University of Missouri where she joined Kappa Alpha Theta sorority. She placed second at nationals for diving during college, was the president of . . ."

Stanley knew all of this, though he hadn't attended many of Gwen's important events, like graduations or birthdays. For years he'd been too busy; then, when he wanted to be there, his ex-wife asked him to stay away. Now it was Gwen who did the asking.

"When Gwendolyn Hubert sets her mind to do something great, she accomplishes it. She's ready to take on Washington next. Let's welcome the next senator from Missouri . . . Gwendolyn Hubert!"

Stanley couldn't keep his eyes off his daughter as she made her way up the stage to the hearty applause on the ground around him. She walked with confidence and welcomed the crowd with an air that exuded capability, power, and warmth. Stanley hadn't come up with this description; he'd read it in one of the many publications that had been tracking Gwendolyn's political rise for the past few years. But now she was running for US Senate. Someday his only child might just sit in the Oval Office. She may have changed her name from Blackstone to Hubert, but she was his daughter and he was proud of her. Even after all these years, he remembered what it felt like to hold her against his shoulder when she slept and how she used to cry when he left. Even if she was conflicted about his role in her life and the danger he posed to her political career, they were father and daughter. Time didn't change that. Nothing could.

Leave now, he told himself.

But something kept him planted there.

A couple beside him talked loudly as Gwen spoke about opening avenues for small businesses. Before he decided between leaving, staying, or slamming his fist into the man's stomach, Gwen's and Stanley's eyes connected.

For less than a millisecond her voice caught, then she recovered and moved through her points on how to make that happen. But even from the distance between them, Stanley could see the red flush rising from her chest up her neck, just as it had whenever she was upset as a child.

The one skeleton in her closet was standing in the audience. Stanley understood how detrimental he could be to his daughter's political career. Her campaign manager might spin it that they were estranged, but he was still her father, and his past had become a liability.

While most viewed him as an heir to success who had built an even bigger empire through real estate and imports, Stanley was plagued with rumors of corruption, illegal activities, and shadowy actions against civil rights groups. It hadn't hurt him, but it could harm his daughter's run for office. She had a proud Southern heritage that went back to Confederate officers and slave owners. She'd never been proud of it herself, at least not yet.

Stanley saw a TV news cameraman move closer toward the stage with a reporter beside him. That moved his feet away.

He'd come to Missouri to talk to her. She'd been out of the state until early this morning and had let him know through some assistant that she had a full schedule.

Stanley walked toward the black town car idling in the parking lot. He needed to get back to Miami anyway. There was a situation there he needed to resolve once and for all. As he wove through a stand of bushes, he felt the buzz of his cell phone in his pocket.

"Marcus," Stanley said, wondering why his nephew and company VP was calling when he was supposed to be in a meeting.

"Some information came in that you'll want to hear."

"What about?" he asked without slowing his pace.

"I got a call from a contact at the Texas State Prison. You must have set this up before I came in, because I didn't know anything about it. Do you know what I'm talking about?"

"Leonard Dubois?" Stanley asked.

"Yes, yes, exactly. You'll have to update me when you get back, but apparently Dubois is scheduled for execution."

"I know that."

"Okay, well, the contact also spotted correspondence from Dubois to a retired FBI agent. Name is . . . let me see here."

"Special Agent James Waldren."

"Yes." Marcus didn't hide his surprise.

"What else?" Stanley asked.

"That's all I know. Who is this FBI agent and what does it have to do with you?"

"It's a lesson, my boy. A lesson to always tie up loose ends."

"O-kay," Marcus said with a long pause. "Should something be done?"

"Something will be done, but I also have that other matter to attend to in Miami. I'll fly home today. Call the pilot and make the arrangements."

"Sure," Marcus said, and Stanley could hear his nephew's curiosity. The boy really needed to build a tougher exterior. Sometimes he was transparent as glass. That was never good in business, gambling, or relationships.

Stanley leaned against the outside of the car, feeling the rumble of its engine through his back. He could see his daughter waving to the crowd as they cheered at the closing of her speech. The execution of Dubois was less than two months away. Gwen's election was in six.

"You don't want me to do anything?" Marcus said.

"I'll be there tonight."

This was a loose end. Stanley notoriously wrapped up all loose ends, but in this instance he'd been young, and everything had gone wrong. Now it was coming back to haunt him. It could haunt his daughter as well, could end her political future. Stanley wasn't about to let that happen.

CHAPTER THREE

Dallas, Texas

James Waldren stared at his phone, pushing at different buttons and shaking his head.

"Want some help?" Rosalyn said from behind the wheel of the car. Her eyes bounced to him and then back to the road.

He squinted to study Rosalyn with her quirky green glasses and dark hair caught up with brightly colored pins in a loose bun. She chewed on a piece of gum with a vengeance.

"Lisa wants me to text her a picture, but I hate this phone."

"You hate every phone."

"Not the one at home on the wall."

"Because the one at home is over two decades old, and you only like technology if you don't have to learn it, which means no technology. Am I right?"

He chuckled, and she said, "Why are you staring at me?"

"How did you know that?" James had thought almost those exact words. He'd begrudgingly learned how to turn on a computer and how to use e-mail and search engines. They were helpful, he had to admit. But all these text messages and video chats and sending pictures, it was too much. He'd nearly returned a flat-screen TV because of the complicated remote.

"You're easier to read than you think," she said with a wink.

No woman had ever said that to James. Not his ex-wife or his daughter or the few women he'd dated after his divorce or his former secretaries, who were now called personal assistants though he never understood why. What was so demeaning about being called a secretary? Now perfectly good positions were renamed. Secretaries were executive assistants, stewardesses were flight attendants, and housewives were homemakers or domestic engineers. He didn't understand, but perhaps that was why the women in his life claimed he was always disconnected—except for this eccentric woman behind the wheel.

"I'm dying to hear how the call went. Will I be meeting your daughter soon?" Rosalyn asked with her usual inflated enthusiasm.

James shifted in the seat. "Lisa is about to go on vacation. We'll see what happens . . ." His voice trailed off. He hadn't told Rosalyn the main reason he wanted Lisa involved—to keep her close. The last time he started digging around about the Benjamin Gray shooting, the threats had pulled him back. Threats had never slowed him down until his daughter was the target.

"I'm sorry, Jimmy. Really. It would've been a great way to spend time together."

"Well . . . that's not what I was doing," he mumbled, knowing Rosalyn had envisioned a touching reunion. He did wish to know Lisa better, as long as they could start with a clean slate. Why rehash a past that couldn't be changed?

"Whatever you say," she said. "But, hey, before I take you home, I need to stop by the office real fast. I want to show you something."

James closed his eyes, ready to be in his own abode. He wanted something hot to drink and needed to review something from his files.

"You'll be glad that we did," she said slyly, but James wasn't convinced. For the next twenty minutes, Rosalyn chatted about her car acting up and how the mechanic said a mouse had chewed up the wiring.

"It cost me almost four hundred bucks, and I still might have a mouse running around in here. Why do I have three cats?"

James made the appropriate concerned responses as his mind replayed the conversation he'd had with his daughter.

Rosalyn parked in front of a small office nestled in the back corner of an old brick building. On the door, a sign read "Rosalyn Bloomquist, Private Investigator." Beneath the words was a caricature of Rosalyn with Texas-sized hair and horn-rimmed glasses, holding a giant magnifying glass.

The first time James had walked into this office after agreeing to a preliminary meeting, he'd been certain he wouldn't help this amateur. As a retired special agent from the US Federal Bureau of Investigation with awards and commendations and, yes, one black mark on his record, there was no way he'd work as a consultant to this wannabe, no matter how bored he was in retirement.

He had sat across from Rosalyn at her antique white desk wanting to laugh at the absurdity of the moment.

But then Rosalyn had proceeded to impress him. She was quirky, bordering on weird, but she was sharp, understood the law, and had a keen sense of knowing how to get information. Her father had been an agent, her brother was a detective in Chicago, and she had retired from a police force outside of Houston to open her own PI agency.

Now James followed her inside to her office in the very back of the building. She moved around her antique desk, pulling a stack of papers from her overflowing side table. She dropped the papers onto the desk in front of him and waited with an expectant look.

"What are these?" He picked up the stack and flipped through the copies.

"I found it."

"You're going to make me guess when I'm this tired?" James asked wearily.

"I won't make you guess. What have you been searching for?"

James sighed. She was going to make him guess.

"Evidence to free Leonard Dubois."

"No, not that. The other thing. The historical item?"

James grabbed the pile of papers. "You found the key?"

"No, not the key, but the other half we needed to find. Oh, I'll just tell you." Rosalyn shook her head as if completely exasperated with him. "I found the Kennedy cabinet."

"It's not at the JFK Presidential Library?"

"No. It's in a secret vault in Washington, DC. If we can find the key, now you'll know where to find the cabinet. Then you can open all its secrets." Rosalyn had a flair for the dramatic.

James flipped through the printouts, then rubbed his forehead. This all sounded like a rabbit trail to him.

"We have no clue where the key is located. And we don't even know if there's a connection to the Benjamin Gray case."

"But once we get the key, we'll know where to find the JFK cabinet. It's progress. The key is worthless without the cabinet."

James grinned at her enthusiasm. "You did good work, you're right."

"Darn right I did. What exactly did your daughter tell you after the man was shot?" Rosalyn used her patient voice with him.

"She doesn't recall much from that day now. But I remember on the day of the incident, she saw my old partner."

"What exactly did she say?"

James hated to remember this part of the incident, when he'd scooped his little girl into his arms, fearful that he'd feel blood or hear more gunfire. He'd wanted to wrap her safely against his chest where nothing could harm her.

"She pointed behind me and kept calling for Uncle Peter."

"So Peter was directly in line with where the shooting occurred. Peter told you about the key and the cabinet. Peter could have cleared this all up if he were still alive."

James didn't want to talk about Peter. He didn't want Rosalyn on the train of thought that Peter might be involved in the shooting.

Rosalyn studied him as she spoke.

"We have numerous possibilities here. Benjamin Gray might have been in the center of a shootout between two other people. He might have been shot by mistake. Or he was the intended victim and the shooter was injured or the shooter shot someone else. Or someone protecting Gray was injured. We need to explore all of these."

James knew she was right, but the effort seemed beyond what was really necessary. Right now they needed to find the evidence to free Leonard Dubois before his execution.

"And then, of course, we need to explore the other element. The key." Rosalyn sat on the edge of her desk. Her rapid-fire thoughts drove him crazy at times.

"Yes, the key," James repeated, feeling the weariness of a long day creep over him. Why had he confided so much in Rosalyn? James had never told anyone else about the key or his gut feeling that the shooting of Benjamin Gray had some tie with the Kennedy assassination or Oswald or politics or something much higher up than what was going on in Fort Worth, Texas. He had some leads on it, but they'd been shut down cold.

A strong cup of coffee sounded incredibly desirable at the moment, making him question why he'd given it up. He wondered if he had any at home and what had become of his coffeepot.

"I've been doing research on objects owned by JFK and Robert Kennedy, also Jackie and the children in case they inherited something out of the norm. I'll keep you posted on that."

"I'm sure you will."

"Back to the shooting. I highlighted all the places in those newspaper printouts where another shooter was mentioned. All said that he was white. And the white cops ignored them because everyone was black."

"Sounds like 1965," James grumbled. "But how does any of this get us hard facts to free Dubois? That's the important question. I know you've picked up a scent in all this, but we're going in a lot of directions. Everything is hearsay. Why don't we work the hard evidence?"

"This is how I do it, you know that. I gather all the pieces, even those that don't appear useful or relevant, and I put the pieces together. That's why I'm good." Her grin was laced with both humor and arrogance.

He grimaced. She was good, he had to admit.

"Let me catch up on sleep and read through all of this. Can I please go home now?"

"Yes, just one more thing," Rosalyn said, sitting in her desk chair instead of heading to the door like he'd hoped.

"What is it?" James said with a sigh.

"I think you're being followed."

CHAPTERFOUR

Dusk had fallen over Boston Harbor. The yachts, visiting vessels, and sailboats docked in the bay right up beside the high-rise buildings reflected lights like stars across the darkened waters.

From her upstairs office in Moakley Courthouse, Lisa stared out the window, phone cupped in her hand. The hallways and offices that made up the US District Attorney's Office were quiet, with nearly everyone gone to their homes throughout the Boston area.

Lisa had promised her father a return phone call, but with the press conference, final paperwork to submit to the court, and numerous calls and visits from Radcliffe's victims who wished to thank her for putting the man away, the afternoon had slipped by.

If she was honest, though, Lisa knew she had avoided the call, watering the plants in her office and stacking new case files. Piles of the latter waited in stacks on her desk, with those nearest her right hand organized into the highest priority. The ones on the floor were the least urgent. She'd skimmed through every stack, even those on the floor, as evening deepened, until her father's texts beeped onto her phone.

She clicked them and found two images from long ago. Fort Worth 1965, Dad had written after the pictures.

Lisa tried to zoom in for a better view, then sent them to the printer sitting in the corner of her spacious office. The printer hummed and flashed as it spit out the black-and-white pictures.

Lisa set the grainy printouts over an open file about mail fraud. She leaned forward to study her four-year-old self in the snapshot. Her blond hair was cut short after she'd tried to trim it herself. She was sitting on a short cylindrical seat of concrete with another little girl beside her. The other child had deep dark skin and wore a white dress.

In the second photograph, the black girl was approaching Lisa, studying her curiously. In the background Lisa could see the civil rights parade with onlookers facing away from the two little girls. Two women sat near them, one with a large white hat on her head. The photographs were compelling in their contrasts, especially considering the year and location, and full of stories anxious to be told.

She dialed her father's house number, and he answered immediately.

"So you can send text messages after all," she said.

"I had to get help. So it really worked?"

"I received two photographs and printed them. They aren't the best quality, but yes, it worked."

"That's interesting." Her father sounded more surprised than pleased.

A frame sitting on her desk caught Lisa's eye. She didn't keep recent pictures of her son at the office, just as she didn't write anything personal or share photos over social media. Her job brought enough disreputable characters into her life to make it wise to take precautions.

John was nine in the picture and wore his rugby uniform. His smile was as wide as the Grand Canyon, and it made her heart ache now with missing him. That ache turned cold as she thought of her father choosing to miss out on such an amazing kid. Yet now he wanted her help.

"Tell me about the case and what you had in mind for me to do."

"Sure, let's get right to it. First, do you remember anything new from that day, anything you might have told me or that you saw?" Dad's voice grew louder, as if he was pressing the phone against his mouth. Lisa pictured him in the old kitchen, maybe leaning over a list of hand-written leads or a file folder from the investigation.

"I don't remember much of anything. Nothing that would help acquit someone on death row, if that's what you're asking. I was, what, four or five?"

"Four," Dad said. "Do you remember the little girl in the snapshots?"

"Vaguely. I remember talking to a little black girl. She might have been the first black girl I'd ever met."

"Benjamin Gray was killed right in your line of sight. I'd hoped that you or she might have seen something. I wish I could find her."

Lisa hadn't known the shooting was that close to them. But if she couldn't remember, why did her father think this other girl would remember something after all these years? And how would he ever find her?

"Do you have any leads?"

"Just the photographs. It's a stretch, I know. I have a lot of other information, but I don't know how to get any of it to you."

There it was again. Dad wanted her to go to Dallas. A sudden heaviness came over her. This entire thing sounded like a wild-goose chase. Most likely the right man had been convicted of the killing, but for some reason, her father was revisiting something from his past.

"Dad, I just can't come out right now. Let's see what I can do from here."

"Why don't you start by reading up about Benjamin Gray and the man convicted of the crime? His name is Leonard Dubois."

"I can do that."

"When do you leave for your vacation?"

"I'm not sure. I was waiting until the Radcliffe sentencing before booking flights. I'd like to go see Mom or go to London."

"Ah, okay. That might be good for you, especially to be out of the country."

"Why is that?" Lisa was beginning to really worry about her father.

One second he wanted her help, the next he sounded relieved that she'd be leaving the United States. This from the dad who had once discouraged her from a student exchange program in Europe.

"Just that it's nice to get away. That's what I meant."

Lisa could tell that there was more to it.

"I'd be going to see my son. You know, your grandson, John?"

"Is that where he is? That's nice. Well, I'll call you tomorrow. Is that enough time to do some research?"

Lisa clenched her teeth to control the anger building in her chest.

"Sure. Talk to you then."

Later, in the emptiness of her house, Lisa ate green curry straight from the square takeout box while standing at the granite counter. The late news aired on the television, but she watched with little interest even as they replayed pieces of her press conference. A legal analyst gave her thoughts on Radcliffe's sentence, and the segment was longer than most other news being covered.

Lisa couldn't stop thinking about her father. The Radcliffe case was over. The loose ends would be wrapped up in the next few days, and she could quickly succumb to the new cases awaiting her attention. Her son had an upcoming trip across Europe with college friends that might keep her from a visit.

Despite her father's neglect of them both, Dad was getting older. He wanted her help. She couldn't think of one good reason to do so. Except that he was her father.

Early the next morning, Lisa rose and grabbed her running shoes. Opening a drawer, she caught sight of a faded green T-shirt from a 10K she'd run with her father on St. Patrick's Day several decades ago. The fabric had worn so thin in places it was nearly transparent, but she slipped it on over a white tank top.

She didn't want to run this morning. A night of restless sleep made her feet feel like cinder blocks while her mind jumped from topic to

31

topic. She'd thought of the Radcliffe trial and then her father and on to 1965 and her childhood in Texas.

After kicking off the blankets, she'd wandered to John's room down the hall, where she'd succumbed to mothering fears. Had she been a good parent? Why had she shouted at him when he'd broken the television playing catch in the house? Had her drive to fight for justice and make the world a better place stolen pieces of her son's childhood?

Lisa had nearly called Drew at three, knowing he might be up working on a project, but in the end she returned to bed, where she tossed and turned as the night ticked by.

She walked the first quarter mile, stretching her calves and arms as she went. Then she ran from her exclusive subdivision and moved toward the pathways along the Charles River. The water reflected a pink sky with fat, puffy clouds that were cut by the lines of a Cambridge crew team, the coxswain calling out as the rowers moved in perfect unison. The scent of wet grass and flowers, mixed with a hint of salty sea, filled the crisp morning near the wide river.

Her legs ached before the end of the first mile, and Lisa nearly gave in to the aroma of freshly baked cinnamon rolls and rich coffee as she passed a favorite bakery.

Her father's voice in her head pushed her onward.

Pace yourself. Find your rhythm and then let go.

Dad had coached her during high school. He'd been an athlete in college before an injury ended all sports except fishing and some golf. He hadn't been a father who cuddled with his daughter, read her stories, or told her how beautiful she was. But he'd been a good running coach. He was supportive and dependable, never missing one of their early-morning practices even if he'd been on a case the entire night before.

Hit the ground with the middle of your foot.

Imagine the world falling back behind you. You don't feel weary or any pain. Separate yourself from it.

Set your focus about fifteen feet ahead of you.

Don't keep tension in your arms. Let your arms swing naturally. Don't make a fist.

He showed her how to touch her thumb and pinkie finger together to keep from balling her hands into fists while she ran. That time was probably the closest they'd been. Lisa had been surprised at his interest in her life. He'd come to her track meets and give her advice, and she could always tell if he was proud of her by the satisfied nod of his head. Their hard work paid off when Lisa placed at nationals her junior year.

Her mind slowly unwound as she rounded a corner and headed back toward her house. The cluttered thoughts settled, and she ticked through what she needed to do that day, mapping out a schedule for phone calls, meetings, and events for the week ahead.

This was why she ran. It was the only way she'd found to cleanse her mind. By the time she reached home, she felt ready to conquer the day.

After her shower, she grabbed her phone and did a quick run-through of e-mail and voice messages. Along with numerous queries from the office, she listened to a message from Drew.

"Call me back after your run. I think you need to look at that case your dad is working on. Leonard Dubois might be innocent after all."

CHAPTERFIVE

The photographs offer a lot of information. You brought the originals?" Drew asked when Lisa arrived at his brownstone apartment. She'd forwarded the pictures to him earlier that morning.

"I don't have the originals," she said, following Drew through the cozy brick rooms and up the winding metal staircase to his second-floor studio. The hallway was lined with framed black-and-white photographs from Drew's international travels as a news correspondent. "My father texted these to me."

"They're fascinating images," he said over his shoulder.

"Why do you say so?"

They entered the open studio, divided into stations for his different projects. One was for photography; another area had his computer with printed news stories covering the desk and bulletin board; a third section was piled with books for research; and in the corner was a small counter with a refrigerator, kettle, coffeepot, blender, and hot plate for stretches when Drew barely left the studio for days.

He walked to the mini-kitchen and took a freshly made smoothie from the refrigerator. He set it in front of Lisa and then went to refill his coffee cup.

"You made this for me? I'm impressed. Thank you."

"Someone has to take care of you. Have you been eating?"

"I keep snacks in my bag just in case."

"You'd better." Drew shook his head.

He'd taken up the role of food police after she'd nearly passed out at his front door. She'd had hypoglycemia for years, but whenever work or life became extra hectic, her self-management suffered. Now with John gone to London for spring semester, Lisa's refrigerator was often a wasteland of expired yogurt and boxes of old takeout.

Drew flipped a switch that illuminated a long counter beneath the Fort Worth pictures of Lisa at the civil rights parade. His quality printer had blown the images up to 8 x 10. Even pixilated, his printouts depicted more than she'd noticed on her smaller versions.

"These are fascinating because, first of all, you were one cute little kid," he said with a grin.

"What else would you expect?" She took a sip of the smoothie, savoring the taste of fresh blueberries, yogurt, and a hint of honey.

"And there's a history here," Drew continued. "A story beyond what your father is looking into. It's like viewing a slice of American history. This was in Dallas?"

"Fort Worth. It was 1965. We were moved to the area when Dad was assigned to investigate President Kennedy's assassination right after it happened in November '63. He spent a good deal of time interviewing Marina Oswald. But by this time he was mostly keeping an eye on local Communists and those connected to Russia and Cuba, and also keeping files on both white supremacist groups and civil rights supporters."

"Your dad is a living history book." Drew leaned over the photos to study them.

"I suppose," Lisa muttered. She dug her reading glasses from her bag and moved around the table to stand beside Drew. The light brought further definition to the images, giving a better view of the background where the crowd lined the street in front of marchers walking with placards.

"This is a moment captured right before a murder," Lisa said, staring at the photographs. It felt surreal that she was one of the two children in the center. The images could have easily been seen in the pages of *Time* magazine or in a civil rights museum. She touched her finger to the little girls who were lost in the moment of meeting one another.

Drew leaned forward, staring at the faces. "You were innocent of the tension all around you. Just two kids getting to know each other, right in the eye of the storm."

"Yeah, then the storm's eye shifted, and we were in the middle of the terror."

Lisa rested her arms against the cold counter, studying the photographs with the eye of an investigator. Her father believed these images were part of finding the truth behind the Benjamin Gray assassination, but Lisa needed more than her father's conviction to believe that the man on death row wasn't the killer.

"Why did your father take you there? It seems like he'd have known there was potential danger to his daughter."

Lisa caught the edge in Drew's tone. He'd witnessed enough injured and dead children while covering news stories that even after a year back home, he still struggled with nightmares.

"Good question. I don't remember going places with him as a child, not without my mother. This must have been a rare thing."

"Maybe this event ended it."

"I should ask Mom. She might have put a stop to all father-daughter outings after this one." Lisa knew she'd have done the same or more if this had been her son.

"Ask your father too. You told me that he was overly cautious with you when you were growing up. Paranoid at times, even."

"He ran background checks on every date I went on, as well as on the guys' families. I think that's somewhat paranoid."

"Well, if I were your father, I might do the same," Drew said, raising an eyebrow. "But maybe he wasn't like that before this happened. Because a paranoid dad doesn't sound like the same man who would bring his daughter to this particular civil rights rally. The racial tension would've been pretty intense at that time, and in Texas of all places."

"I guess it's easy to forget what it was like back then."

They were silent as they studied the images.

"You know that I encounter racial issues on a fairly consistent basis even now," Drew said, pulling up two tall stools.

"What do you mean—you personally?" Lisa didn't exactly forget that Drew was African American. But he was just Drew. Their friendship had rarely encountered racial subjects. Mostly the topic came up as it pertained to Drew's travels and coverage of people groups around the world—in the Middle East with the Sunni and Shiite, or in Africa with the many racial and tribal tensions. Lisa's time with his family brought jokes and good-natured teasing, mainly from them to her, but that was all.

Drew settled onto the stool. "It surprises me at times, and it's definitely regional. It's more pervasive in the South or in rural areas of the country. But it's everywhere to some degree."

Lisa rubbed her forehead as she studied him. "*It*? What exactly do you mean? And where does this occur? At work? Here in Boston?"

"It's here, though rarely in our circles. But when I travel, it might be the high frequency of times I'm called out of an airline security line. And I get pulled over more than anyone I know."

"Maybe that's because you drive too fast," Lisa chided.

"Wayne and Jason drive worse than I do, and they were shocked when I mentioned the other day how often I've been pulled over since getting back in the States. And taxis often pass me up for a white guy, or sometimes I'll hear a rude comment."

"What kind of rude comment?"

Drew shrugged. "I'm just saying this to add context to what it was like in 1965. If I get things like that today, imagine it in 1965 Texas. We're talking about real hatred and real danger. And your father brought his little white girl to this black event where a black group was standing up for themselves. They had to be angry, fighting back—even if only with words. It took either guts or anger to stand up for themselves back then."

Lisa had never considered the events of that day the way Drew described them. Why *had* her dad taken her there?

"My memory is almost blank on the entire thing. That's why I don't understand why Dad wants my help. What can I offer?"

Drew was thoughtful for a moment and ran a finger over his thick eyebrow. "And you're sure he's healthy?"

"As far as I know." A tremor of fear coursed through her at the idea that Dad had cancer or some other disease, and this was his way to have time with her and do one last thing before he died.

"He might be trying to reconcile with you."

Lisa took another drink and thought of the years without her father in her life. "This is a strange way of showing it. He didn't ask anything about me. It was total focus on the case, just like I remember as a kid. He'd lose himself in work."

Lisa remembered standing at the door of Dad's den telling him a story he didn't hear, or Dad sitting at the public pool "watching" her swim but immersed in his notebooks. She'd call for him to see her do a handstand or her first back dive, but he couldn't tear himself away long enough to watch. Her recollections were of her father with eyes cast down in books and papers or staring off into the sky or hurrying out the door with his thermos and briefcase. The taillights of his car were an image cemented into her memory.

"Your father is from a generation that rarely shares feelings or confronts emotional issues. If he's like my father, he probably has no idea he's reaching out to you. He didn't plot it out to make this case be his chance to get to know his daughter, but subconsciously that might be exactly what he's doing."

"Or he just needs my incredible legal skills?" she said, hoping to lighten the moment.

"There is that."

Lisa didn't want to dissect her father or their lack of a relationship.

She'd done that years ago in college and when her son was younger. Eventually she had stopped caring that he wasn't part of their lives.

Drew studied her face. "So what are you going to do?"

Lisa didn't answer. She stood up from the stool and noticed Drew's double computer screens with different shots of city streets. "Is that Fort Worth?"

"Yes. I was searching for the location."

"Maybe *you* should help my father. You'd have that guy freed in no time."

"There was a lot of controversy about the killing of Benjamin Gray. A lot of people believe that someone other than Dubois shot him." Drew took another drink of his coffee. "I stayed up late last night."

Lisa couldn't stop her smile at Drew's weary expression. He'd stayed up late for this, and he'd made her a smoothie. They'd been friends for years, though he was often out of the country covering areas of tension and war in Korea, Afghanistan, Somalia, Libya, and Chechnya. Between their two full schedules, they would go for months at a time not seeing each other, yet their friendship was valued by both of them.

Then a year ago Drew traded in his khakis and combat boots for a suit and tie, or sometimes his sweats and T-shirt when he didn't leave his studio. His documentary film about the history of war correspondents was now fully funded, and he filmed interviews with former colleagues, retired newsmen, and historians.

During his last years in news, he had expressed how the overseas work was for younger reporters who had the zeal for it. His passion had waned. He'd seen too many dead women and children, and usually they had died for the greed of someone else. He had made the decision to quit after he was filming a small village in Afghanistan where a school full of children had been bombed. Parents and villagers were sobbing as they frantically dug through the rubble with their hands. Drew filmed but felt nothing until he saw a small foot sticking out from beneath a pile of brick. He stared at the child's foot and no emotion came to him: nothing for the child, nothing for the families, nothing for the story.

"I knew at that moment that I better find my soul again before it was lost forever," he had told her.

His words had come to Lisa often over the past year, bringing her own toughened soul to light. Survival as either a war correspondent or a federal prosecutor demanded strength. Sometimes it was tough to gauge how much to harden her heart and soul.

Drew was finding his soul again, and she noticed the change in him nearly every time they met now. A year ago he seemed a decade older, from his haggard voice to his bloodshot eyes. Now he helped fund-raising efforts for war veterans and charities that worked with AIDS victims in Africa and uneducated children in the Ozarks. Lisa no longer even tried to keep up with all that he was doing. Though his job now could seem menial in comparison to his previous work, Drew said the time home was like rubbing his foot awake after it had fallen asleep.

Lisa blamed him for the Radcliffe case hitting her so hard. She had forgotten how painful it was to care deeply for the victims of crimes.

"Do you think my father has this right?" Lisa asked as her phone buzzed with new messages. She looked at the screen and did a quick preview—all were work related.

Drew pulled off his glasses. "Well, Texas has exonerated more than a dozen death row inmates who were wrongly convicted. That's a lot of innocent men who would've been executed. Do you trust your father's instincts?"

"I did as a child. He was a superhero in my mind, and it sounded exciting to my friends that my dad was FBI. But as an adult . . . I don't know. I don't really know him."

"You should do this," Drew said.

"Do what exactly?" she asked, avoiding his gaze.

"You should help your father."

"And be part of an old man's obsession?"

"Yes. And maybe save a death row inmate, even if it isn't your usual line of work. Two years ago, what did you write me when my dad was sick?"

"I don't remember," she said, giving him an upward glance at her lie.

"I didn't want to leave Greece because I was on a story. You said to get on the next plane. You said, 'There will always be a story.'"

Lisa didn't comment. Drew had not taken her advice.

"I have to live with regret. I'd give anything to spend those last days with him. My brother told me that Dad asked for me every day, and that he talked about his childhood and shared stories he'd never told before."

An ache for Drew welled up in her chest as she stared at the images on the table. There she was, a little girl, so long ago, and behind that camera was her father, capturing a moment in time. She sighed and leaned into her hands.

"I can drive you to the airport," Drew said, and Lisa knew he was smiling with the belief that he'd convinced her.

She straightened with a sudden sense of panic at what that actually meant. "Hold on. I can't just run off to Texas right now. Maybe I can help from here. I need to see what kind of caseload I've got at work before I say yes."

"There will always be a case," Drew said as he reached over and pushed back a strand of hair that had fallen across her face.

"Did you become a psychologist since I last saw you?" Lisa pulled away from his touch.

A week later Lisa and her suitcase were in Drew's car, heading toward Terminal B at the Logan International Airport. The morning was cold and wet beneath dark gray clouds. She couldn't release the underlying irritation that had plagued her since she decided to fly to her father's house in Dallas. With the Radcliffe case over, she had plenty of work piled up, but it was also the best opportunity to take some time off.

"I should be heading to Bali with my swimsuit. If John and his friends weren't off traipsing around Europe, I'd be in London."

"That would have been nice," Drew said. There was no sympathy in his voice.

"I haven't really relaxed since John and I went to my cousin's

41

wedding in Maui six years ago." The image of warm sand and sunshine filled her with longing.

"We could be doing this together," Drew said.

Lisa squinted her eyes, trying to understand his meaning. "You would give up vacation time for a disaster trip to Dallas?"

Drew didn't respond.

"Hello over there?"

He stared at the road, gripping the steering wheel.

"I shouldn't say this now, it's bad timing. But talking about my dad and your dad, and you leaving today . . . I don't know, Lisa. I need to keep moving forward. I'd like to move forward with you." He turned to see her reaction, then returned his eyes to the road.

Lisa stared at his profile. He glanced at her again.

"Don't look so shocked. We've talked about this," he said.

But Lisa couldn't respond. He had said it, actually said the words that had hung between them so often. Lisa believed they felt the same way, that they loved one another as more than friends but that it would never go beyond friendship. That kept them together. There'd be no messy breakup, no loss of one another, ever.

"You've joked about it. I thought you were flirting or teasing me."

Drew shook his head and muttered under his breath, "This wasn't how I planned to say this."

So he'd planned this discussion? He really wanted more? Drew was her closest friend. The person she could count on for solid advice, even if she didn't like it. Now he was pushing the boundaries beyond what kept them safe.

"We aren't getting any younger. Do you want to spend the rest of your life alone?"

"We aren't that old. And this is a lot to take in on the way to the airport."

Drew pulled up to the unloading zone and turned to face her.

"I'm sorry for saying this right now. But the truth is, I don't want you to go."

Lisa stared at him. She knew his face so well, but he was suddenly not making any sense. "You're the one who told me to go."

His jaw tightened as he nodded. "You need to go. But I don't want . . . This is not coming out well."

"Drew, please stop. We have a good thing here. I don't want to lose it." Lisa wanted to patch this up before the seams were pulled too far apart.

"You keep me at arm's length because you think our relationship is best that way. For such an intelligent woman, sometimes I wonder about you." Drew's face held a sadness that tugged at her heart.

"What does that mean?" she whispered.

"You're running. Not from commitment, not from fear of losing me. You fill your life with work to avoid the truth."

"What truth?"

"That your life is empty."

Lisa's heart raced as everything in her protested against his words. Her life was anything but empty. Her career was flourishing. She'd finally earned respect in a field where a blond, attractive woman didn't garner it easily. She had some good friendships, and while her relationship with Dad was mostly estranged, Lisa and her mom were close, talking or visiting as much as they could when Mom wasn't off traveling the world with her new husband.

Lisa was also close to her son. John already had a list of places to take her when she visited him in a few months. She'd traveled all over the world. Her career made a difference in tilting the balance of good and evil back toward good. How could he say her life was empty? Her face burned with anger. She opened the car door.

"Lisa, wait a minute." He took her arm—gently, but she could feel the strength of his fingers.

"I need to catch my plane."

He looked at her directly, not speaking until she looked at him. "I don't want to say this. I'm here, you know that. But maybe it's time to stop running away from everything that you think might hurt you."

She wanted to yank away and tell him that this was hurting her, his words, his sudden demands out of the blue. Why couldn't they keep things as they'd been for so long? It worked for her, and it seemed to work for him. This thing between them, friendship she called it, wasn't broken.

Lisa stepped out into the cold morning.

"I'll call you from Dallas."

CHAPTER SIX

The end of the fishing pole plunged downward, bending almost completely in half.

"It's a big one!" Stanley shouted as he gripped the pole. He reeled hard and fast as the fish turned beneath the boat, making the taut line go slack.

"Not another," Frank said, groaning as he held his pole on the other side of the boat. Frank hadn't caught a fish all day.

Billy grabbed a large net and then motioned with his head at the smaller fishing boat skimming along the waves toward Stanley's forty-foot fishing yacht.

"Better help him aboard," Stanley said without releasing his grip on the rod and reel.

Billy hurried to the back as the smaller boat came alongside. The driver cut the engine and tossed a rope for Billy, then dropped bumpers down the side of his boat, which sat a good few feet below the yacht.

When Stanley saw his nephew Marcus with the orange life vest secured around his neck, he had to stop himself from the string of humilating jokes that lined up in his head. His nephew had been afraid of the water since he was a timid, nerdy boy, but he looked ridiculous in his crisply pressed slacks with the white straps secured tightly around his waist and groin.

Stanley kept reeling in the line as he watched Marcus grasp the boat seats with his briefcase sliding from under his armpit. Despite hunting and fishing trips, hikes and dirt bikes Stanley had provided over the boy's adolescence, Marcus had never become comfortable in the outdoors. During the few summers when his daughter had visited, Gwen easily outshot, outhiked, and outmanned her older cousin. Stanley couldn't have been prouder. His daughter had fight.

Marcus waved at him, nearly losing his balance as he reached out to climb aboard the taller boat. Stanley had come to accept his nephew's weaknesses only because of his strengths. Marcus had a head for business, and though fearful of some of the darker sides of their activities, he never turned away from anything Stanley asked him to do. He might flinch some or throw up, but the kid wouldn't run from anything. Stanley had to admire such grit, not to mention that the boy had brought the company into profits three times what Stanley had done. That earned Marcus respect, even with a too-small orange life vest tight around his neck.

"Get over here, my boy," Stanley shouted, cinching the reel up another inch as the fish fought far below the surface.

Marcus duck-walked across the boat, holding the railing as he moved while the yacht rocked on the waves.

"Take this a moment. This is what a real fighter feels like," Stanley said.

"I don't want to lose your fish." Marcus set his briefcase onto a cushioned seat. When Stanley shoved the pole in his direction, Marcus took it like a trouper even as he pitched forward from the strength of the fish.

"Hang on with all you've got. You can do this," Stanley said, shouting over the sound of the smaller boat racing away from the yacht.

Marcus struggled, sweat gathering on his upper lip and brow. He tried turning the reel.

"What news do you have for me?" Stanley asked as Marcus strained to keep hold of the fishing pole.

"Well . . . um . . . I . . ."

"Want me to take over?"

"Please," Marcus said, nearly tossing the pole to him.

"Watch this. We'll get you out here next time. Billy, she's coming in," Stanley shouted, and the old man set his pipe down and grabbed up the net again.

Billy leaned over the side of the boat and scooped up the fish that looked to be at least five feet long.

"Will you look at that?" Stanley whooped.

"Is it a shark, or . . . what is that?" Marcus asked, stepping back.

"Bar-ra-cu-da," Stanley said, enunciating each syllable with triumph.

He lifted the fish as it struggled, with Billy holding the other half out of the net. Stanley grabbed a wooden mallet and popped the writhing fish in the head. It stilled immediately. Stanley squeezed its long jaw to show the line of intimidating teeth, then he kissed it smack on its cold, scaly cheek.

"It's good luck to always kiss your kill," he told Marcus.

"O-kay," Marcus said.

Stanley chuckled at the green tint in his nephew's pale face. He'd be over the side any minute. He handed the barracuda to Billy to pop into the fish well with the rest of the catch.

"What have you got for me?" Stanley knew it was time to get down to business before his nephew spent the rest of the fishing trip seasick and worthless to him.

They moved toward the large cabin of the yacht as the boat pitched on the waves. Stanley jumped into the captain's chair, and Marcus pulled an electronic device from his leather briefcase. Stanley loathed all the high-tech gadgets they had these days. He wasn't fully comfortable with a computer, and now they had all these different phones and i-things. But he couldn't ignore their effectiveness as long as someone was around to operate them.

"I put someone on both of them—the former agent and the daughter. She just completed a big case in Boston."

"Yes, the Radcliffe trial."

"Yes, that's it," Marcus said with a surprised expression.

"You aren't my only source of information," Stanley said with a condescending look.

"Agent Waldren contacted her in Boston, and now she's flown to Dallas."

"Interesting." He stared through the captain windows toward the unending line of blue sea. "When was the last time the father and daughter had contact?"

"Before last week, it seems to have been years."

"And none of these people trailing the Waldrens and digging for information can be traced back to us, correct?"

"Absolutely not. I used our affiliate corporation and covered the contact."

"You better be sure of that," Stanley said.

"I am, yes, completely. But should I be watching for something in particular?"

"Just be on the lookout for any connection to me, the family, the company, anything like that. Watch their moves, the people they meet with, and where they go. That's all you need to do or know for the time being."

"All right," Marcus said, biting back an obvious desire to ask more questions and know exactly why Stanley had earmarked a federal prosecutor, a retired FBI agent, and a death row inmate for any activity in the first place.

"So my next move is simply to keep my eyes out there?"

Stanley considered this for a moment. "Yes."

"That's all?" Marcus said.

Stanley knew this surprised his nephew. Marcus had mostly witnessed his uncle act, not wait. But Stanley knew to be wary about this one. After the end of this fishing trip, he'd most likely catch heat from local police. It would die down soon enough, but he needed to proceed with caution. The deaths of a former FBI agent and his federal prosecutor daughter would make an impact. Despite what Marcus believed, there were always risks and links to be wary of. Nothing was ironclad. Not even after decades.

He slapped Marcus on the back hard. "You're doing well. It was a good move to use our affiliate. Keep up with that kind of initiative, it makes me proud."

"Thank you." Marcus pursed his lips and squared his shoulders as he did whenever Stanley doled out praise.

"You're a good . . . man," Stanley said, stopping himself from calling Marcus a kid.

"Did you get to see Gwen?"

"I did. She wouldn't meet with me, but I stopped by her rally to make sure it looked safe enough. I hired her a bodyguard. I've known Lancaster a long time. She'll be in good hands."

"How'd she take that?"

"Doesn't know about it," Stanley said with a laugh.

"That's probably for the best. And . . . the other business. The local news reported this morning on Augustus Arroyo's disappearance."

"That was fast. I guess we better get this wrapped up, and I'll get us back to the marina. We're having fish for dinner." Stanley leaned out of the cabin and yelled to Frank and Billy.

They hurried to one of two long white coolers near the cabin. The two men grabbed the handles at either end and grunted as they slid the cooler down the fiberglass deck to the back of the boat.

Stanley jumped down the stairway to the deck with Marcus following.

"Open 'er up!" Stanley stood with hands on hips as Frank unlatched the cooler and swung the lid open.

Augustus Arroyo was in his pajamas, not the tailored suits and silk kerchiefs he was so proud of wearing. His tanned skin was beet red from the heat of the confined space. He'd vomited, and the stench might have toppled Stanley's stomach if not for the pleasure it brought him. Arroyo squinted in the stark daylight, groaning as he pulled a hand up to cover his face.

"Do you remember what you told me the first time we spoke in person?" Stanley asked him.

Arroyo blinked and stared at him, turning onto his back and adjusting his legs that were surely numb from being compressed in the cooler for hours.

"You said that you would take me down," Stanley said, studying the man for a reaction. "Would you like to say that to me again?"

Arroyo cursed at him, which only made Stanley laugh. They'd been business rivals in South Florida for nearly a decade. Arroyo was powerful, with strong ties in Mexico and South America. But he underestimated Stanley's own ties, and his ruthlessness.

But from the look of him, Arroyo knew when he'd lost. He knew no amount of appeasing, pleading, bribing, or begging would change what was about to happen. It always irked Stanley when someone went down that path, thinking they might save their own life by humiliating themselves. But Arroyo retained his defiance. At least Stanley could respect the man for knowing the stakes, knowing he'd lost and accepting the outcome.

"Billy," Stanley said, taking his eyes from Arroyo to reach for the gun Billy passed him.

Stanley loved the feel of a gun in his hands even more than a fishing rod. He steadied himself against the rocking of the boat. Marcus turned away.

"Kid, you need to watch this," Stanley said firmly.

Arroyo didn't take his eyes off him as Stanley leveled the gun at his forehead. No matter how tough they acted in regular life, most men fell apart in this moment. Stanley found it the ultimate test of courage, and he often made bets with himself over how a man would act when faced with death. He had guessed that Arroyo would break. But the man held himself together.

Stanley pulled the trigger and hit his mark. He shot several more times into the man's chest, then lowered the gun.

"A worthy opponent," Stanley said with satisfaction, blowing the dead man a kiss. Billy brought a camera and took several photographs before Frank closed the lid. They secured the cooler and tossed it into the water, where it bobbed for a few moments until it filled with water from the bullet holes and slowly sank. Then they lifted the other white cooler with Arroyo's dead mistress inside and tossed it overboard as well.

Marcus was bent over the railing, retching his breakfast into the sea.

Stanley put the pistol into his belt and slid a rough arm around his shoulders. "Listen, you'll have to do these things someday. Will you be able to?"

Marcus wiped the edge of his mouth and appeared ready to bend over the railing again. But he swallowed hard and nodded his head.

"I can do it," he said.

Stanley stuck a cigar into his mouth from his shirt pocket.

"Lesson number one. A man always takes care of business. Some things you hire out, but some things you do yourself no matter how dirty your hands get. Do you understand?"

"Yes," Marcus said.

"We'll need to be careful for the next month until this Arroyo business fades away. That's a bit tricky with our other problem, but keep me posted, and if a smart idea comes along, don't hesitate to share it."

Marcus nodded, mumbled an apology, and vomited over the edge again. The boy would probably be there the rest of the day.

Stanley glanced back to the rolling waves as the last of the bubbles rose from the sea where Arroyo and his mistress were dropping far beneath the surface.

Wiping his hands on his pants, he headed toward the helm. He couldn't wait to have a barracuda feast for supper.

CHAPTERSEVEN

Lisa was walking toward the baggage claim when her attention was caught by a sign with her name written on it. The woman holding it jumped and waved, a toothy grin stretched across her face.

"Lisa! Over here! Are you Lisa Waldren?" she called.

"I am," Lisa said as she approached.

"I thought so. You look just like the photos on the news stories I've read."

"And you are . . . ?"

"Oh yes, I'm Rosalyn," the woman said as if Lisa should recognize her. "Your dad will be right back. He was checking to see which carousel your luggage would arrive at."

Lisa tried not to stare at the woman. The night before, she'd left her father a message saying not to pick her up at the airport. When she'd first called to say she was coming, he didn't sound pleased. Then his hesitancy turned to acceptance and planning. He'd pick her up and have her stay with him. Confused by the conversation, it took until after hanging up to realize what she'd agreed to.

In a voice message she had politely stated her change of plans. She'd rent a car and settle into her own hotel before going to the old house.

She hadn't been back "home" since Mom had moved out fifteen years earlier. When she tried to imagine what Dad had done with the place, or most likely, not done, it only brought dread.

"I've heard so much about you," Rosalyn said. She looked to be in her late forties, if that old. She wore lime green horn-rimmed glasses, tall faux leather boots, and a poncho. "Oh, here comes your father."

Lisa spotted him moving through a crowd, scanning the room until he saw Rosalyn waving at him. He wore his usual slacks, polo shirt, and sports coat, but he walked with the gait of an older man, not quite a shuffle, but his confident steps were gone.

"Dad."

"You look healthy," he said. It was a compliment for her father, but Lisa couldn't say the same about him. The lines in his face had deepened, and he had thick bags under his eyes.

They briefly embraced, and he seemed smaller or shorter to her.

"Did you have a good flight?" he asked. He took the satchel from Lisa's shoulder as if she couldn't carry it. "You two already met. Good. I can bring the car up, it's way out in a parking garage." He grumbled at the last part.

"Yes. But I'm supposed to pick up my rental car. Didn't you get my message?"

"What message?" He pulled an antiquated cell phone from his shirt pocket.

Rosalyn set her hand on her hip. "Jimmy, I told you that you have to check that thing every day. See, right there, it shows you have new messages."

"What did it say?" Dad asked Lisa.

"I made reservations for a car and hotel."

"Oh, okay," said Dad, again seeming confused.

"We can still drive you into town. I'm sure the rental agency can bring a car to your hotel." Rosalyn stood between them as if to mediate the situation.

"Sure, all right. Let me get my suitcase." Lisa glanced between Dad and Rosalyn. Was she a sort of caregiver or companion? Dad was obviously capable of living on his own and taking care of himself. She couldn't picture Rosalyn as one of Dad's friends. Her father had buddies, not friends—old men from the Bureau, guys who played poker and went fishing, smoked cigars, talked about the "old days." Maybe Dad had gone through AA and Rosalyn was his sponsor, though Mom had never mentioned that he had a drinking problem.

The luggage was already dumping onto the carousel when they arrived. Rosalyn filled in the awkwardness with constant talking, but Lisa also noticed how her father kept casing out the airport as if looking for someone.

"Your father wanted to leave the car running at the curb. He thinks his retired FBI status should hold sway over Homeland Security."

"It should. I worked for this country for over thirty years. I'm not going to bring a car bomb to the airport."

Rosalyn grabbed Dad's arm. "Don't say that word in here. You know they are listening."

They? The look on her face made Lisa imagine this woman with conspiracy theory publications under her bed and a healthy belief in aliens, maybe even an abduction story in her past by the look of her. What if her dad wasn't as healthy as he seemed and this woman was taking advantage of him?

"Your dad always brags about you," Rosalyn said, sidling up to her.

"Really?" Lisa said, not a bit convinced that this was true. If Rosalyn thought she could be flattered into trusting her, the woman didn't know whom she was dealing with. Lisa had met every kind of person during her years as a federal prosecutor—every kind of liar, con man, charismatic swindler, exaggerator, and thief.

"He clipped every news story about the Radcliffe case. Was really proud of you."

Lisa glanced at Dad to see his reaction, but he just walked toward

the churning carousel as if he didn't hear Rosalyn, which was impossible
with her loud, chatterbox tone. Her father talked so little, especially
compared to this woman, that she wondered how Rosalyn knew anything about him.

"I bought him a scrapbook last year, but he's not great about pasting
things in there properly. Maybe I'll do that for him sometime."

"I'll get the car while your luggage arrives," Dad muttered and hurried off before Lisa could protest being left with Rosalyn.

"He can't stand girl talk," Rosalyn said with a nudge of her elbow.

Lisa watched her father totter off. Again he perused the surroundings, stopping to look back at where she and Rosalyn stood before
hurrying toward the exit. She didn't like the way Rosalyn acted as if she
knew Dad better than Lisa, even if that were true. Everything she knew
about Dad was through a childhood lens or from the disappointed view
of a woman whose father never showed up when she needed him. He'd
attended her husband's funeral but left as soon as it was over. He might
show up here and there to perform the expected duties—walking her
down the aisle, visiting when John was first born, a holiday here and
there. But he left as soon as the duty was done. There was never emotional support, fatherly advice, career guidance, or a shoulder to cry on.

Who was her father? Lisa didn't know.

Rosalyn seemed to have all the answers as she chatted away. Lisa
watched the luggage plummet from the conveyor belt, hoping to see
her bag.

"Your dad will be upset that I told you about the newspaper clips,
but you need to know these things. He'd rather just head to the nearest buffet for dinner and then get straight on to the case. But this is a
perfect opportunity for the two of you to get close again, like when you
were little."

Lisa could feel her heart race as she interrupted the woman. "I'm
sorry if this sounds rude, but . . . who are you?"

Rosalyn stared at her for a moment, then burst out laughing.

"Ah yes, of course. You wouldn't know who I am, since your father
doesn't talk about anything without it being pulled from him like a bad

tooth. We are old friends, I guess you might say. Your dad started out as a consultant for me. I have a small private investigating firm. Cheating spouses, custody cases, missing persons, stuff like that mostly. Here and there I get a case that needs a little expert advice, so I found your father. It started there."

Lisa wanted to ask where "it" had gone from there, but she spotted her suitcase rising up the conveyor belt. As she moved to retrieve it, Rosalyn's laughter returned.

"You probably thought I was some crazy woman. Of course he didn't tell you about me. And there I am with my sign and jabbering to you. That's funny!"

Lisa tossed back a wan smile and grabbed her suitcase. As they headed toward the exit, Rosalyn moved to walk closer and spoke in a low tone.

"Listen, your dad didn't want me to tell you this. But you need to know everything that's going on."

Lisa glanced around, wondering why Rosalyn was suddenly talking so softly. Maybe she was worried that *they* were listening again.

"What is it?"

"This case, digging up the past. There's some danger involved."

"What kind of danger?" Lisa said without drama.

"Someone has been following your father."

"Dad knows this?"

"Yes, of course. And it's true. I'm kind of an expert in these things."

Lisa wanted to laugh. In her line of work, she encountered many such wannabe detectives who set up shop in small local areas, usually former cops who had been fired or never made it beyond traffic duty.

"I've kept a log. It started just about a week after Jimmy received that letter from Leonard Dubois. A car was parked down the street. It would follow your dad when he'd leave, but not in any obvious way."

Lisa nodded as she considered this. Rosalyn wasn't convincing, and the motive didn't make sense. Why would someone put in the time to follow Dad—a retired agent who was practically harmless at this point in life? Why would anyone care that Dad had received a letter from

Dubois, and how would anyone other than those in Dad's life know he had received it? The prison surely censored outgoing and incoming mail, but the letter wouldn't flag anything suspicious. It was simply the plea of a death row inmate trying a last-ditch effort to save his own life.

If Dad was being followed, she doubted that it was related to Leonard Dubois. Maybe it had more to do with one of Rosalyn's little cases—maybe an agitated husband who just happened to leave when Dad left. Rosalyn seemed the type to jump to a lot of conclusions.

"Your father won't want to worry you. He still thinks he should protect you, but you're a big-time lawyer, you can handle this."

"So you think we're all in danger?" Lisa said, trying not to sound as condescending as she felt.

"I'm more concerned about your father's health. Ever since he started this Leonard Dubois case, he's not sleeping, he's having heart palpitations—and you know the doctor already warned him about that."

Lisa couldn't bring herself to admit that she didn't know anything about a doctor's warning.

"That's the real danger. In our line of work there are always risks, but that won't stop us, right?" Rosalyn said with a laugh, leaning side-ways to touch her shoulder to Lisa's as they stood on the curb.

Lisa stared at the cars, wishing to jump back on a plane for Boston. If Drew were there, she just might punch him in the arm. This was his fault.

Lisa had a sudden insatiable yearning for warm sand and a tropical sunset.

She'd give it four days.

CHAPTEREIGHT

Lisa studied the black-and-white photograph of Benjamin Gray's body sprawled out on the city street. He wore an expensive suit and shirt with cuff links, and his necktie appeared neat and tight even though splattered with blood.

His body had collapsed in an awkward position, indicating that Gray was dead before hitting the ground. The pool of blood surrounding his body was smeared with footprints, handprints, and dozens of streaks, most likely from people trying to help the man.

"The detectives would've had a hard time working this crime scene," Lisa said.

She sat back in the dining room chair where she'd had hundreds of meals with her mother, and sometimes her father. Dad usually came home after they'd gone to sleep, and ate from the plate Mom had covered in butcher paper and set in the refrigerator for him.

"Yes, that's a textbook example of a compromised crime scene,"

Rosalyn said, scooting her chair closer to Lisa. "I can't believe I found the pics on the Internet."

"Who posted it?" Lisa asked.

"It's a site for official crime scene photos. It was listed as anonymous."

"We should contact the site for more information. Not many people would have this picture other than the Fort Worth police."

"I already e-mailed them, but we'll see. It might help to have some credentials to encourage their cooperation." Rosalyn smiled at Lisa.

Lisa studied the picture again, wondering why Rosalyn was still here. Half the point of Lisa coming to Dallas was to spend time with her father, not with some strange woman who acted as if she were part of the family. Lisa glanced at Rosalyn's left hand—no ring. So she probably didn't have anyone waiting at home for her.

Dad sat across from them with his hands on the table and appeared lost in his thoughts. His face had gained wrinkles in the years since she last saw him. There was still a gruff strength about him like an aging cowboy, and Lisa wondered about how this case might harm his health.

Lisa's arrival in Dallas had continued in a downward spiral after leaving the airport. The Texas dry heat shocked her. Boston was in full spring, but the sunbaked fields and farmland between the airport and Dallas filled the air with a sense of late summer. Perhaps she had subconsciously hoped she and Dad would have a sudden connection and finally grow close as they put together a case that might free a man before his execution.

Instead, there was the Rosalyn surprise, and then a detached father who insisted on fathering her in his odd way. At Lisa's hotel, Dad and Rosalyn waited for her to check in. Lisa hadn't decided on the number of days she was staying, so she tossed out a number to the woman in guest services.

Lisa noticed Rosalyn's surprise and overheard her less-than-quiet whisper to Dad. "Just four days? What are we going to accomplish in four days?"

Dad made no response, but he insisted on carrying Lisa's luggage to her room instead of using the valet. He wanted to save Lisa the money for a tip, all the while gazing around the hotel as if she'd spent her retirement on the stay.

Rosalyn made the situation worse by gushing over the hotel's marble floors, the shops, and every inch of decor.

"I've only stayed in a place this nice when my aunt married a wealthy guy in Phoenix. I felt like a queen."

"You don't have to rent a car. You can drive the wagon," Dad said, interrupting Rosalyn as they rode the elevator.

"You still have the wagon?" Lisa asked.

"There's no reason to sell it."

"She probably likes having a dependable car," Rosalyn said. She raised her eyebrows with a short shake of her head in warning toward Lisa.

"The wagon is dependable." Dad sounded offended.

"Well, I . . ." Lisa tried to come up with a response Dad couldn't counter. "You know, I don't remember how to drive a stick shift very well. I'm pretty comfortable with the newer vehicles."

Dad seemed to consider that. "The clutch can be a little tricky."

"Then it's settled," Rosalyn said in a satisfied tone as they reached Lisa's room.

Lisa wanted to groan when Rosalyn raced inside with oohs and aahs. "Can I have one of these soaps?" she called from the bathroom.

"Sure," Lisa said.

"Would you like to rest after your flight and start fresh in the morning?" Dad asked and parked her suitcase on the luggage rack in the closet.

"I'd like to get started today if you don't mind," Lisa said, not wanting to stretch out these days in Dallas. The allure of the beach only grew by the moment.

"Then it's off to the Bat Cave," Rosalyn said with a wink, holding up a leaf-shaped bar of soap.

Dad and Rosalyn left Lisa to go ahead to the house, which allowed her time to clear her head. After picking up a rental car near her hotel, Lisa drove to the older suburban neighborhood and then into the driveway of her old house. She stared at the three-bedroom, two-bath home as if gazing into a memory.

The trees in the front yard had grown wider and taller with the front lawn manicured as Dad always had it. The house had been repainted from blue and white to neutral beige with white trim, but otherwise it looked the same.

Rosalyn raced outside to greet her, flapping the photograph of Benjamin Gray's corpse as if it were an invitation to a birthday party.

"I've been doing some digging on the Internet every day, and look what I came up with," she said, pushing the photograph toward her as Lisa grabbed her satchel from the car. Before Lisa could even look around the house, she was ushered to a seat at the table to study it.

But what gain could be found from the old image? Lisa wondered. She glanced at her father, who stared out the front window.

"If this were today, we'd have DNA evidence, fingerprints, footprint casts, security camera footage from various angles. Seems we don't have much more than old photographs and conflicting witness reports," Lisa said.

"If it were today, we'd have dozens of cell phone photos and videos from bystanders," Rosalyn interjected, moving close until her shoulder rested against Lisa's arm. Lisa fought the urge to push the woman away, but moved carefully a few inches over.

"What are you thinking?" Lisa asked Dad.

Dad pushed away from the table. "Why don't we go out to the workshop?"

Lisa followed Dad's lead, but Rosalyn scooped up her purse and turned toward the front door.

"You two enjoy the afternoon in the Bat Cave. I need to run down to my office," she said. Before they barely said good-bye, the woman was gone.

Lisa followed her father through the house, taking everything in. The carpet throughout the living room and hallway was a worn brown, possibly the same carpeting from her childhood. The kitchen looked like a faded, out-of-date version of the house she remembered, with the counters a sixties mustard yellow. It hadn't seemed old-fashioned when she lived here.

Dad held the back door for her as she stepped out. She took in the small fenced yard of her childhood with the detached garage and workshop to the side. Her old swing set had disappeared, but the fort in the huge oak tree remained—though several rungs and boards were missing.

"I haven't had a chance to mow back here lately," Dad said as if in apology.

Lisa wondered about the overgrown lawn dotted with brown spots. During her childhood, Dad had been diligent about tending the yard and keeping his cars clean. His days off were punctuated with the sound of the lawn mower or the hose spraying the walkways and cars.

"Rosalyn was a surprise," Lisa said.

Dad paused and glanced back at her. "I should have told you about her before you came."

"You're her . . . consultant?" Lisa asked pointedly.

"Is that what she said?" Dad gave her a sideways glance.

"That isn't true?"

"It is. But I guess it's more than that now."

"More?"

Dad shrugged. "I don't know. I guess it might seem as if she's my girlfriend. We get along."

Lisa pinched the skin between her eyes where a headache was forming. "So is she your girlfriend or not?"

"Yes, I think so."

Lisa didn't want the details to become more personal, so she dropped the questions that bounced in her head.

Dad unlocked the padlock to the workshop door. He flipped a switch, and rows of fluorescent lights flickered on and brightened as they warmed. Lisa stepped inside to what looked like a secret police headquarters. No wonder Rosalyn called it the Bat Cave. The walls were broken into sections and covered with photographs, diagrams, and notes. The counters no longer housed Dad's organized tools, vise grip, and projects, but were covered with files, stacks of papers and books, and file boxes.

"This is . . . extensive," Lisa said.

Dad's setup reminded her of a museum display compared to her resources or even Drew's studio with its illuminated counters, film equipment, and computers.

This wasn't a normal search for answers. This was an obsession. Lisa knew from her years as a federal prosecutor how a consuming passion could blind people in numerous ways. If Dad's doctor was concerned about stress, this certainly was feeding it.

"I have more to show you in the garage," he said. "I'm trying to re-create the story of what happened. Somewhere in all this, I believe we'll find the real killer and the truth."

Lisa followed Dad to the side door of the workshop that connected to the adjacent garage, and her eyes widened. Where the old wagon had been parked, Dad had set up a reenactment of the crime scene.

The cement floor was outlined with duct tape to depict the streets and angle of turns. Several mannequins stood in the street and off to the sides. Dad pointed out how one mannequin was Benjamin Gray, and behind it, the shape of his corpse was outlined on the garage floor. Red poles with strings attached depicted possible bullet trajectories.

As Dad explained this, Lisa realized that there were mannequins outside of the street line representing her father, herself, and the little black girl sitting beside her when Benjamin Gray was shot.

Dad had brought the copy of the photograph of Gray's corpse. He carried it in front of the man's mannequin, carefully avoiding the bullet poles.

"This is where the photographer was standing."

He stared at the printed photo and the outline on the floor, then off toward the left. Lisa followed his line of sight to the mannequins representing them. On the wall beyond, in the dim light, she noticed a poster-sized image beyond Dad's reenactment. The pixilation in such a large format made the image blurry, but Lisa recognized it as the snapshot of herself and the little girl sitting on the round concrete pillar.

She wondered how many hours Dad had spent out here setting this up, staring at it and studying it from every angle. He might not be as obsessed as he was haunted, she realized, but that was little comfort.

She tried to refocus on what they were here to do. A quick solve would clear out the garage and get the old station wagon where it belonged—she hoped.

"The picture Rosalyn found today was obviously taken at least ten minutes postshooting, probably longer," she said. "There wouldn't be as many prints if the blood was in the initial flow stages. It had to have been taken before police arrived, or else it was a crime photo of theirs. I wonder if paramedics were called. How long did you stay on the scene?"

"I got you out of there almost immediately. That's why I know Dubois wasn't the killer. Let me show you."

Dad took a notepad from a workbench and handed it to her. "These are my notes from that day. You can go over them when you get a chance, but everything I've set up correlates with these."

Lisa flipped through the pad filled with her dad's familiar handwriting and the scribbled diagrams and one-word notes he'd scrawled into the edges. The familiarity brought a desire to cherish his written words, though the sudden feeling also surprised her.

"Benjamin Gray had come up the street with the other marchers." Dad pointed to the street behind the corpse. The road veered from straight to a diagonal toward the left. "He stopped with the others gathering here while the rest of the parade concluded. He would have proceeded that way." He pointed the opposite direction from where Gray had walked. "It's not set up because of course I ran out of room, and it wasn't relevant. But beyond the garage door, that would be the platform where Gray would have given a speech if he hadn't been shot."

Lisa reached for a stool in the corner and pulled it closer to her father before sitting down.

"No, don't sit on that, you're too heavy," Dad said, reaching out for her as Lisa heard a distinct crack. She hopped up and looked at the stool suspiciously.

"Gee thanks, Dad," she said with a wry grin.

"I meant the stool is too weak. Sorry. A few years ago I discovered that my retirement dream of doing woodwork wasn't realistic. I'm terrible. That was one of my failed projects."

"Okay, go on," Lisa said and jumped up on the workbench, then thumbed through Dad's notes.

"When I was taking pictures of you, I had my back to Benjamin Gray. Most people were still looking the opposite direction of him, like the two women in the snapshots I took, watching the remaining marchers coming up the street." Dad walked to the workbench and picked up a stopwatch, then moved in front of the mannequin that represented him.

"Bang!" he shouted and pressed the stopwatch. "I reached you before there was another gunshot. We ducked low, then after the second shot I looked around and saw the person down. I almost ran toward Gray on the ground—instinct from the job—then I grabbed you instead and ran down the alleyway behind us."

Dad took one of the mannequins and ran to the back corner of the garage. He then turned and clicked the stopwatch.

"That's additional time for my explanations," he said.

Lisa was amazed at how having the actual setup of the scene made everything clearer. She'd worked with 3-D computerized renderings that depicted crime scenes, bullet trajectories, and blood splatter, but having the scene surrounding her presented a unique perspective.

"When we reached the end of the alley, I spotted Leonard Dubois being arrested. First off, it's not possible that Leonard Dubois shot Benjamin Gray, then ran past us and around to that alley directly opposite the shooting. He would've had to go right by us. I'd have seen him. But let's say that I didn't. Even then, he couldn't have run down the alley, crossed through the parade, and been arrested in that time period." Dad held up his stopwatch. "It was only around thirty seconds. And the police already had him surrounded."

"What does that mean?" Lisa said.

"Leonard Dubois was already being cornered by police during the shooting. In Dubois's testimony, he said he pulled out his gun when he heard gunfire, and immediately the police surrounded him."

"You think the Fort Worth police were in on this?"

"No, not in on the killing. I really don't believe that, at least I hope not. A lot of evidence was buried, eyewitnesses ignored, and my own inquiries hit a brick wall. But I don't see any reason for the police or anyone besides a fanatic to have killed Benjamin Gray. He was impressive and growing in power but not overly controversial."

"Then the police were already following Leonard Dubois?"

"Yes. I think they were after Dubois for some reason. He was part of early Black Panther groups. I'm not sure what else. But how could the police already have him surrounded in less than a minute? Perhaps he made a convenient killer."

"That makes our job a lot harder, unless we can find a guilt-ridden retired policeman who wants to confess to a cover-up or to smudging evidence. That would get Dubois free without much more effort—if we could prove the conviction was tainted with false evidence and a police conspiracy."

"I have the names of every guy there written in that notepad. Three are dead, one is in a home with Alzheimer's, and that leaves Sergeant Ross. He won't answer my calls."

Lisa knew it was a stretch but made a mental note to do some more digging about Sergeant Ross.

"The real shooter would have escaped in that direction." Dad pointed behind them, the opposite diagonal from where their mannequins were placed and beyond where Benjamin Gray was shot.

"There were fewer marchers that way, plenty of exit routes. A car could've easily been parked on one of the streets beyond here because there weren't parade roadblocks that way. Not only does it not work logistically for the shooter to run in the direction where Leonard Dubois was captured, it makes no sense. He was running *into* the marchers, toward road blockades, and into an even denser population of police officers."

Lisa nodded. "This other direction makes sense. Unless he was a complete imbecile, he would've gone that opposite way. I see in your notes that this is where most of the eyewitnesses said they saw a white man running from the scene?"

"None of those reports was taken seriously by the police."

"Interesting," Lisa mused.

"I want you to see something that I noticed recently." Dad went to a shelf and handed her the two snapshots he'd taken of her and the other girl. These were the originals that Dad had kept in pristine condition for decades. He positioned them in the place of his mannequin, moving it aside.

Lisa hopped down from the edge of the workbench.

"I was taking pictures here." He held up his hands as if holding a camera. In the first image, the white girl, Lisa, was walking up to see the little black girl sitting on the stone round.

"The second photo was taken at the precise moment that I heard the gunfire behind me."

In the second image, the girls sat together and appeared to be looking into the camera as if Dad might have gotten their attention.

"We're both looking at the camera in this one," Lisa said.

"Are you? That's what I thought, but look closer," Dad said. He motioned for her to follow him to the workbench, where he turned on a lighted magnifying glass over the image. Lisa pushed the elbow of the magnifying glass toward the paper. The light illuminated the paper, and Lisa could see the girl's dark eyes.

"Oh, she's not looking at you. Not directly. She's looking behind you."

"Yes," Dad said. "That's what I thought, but with these old eyes, even with two sets of glass on the photo, I couldn't be sure."

"And in that line of sight behind you was Benjamin Gray?"

Lisa walked to the mannequin representing the other little girl and faced Dad. Right beyond Dad and a little over his right side was Benjamin Gray. It was nearly exactly the placement of the shooting.

"The street was crowded with the parade, but that girl was looking in the exact direction of Gray before the shots were fired."

Dad nodded. "We need to find that girl."

"Uh, that should be easy," Lisa said. They had an old photograph of a young black girl in Fort Worth from 1965. How would they ever find her?

"You have people looking at the photo?" Dad asked.

"Yes, a friend of mine. He sent a copy to a forensic photo expert he knows. But I can't imagine that he could find that little girl from these snapshots."

"Maybe they will turn something up," Dad said, studying the layout in the garage again.

"And you don't have the police report or crime scene photographs?" Lisa asked.

"The Fort Worth Police Department was less than helpful, as I said. My boss said it was because of that old grudge against federal officers."

"What's the grudge about?"

"The JFK assassination."

Lisa frowned, trying to catch the connection.

"There was sort of a fight over the still-warm body of our president. Dallas police wanted to keep President Kennedy in Texas. Secret Service, the Feds, Jackie, and the family wanted him out of there. Vice President Johnson needed to get out of Dallas; they were worried about him being killed too. No one knew Oswald was the shooter. It could've been the Communists or Mafia or a government coup. But Jackie wouldn't leave her husband here. It nearly came to blows, and by all rights the jurisdiction was Dallas." Dad chuckled. "But the Secret Service pushed through and loaded the president's coffin into Air Force One, and they got out of there."

Lisa watched Dad, realizing he'd never told her any details about the assassination or his investigation. She only knew the generalities.

"Lyndon Johnson was sworn in as the new president before they left the runway. It was pretty dramatic, from what my old buddies tell me, though of course everyone was in utter shock that President Kennedy was leaving in a coffin after arriving at Love Field only hours earlier. Awful times, those were. But the police in Texas were livid about the move. Not just in Dallas, but Fort Worth, everywhere."

"So they were never cooperative in your investigations afterward?"

"Not very," Dad said with a grimace. "But it was more than being uncooperative when it came to Benjamin Gray's death. They were a roadblock."

The door suddenly creaked open, and Lisa saw her father make an involuntary reach for his belt as if he were armed.

Rosalyn leaned in, looking flustered. "It's the Ripley case. I found out the wife and kids are on the Arizona-Mexico border. I need to get over to the house."

"Need me to help?" Dad asked.

"I can handle it. Unless you want to?"

Dad turned to Lisa. "I've been helping her with this domestic case. Rosalyn was hired to find a wife who cleaned out the couple's bank accounts and took the kids. She crossed state lines, making it a federal offense, but we thought she might make a run back to Mexico where she's from."

"Go ahead, Dad. We'll do this tomorrow. I'm a little tired anyway," Lisa said, though she wasn't. There was a lot to process, and she did that best alone.

"Oh, then get some rest. You'll be all right tonight? I could meet you later for supper?"

"I'll be fine. I'll make some calls, and tomorrow morning I think I'll stop in at the Fort Worth Police Department before coming here," Lisa said.

Dad raised his eyebrows. "That should be interesting."

Lisa smiled. "We'll see if I can get anywhere."

"Good luck," he said, and she caught the doubt heavy in his tone.

Lisa always took doubt as a challenge . . . especially when it came to her father.

CHAPTER NINE

James stood to the side of the window in the darkened dining room and parted the edge of the curtain. Across the street, he could make out the bumper of an automobile. It had parked in that location within minutes of his evening arrival. The foreclosed house where it was parked had been vacant for six months, and few other cars lined Oak Street.

"That's a professional?" James said under his breath. He'd noticed a similar sedan parked near the PI office that afternoon. Yet now, this obvious move could mean they wanted him to know he was being tailed.

Opening the curtain farther, he squinted to make out any details, but night was falling too fast.

The questions remained. Who would be following him? And why?

A vehicle moved down the suburban street, and the headlights flashed over the parked car. The color appeared light, maybe gray or silver. He strained to see more.

The timing was suspicious. They weren't following Rosalyn. The only thing different from his work with her was his digging around in the killing of Benjamin Gray and the Leonard Dubois trial.

Thirty years ago James would've approached the car or sneaked over neighbors' fences until he could get a license, make, and model on the car. It would've been a matter of whether or not he wanted the perpetrator to know he was onto him. Today his considerations included a bum knee, diminished speed, and recent inconsistencies at the shooting range.

The house phone rang, piercing the quiet. James moved along the wall as he hurried to grab the kitchen phone.

Rosalyn sounded out of breath and jumped right into talking before he'd barely said hello. She was probably hurrying to her car or popping into the office and had called him as she raced around. The woman had more energy than he'd had as a teenager.

"Can you believe we got her? I'm so thrilled! If she'd crossed that border, Matt would've never seen those kids again. They just found her loser cousin hidden inside the car—he was trying to get through the border with them. Who has trouble getting *into* Mexico?"

"You did good work," James said. He flipped on the kitchen light, pulling out the phone cord as he took a bottle from a grocery bag on the counter and put it into the refrigerator.

"We did good work."

"I barely contributed. I'm giving you the credit for this one, so take it."

James could actually hear her smile through the line.

"Well, tonight deserves champagne either way," she said in that silky tone she only used on certain occasions. James felt his ole ticker pick up a few beats.

"I just put some into the refrigerator," he said with a chuckle. What this woman saw in him, he didn't understand. He kept expecting her to grow tired of him, move on, open her eyes, get her head examined. But as long as she was around, James would try to enjoy it.

"Should I grab some takeout from Giovanni's?" she asked. He heard the ping of her car door opening.

"Got that too," he said. He'd bought enough at Giovanni's for three, on the off chance that Lisa would still be at the house when he arrived. As expected, his daughter was gone, but he held a slight hope that she'd change her mind and move her luggage from that ridiculously opulent hotel to her old room down the hall.

"Jimmy Waldren, I am impressed. I'm on my way now."

As happy as Rosalyn sounded, perhaps he was glad his daughter wouldn't be staying at the house tonight. His eyes swept the room for one of those fancy candles Rosalyn had brought over on a night she'd cooked for him and stayed over.

"Great," he said, then suddenly remembered the vehicle outside. Another thought occurred to him—what if the house was bugged? "Wait, will you bring home that little computerized thing that we used in the Brickman case? You know what I'm talking about, right?"

Rosalyn was silent for a moment. "Yes, I know exactly what you're talking about."

"And be careful driving home. There was an accident pretty close to the house," James said.

"So you believe me now . . . that the roads are dangerous out there?" she said. James knew she understood perfectly.

"I should never doubt you."

"You know, most women wouldn't find it at all romantic to have work suddenly ruining the moment."

"Did I ruin the moment?"

"Of course not. It makes it even more romantic to me."

James laughed loudly. "Of course. I am a lucky man."

"You're trying to get lucky," she said, laughing with him. "And it's working. I'll see you in thirty minutes."

James hung up the phone and shook his head at himself. Special Agent James Waldren searching for candles, chilling champagne, and shamelessly flirting with a younger woman? His buddies would fall off their chairs laughing. And yet the thought of that car parked across the street brought an old fear creeping over him. He was getting too close to Rosalyn. And his daughter was back in his life, even if only for four days or so. No one was in danger when he kept those he loved at arm's length.

He reached into a high cabinet over the stove and pulled down a pistol and box of bullets. After loading the gun, he opened a drawer in a more strategic location close to the kitchen entrance. Two long candles rolled toward him.

James pulled out the candles and placed the gun inside. This could all be a chance to finally get things right—or an enormous mistake.

CHAPTER TEN

I have an appointment with Detective Newcomb. I'm Lisa Waldren," Lisa said to the woman at the intake desk. From her wallet, she pulled out her "Fed Creds" and slid the ID badge through an opening at the bottom of the wall of bulletproof glass that separated them.

The receptionist looked at the federal badge, then up to Lisa and raised a penciled eyebrow.

"I'll let him know. You can wait there," she said as she slid the badge back through the slot with a red fingernail.

Lisa sat two seats down from a woman holding an ice pack against her forehead and talking in rapid Spanish into her cell phone. Lisa opened her satchel and pulled out her iPad to check her e-mail while she waited.

A moment later an older man in a white shirt and black tie opened a door to the side of the room.

"You must be Miss Waldren," the detective said with a wide grin. "Come on back to my desk. This is quite a pleasure."

"Thank you," Lisa said, following him inside and choosing to ignore the "Miss Waldren." She'd worn a skirt and jacket for this meeting, and her heels joined in the cacophony of voices and sounds along the tile hallway that appeared to be the main vein into the station. The detective turned at the elevator and motioned her inside.

"I did a little search on you after we talked this morning. Congratulations on that Radcliffe trial. They've got your picture and name all over the Internet." Newcomb pushed the button for the third floor.

"It was a relief to win. He hurt a lot of people. And my search on you showed an impressive record of arrests," Lisa said with a touch of her old Texas accent leaking through.

"I do what I can. Surprised me, though—such a pretty thing like you being a federal prosecutor?"

Lisa shrugged and smiled as if this too were a compliment. "I am, and enjoy my job."

"Cold up there in Boston, but great seafood. My brother lived there for a time, but it was too wet and dreary for me. Not enough open spaces."

"It's different from Texas, that's for sure."

The elevator doors opened, and Lisa followed his lead down the hall.

"I bet you miss living here with those awful Boston accents and bad manners. No hospitality to be found in cold New England."

They walked past a row of small rooms with windows exposing interiors that held only a table and chairs. Inside one, an interrogation appeared to be in progress.

"I miss some things out here," she said and hoped he didn't ask her what those things were. She'd made a home in Boston, and Dallas seemed so long ago and with enough bad memories to make it hard to remember the best parts.

Newcomb entered a large room packed with desks and people.

"Right over here," he said, motioning to a desk by a large window. Lisa caught him looking her up and down as she pulled up the chair by his desk. He then grinned at another detective a desk over.

"Now what's this all about again? You're helping your father out on a book he's writing? He's former FBI, you say?"

"My father is retired now. He was assigned the Dallas/Fort Worth region in the sixties. In his retirement he's going over old cases, putting together his memories. It's kind of a pet project. With the Radcliffe case over, I came out for a visit and got recruited to help with some research. It might make a memoir, I'm not sure." Lisa didn't want to use Rosalyn's idea, but it was a good excuse to poke around for answers. The truth was, her father could write a great memoir, and maybe he would when this was over.

"Everybody seems to be self-publishing these days. But the sixties were tough times, especially 'round here."

"I'm sure. But my father has a pretty interesting past, with his investigations after the JFK assassination."

"Ah, yes, that. Was he on duty that day?" Newcomb drummed his fingers on the desk.

"No, he was moved here immediately after and did a lot of interviewing around Oswald, his wife and friends. Things like that."

"So what are you looking for specifically? I think the JFK thing has been done and overdone. And of course that was Dallas, and this is Fort Worth."

"My father is missing information on an event that happened a little over a year later. But he needs to fill in some holes. He gave me these old photos." Lisa pulled the parade snapshots from her satchel and pointed to herself in the photograph. "That's me."

"Cute, and I wouldn't have mistaken you for the other," Newcomb said with a loud chuckle.

"This was a civil rights march here in Fort Worth. These pictures were taken right before a man was gunned down about ten yards away. Dad has a lot of information about other events and investigations in the sixties, but not this one. You guys had jurisdiction, so I hoped you might help me dig up a little more for him." Lisa smiled graciously, hoping a little Southern charm and asking for assistance might stir his sense of chivalry.

"The shooting was here in Fort Worth?" Detective Newcomb pulled the photographs closer.

"Yes, in April of 1965. I know that's way before your time," Lisa said. "But if there are any old case files?"

"Yeah, I joined in the late seventies. But there are a lot of local retired PDs still around. Not sure if any would remember this case, though."

"Where are old crime reports stored?"

"We keep our archives right here. And you're sure it was this station that responded and did the investigating?"

"Yes. I believe it was under Sergeant Ross's command. Would it be possible for me to get a copy of the report? And if you have names of anyone who might talk to me . . . I'm not in town long, but I'd really like to do what I can for Daddy." Lisa never used the word *Daddy* in reference to her father, but the subtle damsel-in-need act seemed to be working.

"I can't see why not. Even though this is personal, not criminal, I'm always happy to help out a fellow servant of the law. Especially a female one." He winked.

"I would really appreciate it," Lisa said, grinding her back teeth together. Newcomb would never get away with treating her this way if they were on a real investigation, or not in the South.

"With that smile, how could I refuse?" he said.

Lisa heard a low chuckle from the detective a desk over.

Newcomb escorted Lisa back to the elevator and down to the basement while telling her about a recent murder investigation he'd solved.

"Hey, Gertz, I've brought you some company," Newcomb called out. He punched in a code to unlock the security gate and strode up to a young man who appeared attached to the computer on his desk.

When Gertz saw Lisa, his face turned bright red and he fumbled with his round Harry Potter–style glasses.

"She's a federal prosecutor up in Boston," Newcomb said as if she were the first female president.

"Hello, nice to meet you," Gertz said, stammering. "I don't get many visitors down this way." He hopped up and smoothed his tie, smearing a yellow streak down the front. A hot dog sat half eaten beside the computer on the desk.

"We keep Gertz locked down here to make sure the computer network keeps running and to protect and catalog our archives." Newcomb spoke about the other man with all the respect of a high school athlete's admiration of the class nerd.

He gave Gertz an abbreviated version of Lisa's mission, ending with the request for old case files.

"That should be easy," Gertz said. He rubbed the top of his computer screen as if it possessed a genie. "About two years ago we went through and cataloged everything. We created key words to make searches easy. We've had several cold cases solved because of it. For example, if I put the details of a murder into the database, then if we have a killing with similar clues, the computer will pick that up and might lead us to the killer. We solved a serial rapist and a string of B and Es that way."

Detective Newcomb's phone at his waistband buzzed. After a quick look at the screen, he said, "Unfortunately I must leave you in the hands of Gertz here. I'm needed upstairs."

"I appreciate all the help," Lisa said.

"And if I can assist you further, Miss Waldren, we can meet for a drink after my shift." Newcomb smiled and set a business card on the desk. He grabbed a pen and wrote an additional number on the back.

"My cell number," he said, and raised his eyebrows.

"Thank you, I appreciate it," she said as if innocent of his motives. It wouldn't hurt to keep the detective as a future reference, but Lisa saw much more potential in Gertz.

Newcomb disappeared down the hall, and Lisa took a chair by Gertz's desk. "Your database system sounds extensive. Is it linked with other agencies?"

"It certainly is. We've cataloged back into the early 1900s, and we're linked into a national database. Just give me some words or names, and I'll show you."

"How about Benjamin Gray? And my father, James Waldren?"

"Do you have a year to narrow the search?" Gertz said with his fingers on the keyboard.

"Nineteen sixty-five, and the surrounding years." Lisa wanted to peer around and see the screen, but she kept herself seated in the chair to the side of the desk.

"Got some hits," Gertz said, leaning forward to peer closer.

"What did you find?" Lisa said, trying not to leap up and see for herself.

"We have one report that includes all three of those words—the two names and the year. Then several other reports with one of those names."

"Can I see the reports? Or do I need some kind of clearance?"

"Federal prosecutor, I think we can stretch the rules for you."

Lisa could feel her heart rate increase as it did whenever she was on the cusp of a breakthrough.

"We have other files that include Benjamin Gray. From 1964, not 1965."

Lisa wondered why the Fort Worth police would have something on Gray before the civil rights march.

"I'll take any info you have. What about Leonard Dubois?"

Gertz typed again. "Yep. Here's a closed case, solved April 1965."

"That's when Gray was killed. Dubois was convicted. Can you print me out the police report on that?"

"Sure can." Gertz leaned close to the screen again. "There's another closed case as well."

"For Leonard Dubois?"

"Yes, but the file itself is missing from what I can tell. There are no pages included."

Lisa wondered if her father knew Leonard Dubois had been attached to another criminal case.

"Does it say anything about the crime?"

"Nope. When we entered the files into the database, we had numerous old cases where the cover sheets were around but the rest of the file was missing. We entered the information we had to keep a record, but there wasn't much data to attach to them. I debated including the cover sheets at all but figured it was better than nothing."

Lisa had encountered the disappearance of police files before due to negligence, and it often smelled of deception.

"Where are the originals? The actual cover sheets and all the other case files."

"Buried around here, but I can get them. I'll need more time. A few days maybe. We scanned everything paper in each case file and photographed nonpaper evidence."

"Copies of what you found would be perfect for now. If it's not enough, I'll come back and check out the originals."

Gertz tapped at the keys until the hum of a large printer started. He crossed his small hands on his stomach as the printing began.

"You know, Newcomb might not be the best detective to work with if you need some help. He's okay, but a tad shady, if you ask me. I can tell you the good men and women who might help you more . . . like Ole Sweeney. He knows everything about this place—the good and the bad."

"He's a detective?" Lisa asked, jotting down the name into her iPad.

"Oh no, not Sweeney. He worked archives for more decades than I've been alive. We worked together awhile down here, but the new computer system was his final straw in going into retirement."

"How could he help me?" Lisa asked.

"He was a walking encyclopedia . . . but he's one of those conspiracy theory–type guys. He'd tell me stories about several of the cops who'd left before I came, and boy, those were some stories. Lots of sixties and seventies stuff. Weren't for his pension, he would've left years earlier. If upstairs had known what he really thought of them, he'd have been canned long ago." Gertz chuckled.

"He sounds interesting."

"I'll have to call him. He doesn't have e-mail or a phone for text messages. But I'm sure he'd talk to you. He loves to talk, that Sweeney."

"I really appreciate all of this," Lisa said with a grateful smile. Sometimes her investigations were like this, a line of bread crumbs she followed till something or someone valuable came along.

Gertz's eyes jumped to her. "Uh-oh," he said.

"What's wrong?"

He pushed back from his chair and hurried to the large printer spitting out papers.

"Guess somebody upstairs doesn't like these searches, or else the news of you being here made it to the wrong person. They're asking me to send you back up and to suspend any archive digging." He grabbed a large pile of papers from the printer and dropped it onto the desk. "I'll say you already left."

"Thank you, and please have Sweeney call me." She set her card on the desk beside Newcomb's.

"Take the stairs. You'll come out at the parking lot. Send a thank-you note to Newcomb to make it look like you didn't get anything. It'll all quiet down."

"I'll do it. I really appreciate this." Lisa picked up the warm pile of papers and her satchel.

"It gets boring down here. I haven't had this much excitement in months." Gertz glanced at his computer again. "But you better hurry."

CHAPTERELEVEN

Stanley leaned back in his office chair, swiveling to catch the view of the wide Atlantic blue before returning his attention to the other man in the room.

Miami's finest, Detective Martin, perused the shelves on his office wall, then studied the spear gun and the mounted sawfish hanging overhead. The detective wore a sports coat a size too large and baggy slacks. Perhaps he'd recently lost weight, Stanley mused.

"Did you and Augustus Arroyo ever go out in your boat? Or should I call it a yacht?" the detective said, leaning close to inspect photographs of Stanley's favorite fishing trips. He remained at the newest one, placed there just that morning—a photograph of Stanley holding a five-foot barracuda.

"Arroyo and I weren't friends. And I haven't seen him in several months, as I already stated." Stanley stretched his arms behind his head.

"Yes, at a charity event for the Miami Art Museum. Witnesses say that you reached out to shake hands, but he refused. His wife threw her drink in your face, isn't that correct?" Detective Martin turned from the wall and moved around the room with an occasional glance in Stanley's direction.

"It wasn't the first drink I've had thrown in my face. She also slapped me—also not the first," Stanley said. He chuckled, recalling the look on Candace Arroyo's face. "I called her by the name of Arroyo's mistress. That bought the drink. Then I asked why he hadn't brought Natasha. She is much more fun than Mrs. Arroyo. That landed the slap."

"You knew Arroyo's mistress, Natasha Marquez?" The detective sounded as if this were new information to him. The guy was crafty.

"I make it my business to know as many people as possible."

"How well did you know her?"

"I don't know her well, and why are you referring to her in the past tense?" Stanley leaned forward as if suddenly engaged. He knew Natasha was dead, of course. He'd watched the ice cooler with her body disappear beneath the sea beside Arroyo's own plastic coffin.

"We believe Natasha may be deceased."

Stanley frowned and stared at his hands. "This is disturbing news. What happened?"

"Your company will profit greatly if Arroyo is out of the picture. The bid for the Hacienda Highland development and shopping center was down to the choice between you two, among other projects."

Stanley shrugged. "I would've profited a lot more before the economic crash if Arroyo were out of the picture, but I like a good rival. Keeps a man on his toes. But I hope it isn't true about Natasha. She was a gorgeous woman."

"Did the two of you ever have a relationship?"

"We've been in the same circles for many years, but I didn't know her personally," Stanley said.

Natasha had been a high-class whore with a very selective and private clientele. The detective wouldn't know this. That information was above his pay grade, so to speak. Natasha's role had evolved as she became Arroyo's mistress for the past five years exclusively—well, almost exclusively. Stanley knew enough of her past to make a call now and then. But during their last encounter, he had sensed her deep affection for Arroyo and a shift in loyalty toward his adversary. Natasha wanted to bargain for her freedom, and his silence.

She had done the unforgivable. She'd fallen in love with Arroyo.

Stanley wasn't sure why that had enraged him. He hadn't loved Natasha. It was business, nothing more. She provided the services he purchased just like the other women. She'd been a willing participant in getting close to Arroyo. The consummate professional, like he was. Or so he'd believed.

Detective Martin didn't consult notes or write anything down. He was the lead investigator in the search for the missing businessman, and Stanley still hadn't obtained the reason the search had begun so quickly. They should've had a few more days before Arroyo was officially listed as missing.

"You aren't married." It was a statement, not a question.

"Divorced. Learned my lesson." Stanley yawned.

"Girlfriend, dating anyone?"

"Here and there. Nothing serious. Why?"

"Just putting pieces together."

Stanley looked at his watch. "I want to help. Maybe I don't have the facts, obviously, but this is the second time I've been questioned today. Everyone says that Arroyo is missing. What makes you certain? And what has it got to do with me?"

"We found blood."

"Whose blood? Arroyo's blood? Natasha's?"

"Perhaps."

Stanley knew they hadn't found any of Arroyo's blood at his house. They'd certainly found plenty of blood residue, but that would be Natasha's. With Arroyo's wife visiting her sister in Greece, Natasha was staying at his estate as she always did when the wife was gone. Her blood had been cleaned up, with enough left in the cracks and grout of the tile floor to appear as if someone had hastily wiped it down. The assumption would be that Arroyo killed Natasha and then disappeared.

Stanley pushed back from the large desk.

"I'm sorry, but I have a meeting with my board in several minutes. Can I answer anything else before I go?"

"Are you taking any trips in the near future, like the one you just took to Missouri, or the fishing trip out into international waters?" Detective Martin studied Stanley as he spoke.

Stanley's nerves immediately turned cold. He had flown his private plane to Missouri to keep his trip under the radar. The last thing he needed was to infuriate Gwen further with his unwanted visit to her campaign rally. And why the mention of his fishing trip?

"I don't have anything planned. Are you asking me to keep you posted or for me to stick around? Am I a suspect in something?" Stanley frowned as if disturbed, and in actuality he was disturbed that he had heat from local police this fast.

"We have numerous persons of interest."

"I'm a person of interest?"

"Not officially."

Stanley and Detective Martin stared at one another, the two men sizing each other up like two bulls deciding if one would charge. Stanley's phone buzzed, breaking the stare down.

"That's my meeting. They'll be looking for me." Stanley raised the phone. "If you have more questions, arrange it with my assistant."

He didn't wait for the detective to respond, but simply walked out. It was somewhat disconcerting having the man still in his office, but Stanley knew nothing could be found there.

Inside the large conference room, only Marcus waited. He turned off the intercom that had allowed his nephew to listen in.

"What could he know?" Marcus asked.

"Nothing. He's probing. Remember, too, it's not what he knows, it's what he can prove. But we're fine right now. We need to watch our step with that other situation," Stanley said.

"The daughter is in Dallas, staying at a downtown hotel. She pulled some old files from Fort Worth PD."

"Interesting. It might be time to distract them," Stanley said. He considered various scenarios.

"I have ideas," Marcus said.

Stanley clenched his jaw, annoyed with his nephew's please-be-proud-of-me tone. He studied his nephew and spoke in a tone that held just a hint of menace. "This may not be the best time, but I do admire initiative. What are you thinking?"

"I'm not sure yet. But are you going to explain what this FBI agent and his federal prosecutor daughter are looking into, and how it relates to that guy on death row?"

Stanley walked to the door. "It has to do with a young man not thinking things through. Just keep the updates coming."

CHAPTERTWELVE

"You're Waldren's kid?" the man asked as he squeezed into the booth across from Lisa. He reminded her of a hardened rancher with his cowboy hat and flannel shirt—not a retired police department employee who'd spent years in the basement of the station.

"Yes, I'm Lisa Waldren. You're Walter Sweeney?" She put out her hand. His grasp was firm, and he studied her with his dark eyes. "Is this the right booth?"

"Sure is." Sweeney's eyes went to the doorway and line of windows they could view from their nearly hidden location at the back corner.

Sweeney had called within hours of her quick departure from the Fort Worth Police Department. She'd stopped back at her hotel to read through the copies Gertz had printed when the call came in. Sweeney said he could meet her right away, at this diner in Fort Worth, and then he gave directions as to where to sit.

On her second drive to Fort Worth that day, Lisa called her father. She was running down a lead and wouldn't be at the house until much later, she told him. Rosalyn's voice came from the background, volunteering to make dinner for all of them.

"Do you know my father?" Lisa asked Sweeney. She studied his movements, the way he clenched his large hands together and how he glanced toward the door and windows every few seconds.

"Not personally. But I know every file in the basement of that police station from the late fifties through the eighties. And Waldren's kid became a big-time federal prosecutor?"

The waitress arrived, saving Lisa from responding. She hated off-the-cuff comments about her career as if she'd magically attained "big-time" status.

"What can I get you, darlin'?" the waitress asked, paper tablet and pen ready for Lisa's order.

"They have great chili," Sweeney said.

"I'll just have tea," Lisa said. The Texas heat outside and the overbearing scent of cooking grease in the diner had sent her appetite packing. The waitress's smile dropped to a frown. "I have dinner plans in a few hours."

"I'll take coffee and the special with extra onions," Sweeney said.

"You got it, hon." The waitress moved on to another table.

Sweeney settled against the back of the cushion and stared at Lisa. "You're looking at information about the Benjamin Gray killing?"

"Yes. My father and I were at that civil rights parade in 1965 when Gray was shot. I was very young."

"You must have been. Gertz told me about you asking for old cases, but not that you were at the parade. Interesting, all this. So you and your dad are working on a memoir at the exact time when the convicted killer of Benjamin Gray is set for execution."

"Something like that."

The waitress returned and set a tall glass of iced tea on the table and a cup of coffee in front of Sweeney. Lisa had meant hot tea, but she didn't correct the mistake.

"Okay," Sweeney said. "Less I know, the better, I suppose. You can't be too careful nowadays."

"That's true."

Lisa's years of interviewing every personality type gave her good instincts for getting the information she needed. Most people were easy to read, others offered a challenge she couldn't help but enjoy trying to decipher. She worked on a strategy to talk to Sweeney without making him suspicious. She'd drive him away if she wasn't careful. He appeared to be the usual somewhat grudging former employee who hadn't found the happiness in retirement he'd expected.

"I appreciate you meeting me," she said, folding her hands around the tall, sweating glass of tea.

"Got me curious. Not every day that someone digs up old cases either cold or closed. There'd be a lot to discover if someone did a bit more of that."

"I can imagine. Gertz implied that you didn't especially approve of everything at your station."

"You mean Gertz said I thought the cops were dirty?"

"He didn't go that far."

Sweeney pressed his fingers together, stretching them out. "They're not all bad, never were. Some real good guys there, actually. But it takes just a couple to create all kinds of problems. You want me to tell you about the Gray case?"

"If you would, yes."

"Benjamin Gray." Sweeney dipped a spoon into his coffee, then opened a container of cream and dumped it in, followed by four other packets. "First I want to know something. Why'd your dad back off this thing all those years ago?"

"What do you mean?" Lisa asked.

"He was on this case for a while. Ticked off more than a few cops. I'm surprised you got through the door over there, but then, guess the years have changed everything. I watched it with interest, wondering what a suit might find out. Then suddenly he stopped pushing, stopped cold, it seemed."

"When was this?"

Sweeney frowned in thought. "Maybe a year or two after it happened, '66 or '67."

Lisa tried recalling the events of that time. She'd started kindergarten with Mrs. Palmer, one of her favorite teachers. Lisa had loved school and her ballet classes that began when she was five. Mom was the predominant memory at that age, as if Dad had disappeared. Later Mom would give excuses for his missing performances and her school's open house. "Dad works very hard," she would say.

"That's something I don't know," Lisa said. "It's not like my father at all."

Sweeney nodded. "Guess that makes sense. Okay then, what I know about the Benjamin Gray case . . ."

The waitress set a giant bowl of chili piled with onions on the table. Lisa settled in to wait for Sweeney to continue. She took a sip of her tea and grimaced from the shock of syrupy sweetness.

Sweeney ate while he talked, taking big bites of chili. "There were a lot of rumors about the arrest of that Dubois. They didn't really run down the other leads."

"What leads?"

"I can't fully remember at the moment. There were witnesses, conflicting ones, and some people in the civil rights movement who didn't like Gray's ideas, and some rumors about a white girlfriend. Those kinds of leads."

"Do you think the cops were involved?"

"In the killing?"

Lisa didn't answer. She wanted Sweeney to give his thoughts.

"No, our local guys weren't involved in the killing. They might have been involved in a cover-up, I can believe that. But the focus seemed on Dubois, not on Gray."

"What do you mean?"

Sweeney wiped his mouth, then took a long look along the windows before he continued. "If Dubois wasn't the shooter, he also wasn't just some bystander who got picked up by mistake. They were watching him. I think it was convenient timing."

Leonard Dubois, a target before the shooting? Based on what evidence? From what Sweeney said, it was all rumors that had trickled down to the guy in the basement. But Dad, too, had mentioned suspicions about the Fort Worth PD.

"So who do you think killed Benjamin Gray?"

Sweeney pursed his lips. "That, I do not know. But not someone from Gray's camp. The authorities would've opened that up right away. Any chance to discredit the blacks, the PD would've been all over that. My guess, someone high up was involved. Someone high enough to influence a good police chief to stop questioning the actions of two dirty cops. Maybe a government hit."

Sweeney had her interested until he mentioned government hit.

"And what do you think happened to JFK?" Lisa asked, throwing that out to see how he'd respond.

"I'm sure your father told you it was Lee Harvey Oswald. But it was undoubtedly a conspiracy."

Lisa considered leaving right then, but there were many respectable people who believed in a JFK conspiracy. And Sweeney had brought up questions she didn't have answers for.

"In the Gray case, is there evidence that can prove any of this?"

"Most is gone now." Sweeney stared at two men who had entered the diner. The waitress waved them down to a booth far from them. Sweeney smiled and gave a slight nod to her. So he was a regular here, Lisa realized. And the waitress knew Sweeney and had either bought into his suspicions or was paid a good enough tip to follow along.

"Where'd the evidence go?" Lisa asked as Sweeney returned to his chili bowl.

"Mostly destroyed. There were interviews, evidence from the scene, things like that. Destroyed by a fire in 1967, but strangely many of the cover letters survived the flames."

"So there wasn't a fire?"

"There was. But I lived a quarter of my life down there. The electrical wasn't faulty, but that's what got the blame. And I never saw much damage. I left on Friday night, and Monday morning the place was cleaned up and reorganized with missing evidence and files."

"So all the evidence is gone?"

"A lot of it. But I kept a notebook. Went over it before we met today to refresh my memory. It's in a safe place, but not going to help you. It's notes from a man who believes the government is after him." Sweeney laughed and scraped the bottom of his bowl for the last bite.

Lisa nodded and took another sip of tea. Sweeney interested her. The fact that he was self-aware made him more believable. It was the ones unaware of their neuroses who were most dangerous.

"My dad mentioned that a Sergeant Ross was at the scene of Leonard Dubois's arrest, but the officer always shut my father down when he tried to talk to him about it. Even today, the man won't return Dad's calls."

"I saw in my notes that Sergeant Ross was there. But I don't have an answer for you. Ross seemed like a good one. I never questioned his cases, except for that one. He ran things by the book most of the time."

"I've known good people, cops included, who've done bad things. Usually there's something behind it. Something to justify the deed."

Lisa remembered one of her first cases where she convicted a female DEA agent of stealing money from a drug bust. The woman had made a desperate move because of her three kids at home, one with disabilities, and a deadbeat husband who had drained their bank accounts. These were the cases Lisa didn't cheer winning.

"I can't help you there. What are you and your father up to? If I didn't know better, I'd think you were trying to get Dubois off."

"We're trying to get to the truth. My father was there, with me. I don't know why he's waited this long, but it's important to him to answer these questions, I guess."

Sweeney set his elbows on the table and stared at her with his intense dark eyes.

"You know that happens with us old-timers. We start going over it all. We try making sense of our lives, and the mistakes haunt us. It's a good thing you're helping him. I never had me any kids. Good thing he's got you."

Lisa couldn't help but smile. "We haven't been all that close over the years."

"You're here now. That matters." Sweeney pushed the empty bowl away from him. "I'd look into people high up who might benefit from Gray's death, who might have wanted him dead. Maybe in Texas or even as high up as DC. But I'd start by talking to your father. He didn't drop this for nothing."

CHAPTER THIRTEEN

Instead of driving straight to her father's house, Lisa returned to the solitude of her hotel room. The day was waning, its events coursing heavily through her body. She needed time to process before confronting her father, without Rosalyn's incessant chatter.

But the stagnant room didn't bring solace. Lisa did several searches, sent off some e-mail queries—calling in favors to get information—and read through some of the papers she'd obtained from Gertz. As she processed the case, she paced the floor, and the walls closed in. She stood for a time at the window staring at the landscape of high-rises and office buildings, then listened to her voice mail, skimmed e-mail, and scanned her text messages. A text from Drew popped out.

Need some info, call when you can.

Lisa stared at each word, seeking for any hidden meaning. After their awkward parting, the sting of his words hadn't been alleviated. Yet he was her favorite person to talk to. She hadn't realized how deeply engrained their habit of sharing their current happenings was until she'd left for Dallas. Not a week had passed without their talking in the year since he'd settled in Boston. The fact was, just two days in Dallas and she missed him. How could she get things back to good with him?

Finally, she pulled on her running shoes and headed down to the hotel lobby.

"Can you recommend a good loop for a run?" she asked the concierge.

"A run? Oh, of course," he said, taking in her exercise clothes. People were more apt to be seeking restaurant and nightlife bookings at this time of day, so Lisa couldn't blame the guy for a moment of confusion.

"Just a few miles or so." Lisa didn't particularly enjoy running, but she needed to unwind her thoughts. The Radcliffe trial had put her in better shape than she'd been in since law school.

The concierge pulled out a city map and highlighted a circular route that would avoid the worst of the evening traffic. The map helped Lisa recall the layout of the city—she'd been away a long time.

She stepped outside the hotel, surprised at the heat still coming off the streets. She tied her light jacket around her waist.

After stretching for a few minutes, she took off at a slow pace down the street dotted with pedestrians. Streetlights flickered on as the sun dipped low toward the horizon and dodged behind high-rise buildings. She caught the scent of honeysuckle as she started running, and the smell mixed with the warm Texan evening reminded her of her teen years on the track team when she'd felt strong and fast. Now her doctor recommended walking with her worn knees. A steady jog was her compromise.

To the rhythm of her feet on the concrete streets, Lisa moved through the information she'd obtained today.

Who exactly didn't want her digging around the archives at the Fort Worth PD? Why would it matter to them after all these years? In her searches, she hadn't found anything incriminating about Sergeant Ross, so why was he so uncooperative toward Dad? Was Sweeney a reliable source or a complete head case? What kind of power could influence the police and DA to convict Leonard Dubois to death row for a murder he didn't commit? There were dirty cops, but this was something much bigger. This went against the deepest ethical codes they were sworn to uphold. It also was more than a moral issue; it threatened every person involved with criminal prosecution. Why would they take such a risk?

Lisa jogged in place as a traffic light changed, then moved forward and down the block of older brick buildings. She caught a whiff of a steak house as she passed people sitting outside drinking beer and eating dinner. Her thoughts moved to Leonard Dubois. If he wasn't the shooter, there had to be a reason that Dubois was targeted. His past might offer some answers.

She came to the harder questions she needed extra courage to ask. Why had Dad stopped pursuing answers in the Benjamin Gray case back in the midsixties? Why had he taken her to the rally in the first place?

Lisa could cross-examine suspects of a crime, but interrogating Dad was a different animal. He'd know instantly what she was doing if she tried a manipulative approach. Dad knew how to get information from people. Lisa didn't delude herself into thinking she was better than he was in that area. A straight-out confrontation could be her only course of action.

At the sign for Houston Street, Lisa stopped. She stared up at it as several businessmen and a family with a baby stroller swept around her. She looked up and down the block, gaining her bearings as she took in the park, a reflection pool, and a brick building at the end of the street.

The sixth-floor window at the end closest to her street was significant. The lawn beyond the building and small rise were often called "the grassy knoll."

Lisa's jog turned into a walk as she approached the building of the former Texas School Book Depository. The sixth floor was now a museum that told the story of President John F. Kennedy's final moments of life on November 22, 1963. From that window, Lee Harvey Oswald pointed his rifle and made the fateful shots.

Lisa had only been here on a school field trip, and when Dad had brought her to one of the anniversaries of President Kennedy's death.

Now the scent of freshly cut grass followed her as she moved by a fountain that bubbled cheerily as if to hide the ugly past. It had taken Dallas decades to escape the repercussions of JFK's assassination. The city was despised by the world, and city officials worked hard to revamp its image and recover from the identity of "The City of Hate." Even the park surrounding the site wasn't dedicated to JFK. The cenotaph for him was a few blocks away, as if again to hide the guilt a city wished to bury.

Only time, the success of the Dallas Cowboys and their famous cheerleaders, and the drama of J. R. Ewing on *Dallas* had helped to subdue the city's bad reputation.

Standing with all of this surrounding her, the past and the present, Lisa felt an odd connection to her father. He'd spent much of his life trying to know the truth of what happened to his favorite president. When new reports, studies, or movies about a conspiracy came out, he'd pore over the evidence again. Lisa's mom once told her that Dad had spent years at this very location, studying and thinking.

But the Benjamin Gray shooting that occurred so close to Lisa and Dad had faded quietly into their past, as well as into Fort Worth's history. Of course, Gray wasn't the president of the United States. Yet Dad had chosen to walk away from that mystery. Only now did the obsession for answers consume him. What had changed?

Lisa shivered as the sweat on her back chilled. Night was coming on fast. She turned away from the quiet Dealey Plaza and street where violence had long ago ended the life of a US president.

When Lisa returned to the hotel, she called her father to say she was exhausted and would come to the house the next day. Concern shaped Dad's voice as he asked to take her to dinner. Instead, they made plans for the morning and said good night.

Next Lisa called Drew before she could talk herself out of it again. "Hi," she said when he answered, feeling terribly junior high.

"Hey. How's it been with your father?"

"He has a girlfriend." She rested against the hotel pillows, relieved to launch into a casual subject that was safely away from them.

"That's . . . a good thing or not?"

"She's much younger, maybe younger than I am. And very different from him, and nothing, I mean, nothing like my mother." Lisa thought of Mom with her pearls and conservative style, her games of tennis at the country club and everything in its place at her home. Since remarrying, her mother enjoyed a busy social life and constant travel. She and Rosalyn were like different species.

Drew was quiet for a moment, then spoke. "Maybe that's good for him. Someone different might be a good change this late in life."

"I don't know. Maybe," Lisa said. Drew never responded in the way she expected. Unlike her female friends, who would've sympathized or been suspicious of Rosalyn's motives, heightening the drama, Drew considered every situation before responding and never told her just what she wanted to hear.

"It would be hard to be alone at that age."

"I suppose so." Lisa pictured the emptiness of her childhood home.

"I wouldn't want that." Drew's voice held a note of something she couldn't quite identify. "It sounds like your dad isn't stuck in one place. He's moving forward."

Lisa knew Drew well enough to catch his implication. She sighed and stared at a Georgia O'Keeffe print on the wall. Did this mean Drew wanted to continue their conversation from the airport?

"You aren't going to let this go, are you?"

Drew chuckled. "Okay, I won't bring it up again. Not until you get back."

"Promise?"

"Only if you promise to talk about it. Really talk?"

Lisa hesitated. "When I'm done with all of this with Dad?"

"Sure," he said.

"All right then."

Lisa studied the hard edges of O'Keeffe's desert flower, trying to think of something to move beyond this sudden awkwardness.

Drew spoke first, in a bad imitation of Lisa's voice. "So, Drew, what have you been up to in the past few days since I vowed never to speak to you again?" He switched to his own voice. "Well, Lisa, I've been researching the assassination of JFK and Benjamin Gray, and the civil rights movement in Texas during the 1960s. And I've been studying the snapshot you gave me."

Lisa laughed lightly. "I didn't vow never to speak to you again."

"You considered it," he said with that old teasing tone in his voice. "But moving on before we get into a debate, I know you said your dad helped in the investigation of JFK's killing, but I didn't realize he was part of the Warren Commission."

"Yeah, he was an integral part. He has notebooks full of his interviews and notes. But since President Johnson was the one who ordered the commission, its factuality has been questioned over the decades. But Dad says the report is completely accurate."

"Interesting. So no secret plot or other shooters?"

"Dad insists there was no conspiracy. Lee Harvey Oswald was the killer, and he acted alone."

"He should know. But how's it going, other than the shock of your father's girlfriend?"

"I have a lot to catch you up on. And I need your help." Lisa heard the creak and roll of a chair that she recognized as the sound of Drew's studio desk chair.

"I expected that was coming," he said.

"And you wanted me to call?"

"Yes, but you go first."

"Can you help me with background info on Rosalyn—the woman my dad is seeing? I'll text you her full name. She has two middle names, of course." Lisa hopped from the bed to retrieve her notes before settling back down.

"You want background information on your father's girlfriend?"

"Well, I can't get it as easily from my hotel. Do you mind?"

"I didn't mean I couldn't do it. I'll say this again, more slowly; do you think you should be running backgrounds on your father's girlfriend?

Aren't you the person who complained about your father doing that to your high school prom date?"

Lisa groaned. He had her there. "I just want to be sure about her."

"I'll do it, but you might understand your father a little better now."

"Uh-huh," she said. "And I'm scanning you a photograph of Benjamin Gray's corpse that Rosalyn found on the Internet. She already contacted the website for more information, but I wanted your thoughts. I'll send that tonight."

Lisa spent the next fifteen minutes updating Drew on her visit to the Fort Worth Police Department, then on her meeting with Sweeney at the diner. As she talked, she could hear the sound of Drew's one-finger tapping on the computer keyboard.

"I have a friend who works at a newspaper in Fort Worth," Drew offered. "Maybe he can dig around for us. But the reason behind a cover-up should be our main focus. That could crack this open. I'll see what I can find."

"Great," Lisa said, feeling better already. He'd helped her process the day better than her run. "And your text . . . you wanted me to call?"

"Yes. I have a lead on your girl."

"My girl?" Lisa rubbed her eyes.

"The other little girl in the photograph."

Lisa kicked her feet to the side of the bed. "Wait, you do? How did you do that?"

"I'm sorry, but I can't reveal my sources. I'm a committed journalist, don't you know?"

"Come on. Are you serious? This is the biggest news of all, and you've waited to tell me. What if I hadn't called you?"

"You'd have missed out, I guess."

Lisa wasn't sure if he was teasing or not. She started pacing the room as he talked.

"I started with the women in the photograph sitting beside you and the girl. I assumed that one was the mother. Your father said that the woman in the hat scooped up the girl after the shooting."

Lisa stopped midstep. "You've been talking to my father?"

"I called him today with some questions. He's in the phone directory."

"What?" Lisa could hardly believe her ears.

"Do you want to hear this or not?"

"Of course." Lisa walked to the large floor-to-ceiling window. The city lights sparkled across the horizon, then stopped abruptly as city met the open Texas flatlands.

"That hat she was wearing isn't just an ordinary hat. It was made by a special local designer in Texas."

"How did you find that out?"

"Intense research—eBay, actually. I did an image search on antique hats, and a similar one was for sale on eBay. That gave me the name of the hat and its designer, which was from a shop in Fort Worth."

"You found the name of the shop? And there's only one?" Lisa moved to the desk and started her computer. Her heart rate quickened as it did whenever she followed clues in an investigation.

"Yes. It was a small shop and changed owners in the eighties, but the designer continued to make hats for the new owners even when it became a little boutique. The designer's granddaughter took over the craft after she retired."

"This is good. I wonder if the hat lady in Dad's snapshot continued to be a buyer. That might lead us to her."

"Exactly," Drew said.

Lisa's mind clicked with other avenues they might follow to discover the name of the woman in the hat, the woman beside her, and the little girl.

"Last year I worked on a case with this college professor who jumped bail. He'd previously been a social media junkie, but he seemed to disappear. I had this idea to use facial recognition software on the major social media sites, and we found him under a different name and living in the Caribbean."

"I remember that. But what are you thinking?"

"Many organizations and clubs are uploading member photographs on their websites or onto other media sources. It's a long shot, but I can call a techie friend of mine to run some facial recognition software over organizations, historic societies, and churches in the Fort Worth area. If they've uploaded membership pictures from the 1960s, we may be able to match the little girl or the woman sitting beside the hat lady. We only have her profile, but it might still work."

"I can Photoshop her profile to create a composite of what she'd look like facing the camera. That would make the software work better."

Lisa typed in her log-in and password to gain access to secure software and search engines accessible only to federal employees with a high security clearance.

She heard Drew's fingers on the keyboard again. He too was on the hunt.

"Most everybody attended church in 1965. I know my Southern black family well enough to know that. It's quite possible they attended a local church that would have archives of members at the church or on their website."

"It wasn't just the black families in the South. But I agree. From your discovery of the hat designer, we can start the search in areas closest to those neighborhoods. People often did all of their shopping and social activities while attending church and school right in their own community."

"This will keep us busy. I'm getting a lot of relevant hits in my searches," Drew said.

"Me too. If the little girl was older, we could search school yearbooks as well. But I think she and I were the same age, so she wouldn't have been in school yet. I'm not sure if my dad told me that or if I just remembered it, but I'm pretty sure she was four too."

Lisa turned on the phone's speaker and worked while talking with Drew. While he re-created the face of the second woman in the photograph, Lisa searched for a list of churches and community organizations in Fort Worth, marking any with images and those that still existed. The facial recognition software searched sites for the little girl and the woman from Dad's snapshots. Lisa only wished the woman with the hat had turned enough for them to have her face as well.

Hours passed as they hit dead ends and kept working. Drew reminded her to eat something, and Lisa realized her fingers were shaking as she dug through her bag for a nutrition bar.

Later she plugged in her cell phone to recharge the battery and stood to stretch several times. They were getting close to something solid, she was sure of it. Then she heard a beep from the software program indicating a hit.

She switched to the program and saw the face of the little girl from the Sunday school directory of a Southern Baptist church.

"We may have found her," Lisa said, leaning close to the screen and comparing the girl's face in the two photographs.

She sent the images to Drew, knowing he had a better eye.

"Molly Carter."

"Yes, and it's from 1965. Look at the directory for 1964. Molly Carter is there as well."

"Yes, but look at the directory for 1966 and 1967. The girl isn't there."

"You're faster than I am. I was just opening that link."

"It's a sad day when you get beat by a single-finger typist."

"Well, I just found the rest of the Carter family in the member directory." Lisa typed and clicked through the church's historical sites. "The whole family left the church after 1965."

"Let's find out where they went," Drew said.

Another few hours searching through employment and school reports, and Drew announced, "This has to be her. Pastor Molly Carter. She's the same age as you, and until four years ago she was living in California."

"She's a minister?" Lisa couldn't imagine that little girl as an adult, let alone a pastor. "And where is she now?"

"She went to seminary in Southern California and served at several churches around Los Angeles and San Diego. But two years ago she took a new position. I found medical bills in collections that indicate her mother is sick."

"Where is she?" Lisa said, knowing Drew was dragging this out on purpose and enjoying it immensely.

"In a little town right outside of Dallas, Texas."

Lisa could barely believe it. "She's here?"

"That's right. Molly Carter is right under your nose."

CHAPTERFOURTEEN

James stared at his daughter.

"You found the other little girl in the snapshot?" Rosalyn said with her hands cupping her cheeks.

They sat in the workshop surrounded by stacks of research and bulletin boards of information that James had spent weeks organizing. In such a short time, Lisa had added much more to the collection.

Yet James was distracted by his daughter's presence. At times all he could see was his little girl sitting on the stool with those big blue eyes, not the sophisticated woman discussing archives, old police reports, and secret meetings.

"It was a joint effort. And not possible without a lot of help from modern technology."

"Still, I'm impressed," Rosalyn said. She glanced at James as if to read his reaction. "That could crack this whole thing right open. Molly Carter might have seen who really killed Gray. How will you contact her?"

Lisa picked up one of the pages she'd brought that morning. His daughter had dark circles under her eyes, as she always got when lacking sleep. James wondered if she'd been managing her hypoglycemia and how late she'd worked to find this information. He couldn't deny that her methods had uncovered quite a find, but he hoped she'd still learn that relying solely on modern techniques and technology could fail an investigation. The old ways weren't completely obsolete.

"I'll try meeting her tomorrow at her church. It's Sunday, so I assume she'll be there. Unless you want to come as well, Dad? Or . . . both of you."

Before James weighed in, Rosalyn spoke. "It might be less intimidating with only one person. But your dad or both of us can come if you want us to."

"Dad, what do you think?" Lisa asked. She sounded annoyed with Rosalyn, and not for the first time.

But he couldn't read whether Lisa wanted to go alone to meet this Molly Carter or not.

"It's whatever you want. You may get more by approaching her alone," he said.

"I think so too," Lisa said.

James had plans of his own for the next day. Mainly, he wanted to address the issue of the person trailing them. That morning the car wasn't parked across the street until Lisa arrived. James would find out tonight and tomorrow if his daughter was the new target. If she was, he wouldn't delay in taking action. He wouldn't allow Lisa to be in danger because they were trying to save Leonard Dubois.

"We need to add all of this to your dad's walls," Rosalyn said, studying the different bulletin boards and seemingly oblivious to the tension. James knew she perceived it; she just chose to ignore that Lisa didn't like her. Rosalyn eventually won people over with her odd personality—it had worked with him.

But there was something else. Perhaps she was only annoyed by Rosalyn's presence, but his gut told him that Lisa was holding something back. Did she get information from the police or from the retired archivist that she wasn't sharing?

His daughter's attention had moved to the bulletin boards sectioned off around the workshop.

"What's this wall about? What's the key?" she asked, leaning forward to read his notes.

James came to her side, studying the images on the wall. He hadn't planned to address this part of the story, had even considered taking it down before Lisa arrived.

In the center was an image of a key, surrounded by photographs and notes about President John Kennedy and his brother Robert; President Lyndon Johnson; his own former boss of the FBI, J. Edgar Hoover; Hoover's secretary, Miss Grady; Kennedy's assistant, Evelyn Lincoln; and numerous other notes that wouldn't make sense to his daughter.

He'd reluctantly included a photograph of his former best friend and partner, Special Agent Peter Hughes. James hoped Lisa didn't ask why Uncle Peter was included in this section.

"All of this is a hunch," James said with a shrug. Lisa glanced at him, studying him in that moment, and then returned to the images. She focused on the picture of Peter longer than he'd hoped, but she didn't ask about it.

Rosalyn moved to the other side of Lisa. James noticed his daughter tense at her closeness, but he couldn't help but appreciate Rosalyn's assertive chatter that bridged the gap in his awkwardness with his daughter.

"It's more than a hunch. Your dad believes, and I do as well, that there were higher powers at play in all of this."

"Higher powers? What do you mean 'higher powers'?"

Rosalyn laughed. "I guess that wasn't the correct word. Higher authority. Someone in government, or in the Bureau, CIA, or military. Someone with power, and a lot of it."

Lisa was silent for a moment. "The man I met at the diner, Sweeney, believes that as well. He also thinks Leonard Dubois was targeted by the Fort Worth PD. So this person is the key?"

"Oh no, there's an actual key—it goes to an antique cabinet that was in the White House. A key that's been missing all of these decades." Rosalyn loved historical clues. One of her side projects was a mystery surrounding a bank robbery in the mid-1800s in her hometown in north Texas. She'd dragged James along to old museums, libraries, and archives for the past two years seeking information.

"A key to a cabinet that has what inside?" Lisa asked.

"Jimmy, I'll let you explain," Rosalyn said. She winked at him and moved off to the side.

James wished Rosalyn hadn't passed the baton. She'd become somewhat obsessed with the key, while he still doubted its significance.

"So there's a missing historical key in the middle of all this?" Lisa asked.

"Possibly. It started with a rumor. I need to give some background."

"Go ahead." Lisa sat back on the stool in front of everything he'd compiled on the key.

"As you know, I was a young agent during President Kennedy's three years in office. There were many tensions. We nearly went to war with Russia twice, over the Bay of Pigs and then the Cuban Missile Crisis."

Lisa nodded, but James knew she didn't fully understand.

He frowned and tried to explain. "This kind of a war meant cities being wiped off the face of the earth. Maybe even most of the world destroyed. The USSR had a leader unafraid of using nuclear bombs. I guess everyone at the Bureau believed we were trying to save our families and everyone we knew from a horrible death."

James wanted Lisa to grasp what he was saying. How many years had he wanted to explain it to her? He'd missed her childhood, been absent from her school events and activities. It was work, duty, but also the guilt that started the day of that civil rights rally when he'd nearly gotten his daughter killed.

"We were still in Chicago, but I was immediately relocated here when our president was killed."

"It must have been a shock," Lisa said.

James nodded, but he remembered his father sharing stories from WWI and his childhood. A parent's history sounded ancient, and James wasn't the storyteller his father had been, nor was he able to put words around the thoughts that rolled through his mind.

"President Kennedy was shot, Vietnam began, Martin Luther King Jr. and Bobby Kennedy were assassinated—all in a matter of years. The Communists were taking country after country. It seemed the world was falling apart. But that's getting off the subject."

James cleared his throat. He wasn't used to this much talking, especially to his daughter, who listened to him attentively.

"The key." He pointed to the image of an etched brass key tacked to the bulletin board. "It's a matter of record that after JFK's death his brother Bobby changed the locks on file cabinets in the Oval Office. It was a condition the brothers had discussed in the event of such a tragedy. They didn't want the vice president to obtain certain sensitive information they'd compiled. Johnson became President Johnson on Air Force One before leaving Texas, just hours after Kennedy was pronounced dead."

Lisa nodded, taking in the information. James knew his daughter might know much of this already, but he needed to go through it for her to understand his hunch.

"Lyndon Johnson and Robert Kennedy hated one another. It was rumored that inside these file cabinets were secret documents that the Kennedys had gathered about various top officials, including Johnson. Within a week, the cabinets were removed and taken elsewhere. However, one of the keys disappeared."

"Just one?"

"From what I've turned up."

"Where are the cabinets located now?"

"In a bank vault in DC from what I can tell."

"How do you know this?"

Rosalyn laughed with her back to them as she typed on her laptop. "You are definitely James's daughter. I can only imagine being cross-examined by you. He can show you the list of trails we've followed to compile the information on the wall."

"But how did you hear about this in the first place?" Lisa pinched the skin between her eyes, just as James did when his head hurt or when he was thinking intently.

James looked away from his daughter's probing stare.

"I first heard about it from a former friend. He was obsessed with it. After he died, I wondered about it. But only now did I return to the subject."

"A former friend?" Lisa seemed to know that he meant his old partner, Peter, but neither spoke his name. "But how do a key and secret file cabinet of the Kennedys connect to Benjamin Gray? The president was dead and the cabinet moved a year and a half before Gray was shot."

"That's why it's only a hunch. Whenever I get into investigating all of this, some connection brings up that missing key. It won't leave me alone."

"It seems pretty thin, but I know the importance of following your gut. That's one thing I learned from you." Lisa smiled then, the first he'd seen from her that day.

"There's someone I hope can help with the key," James said.

"Oh, oh, oh!" Rosalyn shouted.

"What now? You about gave me a heart attack," James said.

His daughter's irritation was obvious on her face as well.

"Sorry, I was just so excited. That photo of Benjamin Gray's body that I found on that crime scene photo website? I found the source."

"Go on," James said.

"It was submitted to the site from an e-mail account at the Blackstone Corporation, a huge sort of veiled company out of Florida. The company does a lot of construction projects, but there's a lot more to it—more than I've uncovered so far. The company, a family business, started in the early 1950s. They have offices in Miami and in Alexandria, Louisiana. The family comes from old Southern money going back to before the Civil War. They owned a huge plantation, which they still have, but after the war, while most Southerners starved, the Blackstones thrived. I'm not sure how, though it doesn't look legal. The family became enormously rich, and in the past decades has continued to thrive." Rosalyn rattled all this information off quickly.

"Wait. Why would someone at such a company post a photo of Benjamin Gray's corpse on an Internet site?" Lisa asked.

While Lisa might suspend some of her belief for his "hunch," James knew she wasn't giving Rosalyn any such leeway.

"That's what I don't know. But the website gave me the information, and I did a bit of digging on this company. I found an article from about fifteen years ago that exposed the Blackstone family's support of campaigns for neo-Nazi and white supremacist politicians. Stanley Blackstone is their aging patriarch. His nephew is VP of his company. There's a string of investigations and accusations against them, but nothing that's held up in court."

"This makes no sense," Lisa said. "Why would they call attention to themselves by posting such an image?"

"That's what we need to find out," Rosalyn said, sounding like a kid asked to go on a scavenger hunt.

James turned to the walls covered with leads and evidences. "We need answers, not more questions."

"The plot thickens," Rosalyn said, rubbing her hands together.

"But Dad's right. We need definitive answers. The goal is getting Leonard Dubois free. So I'll contact Molly Carter tomorrow. If she remembers what happened, she'd be a compelling witness, especially as a minister. But she was four or five years old. For capital murder, we need more to get Leonard Dubois released."

James nodded. "But she might lead us to the real shooter."

"I think we need to look at something else." Lisa returned to her notes on the workbench. "When I'm working a trial, I look at two elements. The victim and the killer. We've been studying the snapshots and Leonard Dubois. But what do we know about the victim—Benjamin Gray?"

Dad's brows lowered. "I have some information somewhere around here about him. But there's a lot we don't know."

"The motive could be racial or civil rights motivated, but it might also be something out in left field."

"This is true. Your dad has some background about him, but we haven't spent much time on it," Rosalyn said.

"I'll research Benjamin Gray starting tonight, and tomorrow I'll go see Molly Carter," Lisa said.

"We have a lot to do." James was overwhelmed by the sudden pride and love for his daughter flooding over him, threatening to be exposed through his emotions. When had he become such a sentimental old man?

Rosalyn jumped in with a flourish. "I'll stay on the Blackstone Corporation and try to find out who specifically posted that photograph. But I was thinking, with such a disreputable family, we may uncover all kinds of criminal activity that our federal prosecutor here could nail them on, even if they aren't connected to Gray. And of course, I'm still on the lookout for more clues about the key. I don't care if you both think that's a stretch, I know we'll find a connection."

James ignored Rosalyn's mention of the key; he didn't think it was relevant at the moment. He always went with the most pressing lead. And his thoughts had been singular—get Leonard Dubois off of death row. But there was much more to this than he'd expected. And some of it touched the deepest portions of his life. From the wall behind where his daughter sat, the face of his former partner, Peter Hughes, seemed to stare at him without compromise. Perhaps all the old secrets were ready to be revealed.

"Let's meet again tomorrow night," he said.

James kept the rest of his plans to himself. He'd get to the bottom of the car following him and possibly his daughter. He'd try just one lead that nagged at him regarding the key. And there were the more personal matters. James knew he wasn't innocent in all of this, but perhaps redemption would come if all the sins were finally revealed.

CHAPTERFIFTEEN

Lisa didn't get nervous.

With years of high-stress situations under her belt through law school, in court standing before judges and juries, in jail cells interviewing killers, and at high-class social events rubbing shoulders with celebrities and dignitaries, she didn't have room in her schedule for butterflies, sweaty palms, or stage fright.

But as she sat in her car outside the redbrick church, her chest palpitated as if she'd had a double espresso and her jaw ached from a night of subconscious teeth clenching—a bad habit she'd previously overcome.

In the satchel beside her, a padded envelope held the snapshots of Lisa and a little black girl. In a few moments, she might meet that girl once again.

Don't analyze, just act, Lisa told herself as she opened the car door.

Music drifted outside as she walked up the steps to the large double doors. The late morning smelled of jasmine blossoms and freshly cut grass.

Except for weddings and funerals, Lisa hadn't been inside a church in years. She hesitated with her hands against the wood, suddenly second-guessing her decision to arrive at the end of the service. It didn't sound like the ending, but Lisa didn't know if music closed or only opened a church service. Perhaps the time listed on the website was incorrect.

She entered a simple carpeted foyer. Glass windows looked out into the main sanctuary full of its mostly African American congregation, standing along the rows of bench seats. The choir sang joyfully from a stage. Lisa moved to the side swinging doors, pushed through, and slid into an empty pew in back.

The song erupted into clapping and "hallelujahs" before moving into an old hymn carried by a soloist. Then Lisa saw the black woman wearing a long robe and standing on the floor below the podium.

Seeing Pastor Molly Carter brought no memory of the day they had met. Studying the woman, Lisa couldn't be certain by appearance alone that this woman was that little girl.

Molly smiled as if filled with a divine joy that rolled outward. Lisa shivered as unexpected emotion welled in her chest.

With her arms stretched outward, Molly said in a rich voice, "The Lord bless you and keep you; the Lord make his face to shine upon you and be gracious to you; the Lord look upon you with favor and give you peace.

"And as always, if you have any prayer needs, our prayer team is coming forward to pray with you."

The pastor kept her arms outstretched and prayed as if talking directly to God. She concluded with a vigorous, "Amen! We have a wonderful God. Now go on and have a glorious day!"

The organ music swelled as the choir disappeared into a side door and numerous people walked forward. Several knelt on the stairs to the altar, while others formed a line around men and women who seemed to be the "prayer team."

Lisa watched as if observing a different culture or a memory from another life. She'd attended Mass with her husband off and on, but that ended with Thomas's death. As a single mom, Lisa fought some guilt that she didn't take John to any religious services, knowing Thomas's mother might curse her from the grave, but with their schedule, church was far down the list of things to do every Sunday.

The truth was, Lisa's world revolved around law and justice. These were concrete and anchored. Churches brought up the mysteries of life and the unknowns of death. She didn't like situations that couldn't be controlled.

The parishioners began to leave as the service concluded, laughing and talking about their plans for the day. She remained in her seat with her eyes on Molly as she prayed with several people who remained kneeling in front. What would it be like to live in this world of prayer, Scripture, and godly devotion? she wondered.

An older couple stopped at Lisa, greeting her with smiles and handshakes, asking for her name and saying they hoped she'd return.

Finally, Lisa rose from the seat when she saw Molly approaching.

"Welcome. I'm Pastor Carter, though I prefer just Molly. I'm happy to have you join us today." Her generous smile lit her entire face.

"I'm Lisa Waldren, and I only slipped in at the end."

"Yes, I noticed. We don't have many white ladies pop in at the end of the service. You stick out in this crowd." Molly laughed.

"I suppose I do," Lisa said.

"But you're welcome here anytime."

Molly waved toward a family leaving the sanctuary. She picked up a hymnbook from the pew in front of Lisa, placing it back in the holder.

"I actually came to meet you," Lisa said, moving to the aisle. Why did she feel like that shy girl again, meeting another little girl? It was as if the years between their first encounter had disappeared.

"Has my fame spread far and wide?" Molly said.

"I was hoping to talk with you. Whenever it's convenient."

Molly nodded with a gentle smile as if such requests happened often. "Now works just fine for me, if it works for you. Would you like to talk here or in my office?"

"Your office, if you don't mind."

Lisa followed Molly from the sanctuary and down a long carpeted hallway, passing classrooms with different age groups posted on signs next to the doors. They reached a simple office, lined with books, that looked out onto a garden area.

"Have a seat," Molly said. She pointed to a small couch. She pulled her office chair around and away from the desk to be adjacent to Lisa. "What can I do for you, Lisa?"

"I believe we met when we were children."

Molly's eyebrows rose, and she tilted her head to study Lisa.

"I grew up in California. I think I'd remember you. What was your name again?"

"Lisa Waldren. But it was before you moved to California." Lisa pulled the snapshots from her satchel, realizing they explained their background better than words. "My father took these at a rally in Fort Worth in 1965."

"What is this?" Molly asked, taking the photographs. Her face registered surprise as she looked at them, then deep concern. She stood with the photographs and closed the office door. "Your father took these?"

"Yes. That's me beside you."

"How did you find me?" Molly studied Lisa.

"Let me explain." Lisa realized she'd approached this completely wrong. "I'm a federal prosecutor, and my father is retired FBI . . ."

"The FBI and a federal prosecutor hunted me down. Are you trying to make me feel really nervous about this?" Molly laughed, but her face reflected concern.

"I can usually interview people much better than this." Lisa shook her head. "But first can I just confirm that this is really you?"

"Yes. That's me, and my mama is in the white hat. Aunt Hattie is beside her. And so this is you?"

"Do you remember?" Lisa asked, leaning forward to view the photos again.

"Sure do. You were the first white girl I ever talked to. Don't you remember?"

Lisa shook her head. "The entire event is hazy, I guess. I don't remember enough that means anything."

Molly leaned back in her chair with her eyes on the images in her hand.

"I remember chunks of it. That shooting and all that."

"You remember the shooting?"

"What is this about? Why did you hunt me down? Why does it matter now?"

A knock sounded on the door, and a middle-aged woman peered inside.

"This is my assistant, Miss Ginny," Molly said.

Lisa noticed that Molly slid the snapshots under a file folder.

"Well, hello, what's this? We got a white lady joining the church?"

Lisa shifted in her seat. She didn't know if Miss Ginny expected her to respond, or Molly. In the Northeast, Lisa was accustomed to being "color blind." There wouldn't be mention of her being white.

"We're just having ourselves a little chat," Molly said.

"Oh, I'm sorry to interrupt. You a friend from California?" The woman stepped inside, filling the doorway with her round shape.

"No, I live in Boston now, but I grew up in the Dallas area," Lisa said. She glanced at Molly, then back to the woman.

"You don't sound Southern anymore. But then, you don't look Southern either." Miss Ginny laughed as if there was a joke Lisa should understand.

"Did you need something, Miss Ginny? Remember, when the door is closed, it means I'm in a private meeting."

Miss Ginny portrayed more embarrassment than Lisa thought she really possessed. "Oh my, I apologize, that's right. I was just checking in before I go on home. My man is making his mama's secret fried chicken recipe, but then I guess your friend here would expect me to go home and eat fried chicken. And look if we aren't doing just that!" She burst into more laughter, slapping her hands together.

Lisa couldn't think of any way to respond. She hoped her mouth wasn't dangling open.

"Thank you, Miss Ginny. I'll see you in the morning." Molly raised her eyebrows at the woman as if to send her on her way.

"All right, I'll leave you two, then. Have a good day, and if you do want to join the church, we'd love to have you."

"Thank you," Lisa said.

Miss Ginny winked at Molly and closed the door with an exaggerated ease.

"Sorry for the interruption. Miss Ginny's mother was the church secretary for decades, and she's trying out the position for the next three months. It's been a challenge," Molly said.

Lisa smiled. "I imagine it is, but she's quite entertaining."

"That's true. Now back to these." Molly picked up the snapshots from beneath the folder.

"Yes. We were searching for you to try to get some information."

Molly appeared lost in thought. "Your father is retired FBI, and you're a federal prosecutor?"

"That's right. But do you mind telling me what you remember about the shooting?"

Molly frowned, then looked squarely at Lisa. "So are you and your father finally going to get to the truth of what happened that day?"

CHAPTER SIXTEEN

I'm trying to reach William O'Ryan," James said into his cell phone. He leaned close to the computer screen at the list of contact numbers for the news conglomerate in New York City.

James had considered different routes to reach the reporter, then simply called the number he found for the cable news headquarters on the Internet. A company receptionist connected him to O'Ryan's assistant.

"Mr. O'Ryan isn't in the office right now; may I take a message?"

"He and I met years ago in the late sixties. I'm James Waldren, a retired special agent with the FBI. Is this the best way to contact him?"

"Yes, Mr. Waldren. I'll make sure he receives this message."

James left his number, wondering if he would really hear back. William O'Ryan had moved up in the world from the green idealistic journalist James had met decades ago. The last time James had seen him was when Peter Hughes had committed suicide.

Now O'Ryan was a big shot living in New York. He hosted a wildly successful news program, offered political commentary, and had authored numerous *New York Times* best-selling books. The pictures of O'Ryan on the website presented him as an intelligent, suave reporter. James last remembered a young man still somewhat in shock at Peter's funeral. The kid had tried to save Peter even with blood gushing from a gunshot through Peter's head.

James set the phone down as he read more about O'Ryan. It made a beeping noise, which probably meant the battery was going dead, though the bars looked fine to him. He moved a stack of papers to cover the noise.

The official FBI photograph of Special Agent Peter Hughes stared up at him from the wall. After all these years, it still didn't sit well with him that his former friend was dead, or that Peter had been a traitor to the Bureau and essentially to James and his family as well. James had believed he knew the man like they were brothers. They couldn't have been closer, and yet Peter had lived a secret life that James's FBI skills never once detected.

"I'm almost done," Rosalyn yelled from outside, tapping on the workshop window. For the past few hours she'd been moving around outside the house on a ladder.

"Are you sure you don't want my help?" he yelled back.

"You'll mess it up!" Rosalyn laughed, and she was probably right.

She had become skilled at installing obscure cameras inside and outside her clients' homes, in their cars, at their businesses, or even on their bodies. That morning she'd decided to check the house for bugs and to wire James's house and workshop with security. Now they'd have monitors in the house and workshop and cameras covering the entire property. James shook his head at the prospect.

His sight fell again on Peter's photograph. They'd spent years not just working together but sharing every detail of life. Peter was family. He had loved Lisa, saying she was the child he didn't have. James had trusted the man with everything.

The bitterness of betrayal had faded with the years. Now he just wanted to know why.

Peter was at the rally that day. James had been surprised to see him and waved at his partner from across the street. Peter motioned that he'd be there in a moment, but they didn't see each other again until after the shooting.

James had never believed Peter was tied to the event. He agreed with Lisa's contact, Sweeney, that there had been a cover-up. He just never knew why. His own boss shut down his quest for answers. Then he was demoted without cause after he pushed for answers surrounding Leonard Dubois's arrest. He might have still sought answers, until the final straw that made him turn his head and look shamefully away, though he still didn't regret the decision.

Now he had to reconsider everything. Peter sat in the thick of it. Friendship may have clouded him years ago, then anger and hurt. Then burying his head took over the rest.

What did you know? And why didn't you tell me? James picked up the photograph. He also needed to rethink the fact that Peter was the person who got him on the trail of the JFK key.

"Hey, Dad, are you out there?" Lisa's voice came from beyond the workshop door.

James pulled off his glasses as the door creaked open and afternoon light beamed in.

"Yes, come in. I didn't know you were coming by."

"I called, but it went to voice mail. Your mailbox is full."

"Darn thing." He groaned as his eyes adjusted to the flood of light. Then he saw that his daughter wasn't alone.

"Dad, I'd like you to meet Pastor Molly Carter," Lisa said as the smaller woman reached out to greet him.

"Just Molly, please. I can't get my congregation to do so, but I prefer it."

James brushed off his hands and strode toward the woman. Her smile faded as she viewed the covered walls.

"You weren't kidding. You two are investigating this," Molly said. She took James's outstretched hand and shook it.

"You really did find her," James said as Molly gazed around the workshop. She grimaced at the wall of crime scene photographs.

"I was as surprised as you," Lisa said.

"We should go inside for tea or coffee," James suggested as Molly glanced at him, then back at the newest photo of Benjamin Gray dead on the street. The woman was a minister, after all, and his workshop wasn't the best accommodation for such a guest.

"Good idea, Dad," Lisa said.

They made small talk on the walk back to the house. James asked Molly where her church was located. She asked if they attended a house of worship.

"I've been dragged to services by the woman I'm seeing," James said. He noticed Lisa's glance of surprise.

James wanted to get to the real questions with Molly. Had she seen who shot Benjamin Gray? Did Lisa already know that answer?

He opened the gate to the backyard and walkway leading to the house. As the women passed him, James was struck by the presence of the two little girls in the snapshot he'd studied for countless hours. Here they were walking with him as grown women. A week ago he'd have never imagined this moment would occur. But the big question loomed: What did Molly Carter remember?

Once inside the house, James invited the women to the living room. He checked the front window and grimaced at seeing the car parked across the street. It hadn't been around all morning, nor had James seen it outside Lisa's hotel when he'd driven by there late in the night and again before sunrise.

"Let me get the teakettle on the stove," he said, hurrying to the kitchen. He returned a few moments later with a basket of individual teas and teacups.

"Dad, sit down with us. I can help with all of that," Lisa said. "My father is trying not to go into interrogation mode."

"This is an interrogation?" Molly said it lightly, but James caught a trace of suspicion.

"No, I didn't mean that. Just my father and I find it difficult to make small talk or polite conversation when we want answers. My son and his friends call me Bad Cop."

This wasn't going well. James could see the unease growing in Molly. With all Lisa's training and experience, she wasn't helping Molly gain her trust. Lisa sat at the edge of the couch, back straight and obviously uncomfortable.

"That must make you Good Cop," Molly said to James. "Lisa said you've been looking for me, and I'm still a little creeped out that you two found me from that photograph. My cousin thinks the government is keeping secret files on Americans, and it appears to be true."

"I was surprised it was possible myself," James said.

The teakettle whistled from the kitchen, and Lisa went to retrieve it.

"What does it say about my belief in people that I jumped in the car with your daughter when she told me about your mission to free that inmate on death row? Then I ended up in a strange workshop with people who have Big Brother accessibilities."

"Want to see my badge?" James asked.

"That's okay. Your daughter showed me her credentials. But I don't understand why you're both doing this."

Lisa returned with the kettle and poured hot water into each cup, then disappeared from the room.

"In my gut, I've known that Leonard Dubois didn't kill Benjamin Gray. I've known it for almost fifty years. He has an execution date now, and he wrote to me. Somehow he found out or maybe he's known since the trial that I didn't think he was guilty of killing Benjamin Gray. This is his last chance. If we fail, the state of Texas will put Leonard Dubois to death in a matter of weeks."

Molly stared at him with black eyes probing him. Then she dipped a bag of tea into her steaming cup of water, swirling it around. Lisa returned from the kitchen with bowls of cream and sugar with tiny spoons he'd last seen in the back of the silverware drawer.

"I wish I could help," Molly said.

James was surprised by the disappointment he felt.

"What do you remember?" he asked.

"The dress I wore that day. It was pretty and brand-new. As was my mama's new hat. I wanted a hat too, but Mama said I didn't need

123

one with such a fancy dress. Then I remember meeting Lisa. I'd seen white girls before, of course, but this was the first one I talked to. I liked her dress as well." Molly smiled at the memory. "In my recollection we looked more like princesses than the photos reflect. Then came the sound of a firecracker. My mama and aunt were screaming. Mama grabbed me from a man who was shouting something—I think that was you."

James nodded. "I was trying to get you girls onto the ground, and your mama was screaming at me. I shouted that I was FBI, but I'm sure a white man holding her daughter was terrifying. She grabbed you away and took off running."

Molly nodded. "Yes, we ran down the street. Mama and Auntie were screaming, and I had no idea what was happening. For a while I thought it was our fault." Molly motioned toward Lisa.

"Ours? Why?"

"I didn't know someone had been shot. I thought all the chaos occurred because I was sitting next to a white girl and her father was taking our picture."

"Oh no," Lisa said, sitting in a chair across from Molly.

Molly laughed to herself. "You know how children get confused about things like that. When we got home it was several days before my granddaddy explained what had happened. Even so, it was quite a long time before I befriended a girl who wasn't black."

"I can imagine," Lisa said.

"So you didn't see a shooter or anything like that?" James asked.

"I believe I saw Benjamin Gray on the ground, but I've heard the story enough that I'm not certain of that memory.

"My mother is ill now. She's in her late eighties, but her mind is crisp. Over the years when we talked about that day, she would tell me the same story. We were watching the parade, and we met a little white girl and her daddy taking pictures. Benjamin Gray went by us, and Mama was excited to see him 'cause he was important. But then she was looking for my uncle, who was marching in the parade farther down. We heard gunshots . . . then she saw the white man holding me.

She screamed and tore me away while he was shouting that he was a policeman. Guess she didn't get that exactly right. It's always been the same story, until recently."

James waited, anxious for the point.

"Then last year Mom brought up something I'd never heard before. I was worried about her memory at first."

"What did she say?" James asked.

"She said it was a white man who shot Benjamin Gray." Molly studied his reaction.

"A white man?" Lisa's eyes also jumped to James.

"Why didn't she tell you that earlier?" James asked.

"I asked that. She said she was afraid. My father was convinced we'd all be killed if she came forward or told anyone that story. He was furious that she'd told some cop at the scene. The way the police acted back then, especially that day, there was no way she'd admit that she saw white men with guns shooting up a black event. My daddy made her promise never to speak of it again. He was so paranoid that we left Fort Worth to live with his sister in California only weeks later."

Lisa stood and paced the floor.

"She might have confused me with the shooter," James said.

"Why you?" Molly asked, stopping her reach for her cup.

Lisa, too, paused to hear what he had to say.

"I pulled out my gun as soon as the shooting started. It's an automatic response from training."

"She told me you were a policeman, and that it wasn't you who shot Benjamin Gray. But I will ask her for the story again."

"Or she might have seen Peter," James said.

"Who's Peter?"

"Dad's old partner. Uncle Peter was there?" Lisa frowned.

James knew this was news to her. He hadn't even set out a mannequin in the garage representing his old partner's placement.

"Yes, he was there," James said. He didn't tell Lisa that she'd called out to him that day, immediately after the shooting began. Peter had been close to them. Close to Benjamin Gray as well.

"Why—" Lisa started, but James interrupted her with a question for Molly.

"What brought you back?" He steered the discussion away from Peter, and Lisa surely knew he'd done so on purpose.

"We lived in California for years, but Mom never liked it. After my dad passed in '98, she moved back to Texas. Guess she hoped the danger was gone by then. I only moved back because of Mom's health."

"What are the chances?" James mumbled.

"It wasn't chance, I can tell you that. I love California, never would've left on my own. It was God who brought me back to Texas. And now I see it was for even more than I thought."

"Can we talk to your mother—if she's well enough?"

"We can."

"And maybe we should go see Leonard Dubois," Lisa said. "I checked it out, and we can visit the prison tomorrow morning."

James didn't respond. Instead, he dipped his bag of green tea in the hot water, up and down, up and down. He didn't want to see Dubois, especially not with his daughter or a minister in attendance. Dubois had spent his life in prison. James's silence had sealed the man's fate.

"I would like to meet him," Molly said.

James pinched the skin between his eyes. Now he'd have Molly tagging along with their investigation? He watched as she put sugar into her tea, appearing more relaxed. She explained that her mother lived with her sister now, outside of Dallas/Fort Worth.

How could he not agree to see Dubois with them? James felt Molly was holding back. The visit with Dubois might help her spill everything to save his life. Yet it might also implicate his cowardice in not coming forward earlier.

Rosalyn was his saving grace. He heard her calling from the backyard.

"Jimmy!" she yelled at the door in the kitchen.

"We're in the living room," he called back.

Rosalyn marched in with a rope of wire over her shoulder and a headlamp attached to her forehead. She stopped, mouth dropping open, when she saw Lisa and Molly in the living room.

"You're the little girl. Lisa, you found her! Way to go. Hi, I'm Rosalyn. This is great to meet you. Did she remember anything? Does she know who killed Benjamin Gray?"

Molly chuckled at Rosalyn's questions firing around the room. Before anyone could respond, Rosalyn raised her hand that held James's phone.

"Oh yes, Jimmy, you have a phone call. While I was wiring the workshop, I heard it ringing under a pile of papers. It accidentally turned on when I pulled it out, so I said hello. It's some news guy in New York." She pushed the phone toward him.

James took the phone as if it were a foreign object. "He's on here now?"

"Yes, that's what I just said." Rosalyn dropped the pile of wire onto the floor, brushing herself off as she sat beside Molly.

"Hello?" he said into the phone.

"Agent Waldren. This is William O'Ryan. It's been a long time."

"Yes, yes, it has been. I'm . . . I'm glad you remembered me," James stammered. He hurried from the room to the quiet of the kitchen.

"Of course I remember, though it wasn't under good circumstances. What can I do for you?"

James took a deep breath. It had been a most surprising day, and he needed to switch gears and fast. "I'm looking for some old information about my former partner, Peter Hughes."

"I had a feeling that's what your call was about. You probably know that I have quite a bit of information about him."

"What do you mean?" James leaned against the cold Formica counter.

"Before Peter's sister died several years back, she sent me all of his personal belongings that she'd boxed up after his death. I had closed down my hunt on that years earlier, but I kept it all in case anything ever turned up again. Never even had time to go through it. I have the boxes in storage at my house if you want to take a look."

The death of Peter's sister had seemed another closed door when James started looking back into everything. But she'd not only kept Peter's belongings, she'd sent them to O'Ryan.

"I'd like that very much," James said coolly, trying to keep the excitement from his tone. There was nothing like a clue opening up to set his heart racing.

"Just one catch," O'Ryan said.

"What is it?"

"If there's a story in this, and I know there is, I expect the scoop when you have it."

James chuckled. "You have a deal."

As he hung up the phone, James caught a glimpse of Lisa in the living room talking amicably with Molly and Rosalyn. He knew he couldn't get out of this quick trip to see Leonard Dubois tomorrow. Worse than going with Lisa and Molly to face Dubois was letting them meet the man alone. Dubois might say anything to the women. And he wanted to be there when Molly opened up.

But then he'd get the next flight to New York.

As he watched his daughter and Molly sitting beside each other once again, James wondered if he'd brought them into another dangerous situation. The last time they'd met, someone was shot dead in the street.

He still didn't know who was following him, or why. So how could he assure their safety while he was gone chasing this new lead?

CHAPTERSEVENTEEN

From the backseat of her father's old station wagon, Lisa checked the long, empty stretch of highway behind them. No other cars followed for miles.

After Rosalyn's mention that someone was following her father, Lisa had kept a watchful eye out for anything suspicious.

She'd suspected a tail the night before when she dropped Molly off at the church, and again that morning when she drove from the hotel to her father's to meet Molly and Dad for this drive to the Texas State Prison. If she was followed, the vehicle wasn't behind them now.

Lisa settled back into the seat. With Dad behind the wheel, the flat farmland stretched to an endless horizon as the old station wagon seemed to crawl down the highway. They'd run out of small talk a half hour earlier. Now they rode in scattered silence. In her career, Lisa's interview and interrogation skills were admired. She'd taught workshops to first-year attorneys on the subjects. Yet with Molly, Lisa had failed to establish trust and continued to feel disconnected and awkward around the woman.

"Our denomination has a strong ministry for inmates, but I've never been inside a prison before," Molly said from the front passenger seat.

"They're overrated. Not as much fun as they sound," Lisa said, leaning forward.

Molly tossed a grin her way. Then she pointed toward the sign for the prison as the fields became lined with tall electrified fences topped with razor wire. "It's the size of a small town," she said, taking in the buildings that lined both sides of the road.

Dad cleared his throat. "Higher population than many Texas towns."

He pulled into the parking lot nearest the death row complex set across from the main prison. A group of protestors carrying placards seemed to come alive as they drove up. They hopped up from lawn chairs and shook their signs.

One read "Americans Not Barbarians—No Death Penalty."

Another said, "Stop the Killing!"

"That's for Leonard Dubois," Dad said. "He's getting more press because he's the longest-serving inmate on death row to have an execution date."

Lisa had read numerous articles about Dubois debating the ethics of the government killing a man of his age, or any age at all. None questioned his guilt.

Access to death row inmates was usually restricted to family and attorneys at scheduled times. But with the credentials of a federal prosecutor, a retired FBI agent, and a minister, as well as Lisa's call to a DA in Dallas and Dad's call to whatever powers might be, they'd achieved access to Leonard Dubois without much ado.

As they approached the four-story redbrick building, they were surrounded by protestors shouting their slogans.

They went through the screening process, showing identification, leaving purses, and emptying pockets before going through the X-ray scanner. A correctional officer escorted them through the labyrinth of hallways and checkpoints.

"You all are in Booth 2," the correctional officer said. He led them down a corridor to a room divided by a glass wall from another room. The door closed and locked with the officer remaining inside at the door.

Before they'd settled into the seats, the door on the other side of the glass opened. Leonard Dubois shuffled in with links on his ankles, escorted by another officer.

Dubois's orange jumpsuit hung a few sizes too large except at his wrists, where it appeared too short. He grinned to himself, still not having looked at them, and Lisa saw that he was missing a front tooth. The missing tooth aged him considerably, and Lisa knew if the media got a photograph out, it would win the man some sympathy votes. Yet public sympathy wouldn't save him.

"Well, don't I just have a crowd today," Dubois said with a laugh that turned into a cough. His voice was surprisingly clear through the glass. "Sorry 'bout that. Been feeling under the weather."

"Hello, Mr. Dubois," Molly said. She'd risen from her chair when he walked in and stood at the window. "I'm Pastor Molly Carter, and—"

"Pastor, you say?"

"Yes."

"A woman pastor? Back in my days at church, women couldn't be ministers. Especially not a black woman." Dubois tipped his head to her and sat down.

"It's still like that in some churches," she said, taking no offense.

"Times do change." Dubois rubbed his hands together.

His fingernails needed trimming, and Lisa noticed white lines through the nails indicating that his illness might be more than just a common cold.

Molly looked at Lisa and Dad. "I'm sorry, I just took over. Old habit of being in ministry."

"Go ahead. You're doing well," Lisa said. They hadn't executed a plan for this meeting, and Lisa was intrigued to see how Leonard responded to them.

"Mr. Dubois, I'd like to introduce each one of us," Molly said in a friendly pastoral tone that made Lisa smile.

His eyebrows rose as Molly stated who they were.

"So you're Agent Waldren? Got my letter, my attorney told me."

"Yes," Dad said. He didn't speak further, which surprised Lisa. Her father had given himself to the obsession of saving this man, yet he wasn't going to speak to him?

"And you're related to him?" Dubois asked Lisa.

"He's my father."

Dubois whistled. "Is this about my case or not? I don't know nothing about nobody in here if you're wanting me to testify against someone."

"We're here about your case," Lisa stated.

Dubois studied Dad. "I remember you from the trial. You sat in on part of it, and my attorney wanted you to testify. That was a long time ago. You got old." Dubois laughed, breaking into a cough that wracked his body and bent him in two, with his head falling down by his knees.

"Do you need something? Water?" Molly looked at the officer behind Dubois as if telling him to do something.

"No, no." Dubois put his hand up and coughed into his elbow.

Lisa thought she saw a fine splatter of blood hit his orange suit. Finally, he recovered.

"I'm fine. Guess I'm getting old too."

"We'd like to ask you some questions," Dad said.

Molly glanced at him as if surprised by his lack of sympathy. Lisa sensed a tension radiating from her father. She didn't quite understand what it was, but he'd been especially quiet all morning.

Dubois straightened in the chair. "I'm usually in the other booths. The ones with the telephones. This is nicer, being able to talk. Guess those are the perks of an execution date."

He turned to view the burly correctional officer beside the locked door.

"What do you want to know? And I have some questions for you as well," he said, tapping the glass in front of Dad.

"We were all at that civil rights rally that day," Lisa said. "All three of us."

"You two were there? You must've been little ones."

"Yes, we were very young and only feet away from Benjamin Gray during the shooting."

"If you were there, then you know it weren't me!" Dubois said, jumping up. His chair scraped loudly as it pushed a few feet behind him.

"Dubois," the officer behind him said.

Dubois pulled the chair under him and skidded it toward the glass. He spoke low and urgently. "How come I'm in here if a fed prosecutor, a woman minister, and an FBI agent all know I'm not the guy who killed that Gray fella?"

"We didn't see the real killer," Molly said.

"We have no proof," Lisa added, wondering if coming here was more torture for the man than simply the countdown of days.

Dubois slumped back in his chair. "Then why you come here, bringing all your hope when I'm just fine after all these years? Why are you here?"

"We don't believe you are the killer," Molly said.

"You don't believe? There are plenty of people who don't believe that, and I've still been here all this time. Isn't that right, Mr. FBI Man?"

"If you want help, you need to answer some questions," Dad said.

"Ask what you want."

"Who didn't like you before the rally? What were you doing back then that made you enemies?"

Dubois cleared his throat. "My parents were always afraid. But I was a young man back then, full of excitement and hope. My buddies and me were all fired up to do something about the world. Things were changing in 1965."

"Mr. Dubois," Lisa interrupted. "If you want our help, we need the truth. Not what you and your attorney rehearsed for the media."

Dubois raised his eyebrows. "Is that right? And how can you be of any help, if you don't mind me asking?"

"You have an execution date. My father asked me to help find evidence that might free you. The real killer, evidence that might clear you, or proof of any kind of injustices during your trial . . . there are numerous possibilities. But we need facts, not beliefs."

"What makes you so sure I'm innocent?" Dubois asked. He looked at Molly for the answer.

"I don't know that you are," Molly said. "I just came into this yesterday, but as a child, my family talked about it, saying the wrong man was convicted. People were too scared to talk back then, and what could they have done? Some people say the killer was white."

"A white man?" Dubois laughed long and hard. "A lot of good that's going to do. No white man would ever have gotten convicted of this. Either that's a pack of lies, or it's even more hopeless than I thought."

"You were connected with the Black Panthers?" Dad said.

Dubois's expression became serious. "What's that got to do with anything?"

"It was used to further make you unsympathetic during the trial."

Lisa hadn't read through the court transcripts. There might be a lot more she'd missed besides Dubois's involvement in a black group known in that era for hatred and violence. There was also that other case file in the archives of the Fort Worth PD. Dubois's name was attached to the investigation, but only the cover letter remained. What had that crime been?

"Unsympathetic to who? The jury didn't have sympathy."

"You made enemies before the day of the rally. It would help to know why."

Dubois ran his hands through his hair as he leaned forward in his chair.

"Back then, Black Panthers was just starting. We were mad, really mad, and with good reason. Then comes real talk about a group that might *do* something about how things were. Not just follow the white man's laws and rules. No living under a sense of 'master this or that.' It sounded pretty good for a while. But the Panthers I was around couldn't get along or make decisions. I didn't want to go to that rally." Dubois grew quiet for a moment. "How much time do we have? Seems my time should be up by now."

"We can talk awhile," Lisa said. "Why did you go?"

"Everybody kept talking about that Benjamin Gray. I weren't too interested in him, though—too passive. But I was visiting family in Fort Worth, and they were going. I was late. Didn't get down there with the others."

Lisa knew he'd agonized over the series of events that put him there. She'd seen victims and the guilty alike rehash the path to tragedy again and again like a hamster on a wheel.

"I heard a popping sound. Came a few blocks ahead of me, and I knew it were gunfire. I pulled out my pistol. That was my mistake. I should have just run on away."

"Why did you have a gun?" Molly asked.

"Everywhere I went, I packed a gun. All of us did. My mama was terrified of it, said it would get me killed. I told her that if white men could carry, then I was packing too. But once I pulled out that gun, it was all over."

Lisa imagined the scene from there. He was arrested, hauled in, and maybe there was no other reason than he was a convenient place on which to rest the blame.

"There's no other reason beyond the gun? You don't think you were targeted or being watched? Nothing significant happened before that day?" Lisa studied every twitch and reaction Dubois made as she asked these questions.

He glanced at Molly, then back down at his hands. Slowly he shook his head. "Nothin'. We done here? I'd like to go rest now."

"Sure. But will you compile a list of people you were involved with at that time? Everyone from family members to your buddies' names, every name you can think of," Lisa said.

"I won't snitch on nobody," he said.

"We just want to look for names that connect with other reports and witness accounts to see if we can find some connection that might have been missed."

"Okay, I can do that," Dubois said. He winced as he rose from the chair.

"I'll leave our contact numbers in case you need something."

They followed the officer back through the death row complex to the reception office. Lisa picked up her bag and credentials at the desk and walked into the waiting area where an elderly black woman was struggling to stand up from the chair. Her cane slid from her hand and clattered onto the sterile tile floor.

Lisa bent down and picked up her cane, meeting the eyes of the woman. They were full of tears.

The middle-aged woman beside her reached for the cane and thanked Lisa. Molly and Dad were still collecting their belongings in the room beyond the first security line. Lisa took a seat to wait for them.

"I was given an appointment to see my boy, so why can't I see him?" the older woman said to the other.

"Don't get all upset now, Mrs. Dubois. The man said you'd be allowed inside before long. Some other people were here talking with him."

"I don't have me too much time left with my only child. They took him away from me all these years, and now they're gonna kill him."

"I know, I know. Let's just be patient. You'll get to see him."

Lisa guessed the woman's age to be in the late eighties or early nineties. Her vein-covered hands shook as she wiped at her eyes. Lisa thought of her son, John, her only child. This woman had endured unthinkable pain for almost fifty years of Christmases, birthdays, Mother's Days, and family births and deaths with her little boy always here.

Molly walked into the reception area and approached Lisa.

"Mrs. Dubois, you can see him now," the officer said from the desk. Molly's eyes jumped to the two women.

"Did you hear that? We can take you to see Leonard now," the younger woman said to the older.

Mrs. Dubois put her hands together as if in prayer. "Thank you, Jesus. I just want to see my boy a few more times before he's gone from me. My only child, all these years locked up, now he's gonna be killed, and he didn't even do the crime."

"Yes, I know. You told me. It's okay now, you're going in to see him." The woman tried to soothe her.

Lisa watched the mother of Leonard Dubois with her cane in hand enter the prison where her son had lived for nearly fifty years and where, unless they did something, he would soon die.

Dad had finally reappeared, and as they left the prison, all three were silent.

"That was heartbreaking," Molly said as they reached the car after fighting through the protestors.

Lisa nodded, her eyes connecting with Molly's.

"But Leonard isn't telling us everything," Molly said.

Lisa glanced at the woman and grinned. "Pastor Carter, you would've made a darn good prosecutor."

But how could they get Dubois to come clean about what he was hiding? If his secret was big enough, he might want it taken to the grave.

And after meeting Leonard Dubois, Lisa knew there was another important factor to consider.

"Dad, did you know that Leonard Dubois is sick?"

"What are you talking about?" Dad stopped by the old station wagon.

"You may be trying to save a man who doesn't have long to live anyway. Is it still worth all the effort?"

CHAPTEREIGHTEEN

D idn't you miss the turn?" Lisa asked from behind him.

"You should have taken that last exit." Molly pointed toward the right.

James had set his mind and headed that direction, forgetting that he hadn't told his daughter or Molly his idea.

"I want to make one more stop before going back to the house."

"A stop where?" Lisa asked.

Her annoyance at his driving was thinly veiled, but he'd been behind the wheel decades longer than she had. And he knew she wouldn't be thrilled with his plan.

"I'd like us to return to the scene of Benjamin Gray's shooting."

"Why?" Lisa asked.

Molly's expression seemed to ask the same question.

"It's important to cover all our bases." James didn't say that he hoped it might break loose a memory for one or even all of them. He hadn't been back to the site himself in decades.

"You have the entire crime scene recreated in your garage. What more do we need? I'd like to read the transcripts from Dubois's trial tonight and see if I can reach out to Sergeant Ross."

"This won't take long." James wasn't giving the women a choice. Lisa could argue all she wanted, but he had the steering wheel. Sure, she'd had success with her methods in finding Molly, but this was good old-fashioned detective work that he wouldn't skip over.

Glancing in the rearview mirror, James saw his daughter slump back against the seat. He bit back a smile and focused as the traffic pressed around the car.

Once they reached Fort Worth, James took the exit for downtown. Leaning against the steering wheel, he read street signs with cars honking behind him. Once he almost turned the wrong way down a one-way street.

"Dad, do you know where you're going?" Lisa had kept silent until this point.

James didn't respond, just continued to turn down streets and then back again. After another fifteen minutes, he couldn't deny it any longer.

"I may be lost," he said.

Molly burst into laughter.

"I used to know Fort Worth like the back of my hand, but they've done so much renovating, it's hard to recognize anything now," James said.

"Take the next left," Molly said. She joined in the search with him and rolled down her window for a better view. Then, "Is that it?" she asked.

James pulled over to open the map on his phone. He dropped the phone onto his lap, the worthless thing, and wished for an old tried-and-true paper map. He followed where Molly pointed. The layout, the small square at one end, the massive trees that hadn't been planted . . . it had to be the place.

"This is it."

After parking in a garage, they walked to the small square. James carried a manual camera he'd grabbed from his trunk. He didn't go anywhere without a camera tucked in his car, just in case.

"It doesn't look at all the same," Molly said.

The sidewalks and building fronts had all been refurbished. The area appeared geared for a young swanky crowd, with its boutiques, expensive restaurants, wine bars, and clubs with live entertainment.

"I would never guess that I've been here before," Lisa said.

James turned in a circle, then walked a few dozen yards until he stopped. The old rounded seats were still there.

"Will you two sit down the way you were that day? Like in the snapshot."

Lisa and Molly sat down, then switched places. James could see the location as it was nearly fifty years ago. He took a few shots, advancing the film and trying to get the exact spot where he'd taken the others.

"Is that the same camera?" Lisa asked.

"What's wrong with keeping things? People throw perfectly good things away too easily these days."

"If you use the camera on your phone, we can upload the photos onto the computer and I'll send them to Drew for comparison," Lisa said.

James knew that was a good idea, but he wanted to develop the photographs in black-and-white just like the old snapshots.

Molly rose from the bench, and before he could ask her to return for a few more photographs, he noticed how shaken she appeared. She turned away from them as he said her name.

"I'd like to stop this now."

James lowered the camera to hang around his neck.

"Are you okay?" Lisa asked her.

"I'm not feeling well. Are we done here?"

Molly wiped at her face—was she crying? James couldn't be sure, and she was trying to behave as if everything were fine.

"You remembered something," Lisa said.

Molly shook her head. "I'm not sure. I don't know."

"What is it?" Lisa asked.

James wanted to get in there and question her but remained farther back.

"I don't want to talk about it. Please take me home."

CHAPTER NINETEEN

Someone tried to kill him."

James fumbled with the phone on his bedside table. Not fully awake, he'd grabbed the receiver thinking it was his alarm clock.

"What? Who is this?" He sat up in bed, swinging his legs over the side.

"George Wentworth Jr. I'm down here at Texas State Penitentiary. My client is Leonard Dubois."

"Someone tried to kill Dubois?" James flipped the lamp on.

"Yes, that's what I said. He's been telling me that he believed someone was after him. The prison is investigating, but he's not happy about being in the infirmary. Seems convinced he's going to be killed in there."

"Slow down a minute. Dubois is in solitary confinement. How could someone try to kill him?"

"Poison. His meals have been laced with it."

"You have proof of that?"

"Preliminary proof. The police have been called in. And the prison

141

is holding an in-house investigation. They'll be testing the food for confirmation."

James glanced at the clock. It was five in the morning. Lisa had told him that Dubois was very sick, but he hadn't paid much attention to her assessment. Wouldn't the prison doctor have checked him out if he displayed anything serious? But Lisa had been right.

"Are they treating him?"

"They say that they are. But I haven't been in to see him yet. I could use some help with this."

"What kind of help?"

"I don't know, but I want my client safe. My father represented Leonard before me, and I've known him all my life. He's a good man. If someone in the prison was trying to kill him, how can he be safe while still in the prison?"

"Isn't that a matter for the courts?"

"Will Leonard be alive that long?"

James rubbed his eyes. "I don't have much influence anymore. But I know someone who does."

"Just hurry. I have a bad feeling about this."

CHAPTER TWENTY

Lisa sat at the hotel desk still in her pajamas. She'd been on the phone all morning. Papers with scribbled notes covered the desk surrounding her computer.

Molly had brought coffee, though Lisa's sat mostly untouched until she admitted she didn't drink the brew.

"How will we ever be friends if you don't like coffee?" Molly said. "Please don't tell me you're one of those vegans as well."

Lisa wondered if they might become friends, and if then Molly would tell her what she'd remembered in Fort Worth.

"Not a vegan or a vegetarian. I don't care about all that organic stuff either. But I do avoid caffeine."

Molly sighed. "I might be able to get over that. One perk, I get to drink your coffee." She downed the second cup as she waited to hear the outcome of Lisa's phone calls.

Finally, Lisa pushed away from the desk. "Dubois should be safe now," she said. She ran her fingers through her hair and wondered what she looked like with bed head and no makeup.

"Do they really believe someone tried to kill him?" Molly sat down on the small love seat.

"They're bringing in a federal team to investigate along with the local police. But it sounds like it, and the warden's taking it seriously," Lisa said.

"Will this get him released?"

"No. We can hope for a delay in his execution date. They moved him to a more isolated and secure area." Lisa picked up the papers covered in notes and phone numbers she'd scribbled out and clasped them together with a paper clip.

"Who would want to kill him? I mean, he's set to die soon anyway."

"It makes little sense unless Leonard has information that someone is afraid will get out. At first I was concerned it was due to our visit, but it sounds like the poisoning began at least a week ago."

Lisa wrote down a few additional notes on several Post-its and pressed them onto the front of her small stack, then slipped it into the drawer where she kept all material related to Leonard Dubois. Since arriving, she'd made the hotel desk her own.

"Are you going out to the prison? Should I?" Molly asked.

"I don't think we can see him today. They've got most of the prison locked down. Maybe in a few days, but I know I can't do another drive out there with my father behind the wheel."

"I'm with you there," Molly said with an exaggerated sigh of relief. "I better head over to the church, unless there's anything else—"

Lisa's phone rang. The number was from her house in Boston.

"Jessica?" Lisa said as she answered. Her house sitter never called when Lisa was away.

"Someone tried to break into the house!" The girl's voice was frantic.

"Slow down, Jess. First of all, are you safe? Is the person gone? Did you call 911?"

Lisa had grabbed up the hotel phone, preparing to call the Boston

PD on another line if Jessica hadn't done so already. Molly sprang to her feet and was at her side.

"Yes, yes, the police are here." The fear in Jessica's voice set Lisa's heart racing, though she remained outwardly calm. The girl was a few years older than John and attending college to be an elementary school teacher.

"Tell me what happened," Lisa said in a soothing voice.

"I wouldn't have been here, but I was in bed with a bad sinus infection. I was sleeping when the security alarm went off. The guy took off right away, was gone before the police arrived. But they have him on the security camera. He was trying to get in through your office. But, Lisa, I don't know if I can stay here tonight."

"That's fine, do what you need to do. You did everything right, I'm proud of you. And I'm glad that you're safe. Can I talk to the officer in charge?"

"What happened?" Molly whispered.

"Someone tried to break into my house in Boston," Lisa said to Molly.

Molly clasped her cheeks in dismay. "What is going on?"

The officer introduced himself and already knew who Lisa was. He retold her the facts that Jessica had relayed, adding that they'd found little else except a few footprints near the office door and in a section of landscaping near the street. Lisa's security camera had gotten footage of the intruder.

After thanking the officer and leaving her number, she talked to Jessica again to be sure the girl was okay. Next she called her security company and asked for a copy of the footage to be sent to her as soon as possible.

She hung up and considered texting Drew to ask him to check in on Jessica, but she knew he was in the middle of a film shoot this morning.

"Do you think the two are related?" Molly asked.

Lisa didn't know what she meant at first. "You mean Leonard's poisoning and this? No, I don't think so. I get a lot of threats in my job."

"Seems strange to me, but this isn't my line of business."

"Wait a minute," Lisa said, taking in the room. She stood and walked around. "My suitcase wasn't on the floor. Dad put it on the luggage rack in the closet. I remember because I put it there, always. And I certainly wouldn't put it on top of my shoes."

"What are you saying?" Molly followed her to the closet.

Lisa turned and studied the rest of the room. Nothing else appeared out of place, but she'd been in the room since yesterday evening.

"Maybe it was housekeeping," Molly offered.

Lisa ran through her morning. She'd been at the computer and desk since getting the call about the probable attempt on Leonard Dubois's life.

The night before, she'd been tired after returning from the prison and suffering through her father's drive home. She'd spent the evening reading through e-mails from work and addressing court details she'd ignored, while sitting in bed with her computer. She'd grabbed her silk pajamas and tossed what she'd worn to the prison onto a chair in the corner.

Lisa opened each of the desk drawers. In the Dubois drawer, beneath the papers she'd written that morning, she had the copies from the Fort Worth Police Department, the pictures her father had sent her back in Boston, and other notes, but they seemed out of order. At the very bottom sat the picture Rosalyn had found on the Internet of Benjamin Gray's corpse with her Post-it note that read *Blackstone Corporation*.

"I'm sure I had this in a different drawer," Lisa muttered. The drawer below it held everything she'd researched about the civil rights leader. The photograph had been in that drawer, she felt sure of it.

"Do you think someone was in here?" Molly asked, bending down to check beneath the bed.

"No one can fit under there—I check that every night," Lisa said. "I'm a bit OCD about certain things. My suitcase is always on the rack. And even though my desktop is usually messy, I like my files organized a certain way. Last night I did think my toiletry bag was in a different place as well. I'm going to ask the hotel to look at their recordings. They have cameras throughout the hallways. Can you stick around for a while?"

"If you need my help, I can rearrange my schedule."

"Great, and you can use my computer if you need it. I'll get dressed and go downstairs. Just lock the door behind me, and don't let anyone in."

When the manager heard Lisa's concerns, he went above and beyond helping out. He and the head of security located the recordings of her hallway from the day before. They viewed Lisa leaving the room and the maid coming in to clean. After she moved to another room, a well-dressed man came down the hall and found the housekeeper. The man spoke to the woman, pointing to himself, raising his hands as if frustrated, then looking at his watch and seeming to plead by folding his hands in a prayer and holding up a finger as if to say it would be only a minute. That was Lisa's interpretation anyway, and the housekeeper opened the door.

"She let him in," the hotel manager said angrily, grabbing up his phone. "We have a strict policy about our guests' privacy and safety. She's done here."

"She made a mistake. Please don't fire her," Lisa said. "This guy was probably very convincing."

The older black woman appeared close to retirement. The recording showed her standing for a moment at the door as the man went inside. She moved back to clean the other room, then returned and knocked on Lisa's door. The man came out, smiling and chatting with her, then he hurried off.

The hotel manager was livid, but once he realized Lisa wasn't holding him or the hotel responsible, he calmed considerably.

Lisa returned to Molly and updated her, then called Dad. She told him about her house in Boston and now her hotel room.

"I'll be right there," Dad said and hung up the phone.

"So what now?" Molly said.

"I don't want to scare you, but do you live alone?" Lisa asked.

"I've got two large Labs. Sweetest guys, but not so sweet to intruders. And why would I be in danger?"

"You probably aren't, but we should be careful."

Molly and Lisa made plans to visit Molly's family. As they talked,

Lisa's thoughts jumped around to the numerous elements they were dealing with.

Leonard Dubois was hiding something. Now someone wanted him dead, most likely so he wouldn't talk. But about what?

Sweeney and the reaction from the Fort Worth PD made it appear likely that some kind of a cover-up had occurred.

Someone from a company in Florida had released the image of Benjamin Gray's corpse onto the Internet for no apparent reason. Lisa wrote herself a note to ask Rosalyn to search other websites to see if more pictures had been posted.

There was Dad's hunch about some historic missing key that once belonged to JFK or Bobby Kennedy. That piece seemed too far from what they were doing to matter, but she wasn't disregarding anything at this point.

And in their digging, they'd touched a nerve with someone. It seemed that person wanted to find out what Lisa had uncovered. Why else the double break-ins? Since her arrival, she'd only uncovered more questions and no concrete answers.

It hit Lisa again that a stranger had been in the room. He'd riffled through her belongings, and what if she'd come back when he was there? She had a bedtime routine that included locking doors and checking closets and under the bed. After the horrific crimes she'd prosecuted over the years, this routine helped her sleep. At home, her advanced security system was another nightly sleep aid.

"You do a good job of hiding it," Molly said, studying her.

"Hiding what?"

"When you're worried about something," Molly said with a kind smile.

"Worried? I suppose a little," Lisa said, realizing she wasn't the best at gauging her own emotions. She dealt with the issue or problem that presented itself. How she felt was further down her list of concerns. "But then, I'm not the only one good at hiding my worries."

"I'm a pastor, so I try not to worry but to pray instead."

"Does it work?"

Molly smiled. "When I remember to do it. I prayed last night about this digging up the past. You want to know what happened in Fort Worth when your dad started taking our pictures?"

"Yes. Did you remember something?"

"When your father started clicking the camera, I felt the fear from that day come back over me. I may have seen Benjamin Gray get shot. I remembered blood. Blood on more than one person. But I can't be sure. And I couldn't testify to it in court. Isn't that all that matters right now?"

Dad arrived in a fluster, looking around the room as if the intruder were still lurking in a corner. "We should dust for fingerprints."

"He wore gloves. I already viewed the security tapes. The hotel has been very helpful, and they're giving me a copy."

"You're staying at the house," he said firmly. "Molly, you can stay there too. We have plenty of room."

"I'm perfectly safe here," Lisa said. "Anyway, Molly and I are taking a drive to visit her family, probably tomorrow. And you are going to New York."

"I'll go later."

"Dad, calm down. My security system at home did its job. If I'd been here, no one would've gotten in—I always use the latch when I'm in my room. Molly has dogs. She can also stay here if she gets nervous."

"Nobody's stalking me. I'm a harmless pastor," Molly said with a grin. "I have divine protection, my dogs, and I didn't mention my handy .357. I'm a Texas girl, you know."

"I'm sorry we pulled you into this, both of you," Dad said.

"Don't worry. I was pulled into this back in 1965. I'm fine," Molly said.

"We're okay." Lisa reached her arm over her father's shoulder, and he grabbed her into a hug that took her breath away.

"If anything happened to you," he said with a sharp intake of breath.

Lisa could feel the ragged breathing of his chest. "It's okay, Dad. We're okay," she said as he held on tightly.

She couldn't remember the last time she'd been in her father's arms like this. It felt awkward and frightening. But she didn't want him to let her go.

———

That night Lisa sat in the hotel bed researching Benjamin Gray. In her experience, the victim of a crime was often sidelined in the hunt for justice. But if someone listened, the victim's lost voice could speak more answers than questions and offer more evidence than silence.

Benjamin Gray had grown up in a small Louisiana town. His minister grandfather was Gray's biggest influence, according to his speeches and writings, but most of the family labored in farming positions and never rose above poverty level.

As a young man Gray left school after his first year of college when his father was killed in an unspecified accident. In a speech Gray once implied that his father's death had been a crime, and that he thought of his father's nearly unrecognizable corpse whenever he considered backing down from his cause. His message, similar to that of Reverend Martin Luther King Jr., spoke of nonviolent resistance. He sought to inspire the black community to create change by living lives of integrity, education, innovation, and morality. As Lisa read his speeches, she understood why he inspired people, and also why others would hate him.

Her phone lit up with a text from Molly.

Are you okay there alone? I can loan you a dog.

Lisa laughed at the thought. She preferred being by herself to most people's company. But she was surprisingly comfortable with Molly and could easily have shared her hotel room with the woman, perhaps even with her dogs. Lisa rarely met people she liked to such an extent.

Your dog may not appreciate the offer. But I'm good. What about you?

No worries. See you in the morning. I'll bring the coffee.

Lisa was about to respond when Molly wrote again.

Just kidding about the coffee, but I know a great juice bar on the way out of town.

Perfect. See you then.

Lisa returned to Benjamin Gray, writing down facts and thoughts as she read and tagging articles to print. The name of Gray's hometown in Louisiana sounded familiar, but she couldn't place it. Her research of the area didn't turn up anything. It was a small town in the South, built along a waterway with nothing special to distinguish it from other Louisiana communities.

She read through the names in Gray's entourage, running searches on each of them. Most had continued in the civil rights movement or become prominent leaders in their communities. Nothing suspicious caught her attention.

Next she searched for information about Gray's love life. Before his death he was engaged to a beautiful young woman from New Orleans. Lisa wrote down the name *Madeline Fitzgerald* and was searching for more about her when Drew sent a text. She knew he was en route to Chicago where he was speaking at a media seminar in the morning.

I don't like this. Time to come back.

She smiled at his concern. They were back to daily updates, though something was different between them now. Lisa hadn't allowed herself to analyze whether that was good or bad, but he hadn't taken the news of her break-ins and Leonard's poisoning well.

You aren't even in Boston, she wrote.

I'll be back tomorrow. You can stay with me.

Lisa bit the edge of her lip. What was he doing?

Purely platonic, if you insist, he added.

You told me to do this. I'd regret it if I didn't help my father.

I take it back.

She could almost hear Drew's voice saying it, and it made her miss him. Throughout the evening since her father finally dragged himself away, she'd felt surges of unexpected emotion.

Good night, Drew. Talk to you tomorrow. I'm going to try calling John.

Lisa stretched out on the bed, setting the research aside as she dialed her son in London. Throughout the day John had kept coming into her thoughts. They usually spoke several times a week, but since Lisa's trek to Dallas they'd only communicated through quick messages.

"What's wrong?" John said as he answered.

"Nothing. Why would you ask that?" Lisa asked, enjoying the sound of his voice.

"We make scheduled video calls. Sundays and Wednesdays most often. And my mother does very little spontaneously."

Lisa heard the sound of laughter and music in the background. "Nothing's wrong. Where are you?"

"Eating at a pub. I stepped outside so I can hear you. So everything is really okay?"

"Yes," she said, missing her son with a deep physical ache that surprised her. "But . . ."

"What?"

"Nothing, never mind, go back to your friends. Let's schedule a video call for this weekend."

"Mom, what is it?"

Lisa closed her eyes for a moment as emotion filled her. "It's, well . . . was I gone too much with my job?"

"What?"

"When you were growing up . . . do you feel like I hugged you enough, told you I love you?"

John laughed, not mockingly but with the laugh he used when she overly mothered him.

"My mommy misses me," he said, teasing, but then in a lowered tone added, "I miss you too. Yes, you hugged me enough. And I love you, Mom."

CHAPTER TWENTY-ONE

They were fourteen stories up. Stanley peered over the edge of the rooftop and watched the gusty wind twist into dirt devils and run through the deserted building site.

A memory came to him of a man who had fallen nearly as far. Stanley hadn't done the tossing, and he was only ten years old when he saw it. His father pulled him from bed in the middle of the night and brought him to the rooftop. Stanley had stared at the man twisted on the ground in a pool of blood so dark it appeared black instead of red.

"That is what happens to traitors," his father had told him.

Later Stanley learned that the dead man was a family friend. They'd vacationed together, and Stanley often played with the man's son.

Now, looking at the construction site below, he couldn't remember any of their names, only that the newspapers reported the death as a suicide.

"When is the next building inspection?" Stanley asked, taking in the bulldozer and construction equipment parked where the multistory parking structure would stand in a few months.

His nephew approached hesitantly, keeping his distance.

"Week after next. We're on target now that the lawsuit has been dropped. After we pull permits, we'll move forward with the Hacienda Highland project."

Stanley wondered what his former foe Arroyo looked like now, deteriorating in the ice cooler with his bullet-riddled face bloated from the seawater and eaten by sea creatures. The detective on the case continued to hound Stanley, an annoyance he hoped would soon disappear.

"Good. When do you estimate the ribbon cutting?"

"August," Marcus said, sliding his hands into his pockets.

A long silence between them made Marcus squirm. Stanley breathed in the scent of fresh lumber and sawdust. He could smell the river, though it was half a mile off, and he could also smell Marcus's fear. It was time to find out why he was so afraid.

Stanley sat on the raised ledge of the rooftop, fourteen stories of space behind his back, and motioned for Marcus to sit beside him.

Marcus looked ready to wet his pants, but he did as Stanley requested.

"I'm angry," Stanley said after a few more drawn-out moments.

"If you could hear me out," Marcus stuttered, jumping to his feet.

"Go on. Make your case." Stanley folded his arms at his chest.

"You keep telling me to take some initiative. I've tried figuring out how to do that. Finally, this seemed like a great opportunity."

"I have told you to take initiative, this is true. You are great with money, figures, and running a business. But you doubt yourself in other areas. You also don't think through and look at the wider picture and consequences. Nor—"

Marcus cut in as if pleading for his life. "I thought it would solve everything. If that inmate died, then who would try finding out the real story? We had the contact inside the prison. He could make it look like an illness. The man is old, after all."

Stanley hated incompetence. He hated explaining the obvious. If

Marcus were not his own blood, his impatience with the man would've run out long ago.

"Think things through, Marcus. The prison would've ordered an autopsy. They most likely would have discovered the poisoning, which makes more people than just this Agent Waldren and his daughter start digging into things. And contacts are only loyal when it benefits them."

"The contact has no knowledge of us. None of our negotiations can be linked to you or the company." Marcus set his foot on the ledge as he peered over.

"That's how it may appear, but it's surprising what can be uncovered these days. All this new technology that I don't quite understand. And we have another issue."

"What is it?" Marcus said with a shaky tone.

"Our company files have been hacked, and some of my personal files from the plantation have turned up on the Internet." Stanley rose from the ledge, stretching out his back.

"What?" Beads of sweat lined Marcus's forehead.

"Ricky is going over the computer issues."

"Our financials?"

"Possibly, but for certain my personal files. Yet what's very strange is how photographs I kept in a safe at the plantation showed up on the Internet."

"So someone broke into the safe?"

"They must have, because I've seen the images, but they put everything back. Nothing is missing as far as I know. I'll be going out there tomorrow to be sure. Not only that, but the images were posted from our company—it was an IP address or something. Ricky can explain it better."

Marcus appeared perplexed, but Stanley sometimes wondered if his nephew played up the nervous absentminded professor act. He'd lived long enough to know not to trust anyone, even a bumbling nephew.

"We have a traitor in the company?" Marcus asked.

"Yes, we do." He studied his nephew intently as the wind blew around them.

Molly reacted by praying for their protection. She made them all hold hands in a circle as she prayed aloud. James had never experienced that before, and he'd stood unmoving when she asked if anyone else wanted to pray. Rosalyn jumped in with some words about God's favor upon them—where her prayer came from, he didn't know—then he and Lisa stood in the awkward quiet until Molly wrapped it up. Leaving the three women behind after the break-ins and their being followed, he found that the prayer brought a surprising measure of relief as he said good-bye.

After he arrived at the chain hotel decorated to look like a country inn, James checked in at the front desk, grabbed a few cookies from the welcome tray, and rolled his suitcase into the room that smelled just a hint like cigarette smoke. He sat on the flowery bedcover, still unsure if leaving Dallas had been the right decision. His instincts were out of sorts. He couldn't tell if his apprehension was reasonable or emotional.

Pulling out his cell phone, he saw a missed call and message. His fingers fumbled with the buttons, then he heard the voice.

"Waldren, this is William O'Ryan. I had the boxes delivered to my office here in Manhattan. It'll be easier than your trekking out to the house. We can meet tomorrow afternoon when I'm off the air. Then I leave the next morning for ten days. Hope your flight came in all right. See you tomorrow."

James hung up and slowly tapped out a text to Rosalyn telling her he'd arrived. He wished he knew how to add one of those funny faces Rosalyn would send to him, but she'd get a kick out of the message regardless. He rarely did the text message thing.

His phone beeped a new message back within seconds.

Was just sending you a mental message to let me know you arrived or not. Since you don't answer your phone, I used telepathy. And it worked!

James chuckled aloud. Another beep sounded.

My gut tells me you're going to uncover something big. So quit worrying about us, enjoy NYC a little. Go eat a hot dog for me with extra onions and mustard.

James typed back, OK.

Rosalyn was right. With William O'Ryan leaving on a book tour, this trip was James's best shot to go through Peter's belongings. They didn't have any time to waste, with Dubois's execution date approaching.

The prison visit had only brought that into sharper reality. It also sharpened the sting of guilt. James had backed off from the investigation in the 1960s as instructed, as threatened, and for good reason. But regardless, Leonard Dubois had spent every moment since his arrest in 1965 locked behind the razor wire. A man had only one life.

James paced the room, flipped through the television channels, and finally pulled on his coat. The smells of New York changed at every turn. Espresso, pizza, car exhaust, sea air, sewer, and fragrant flowers took turns assaulting his nose. The scent of hot dogs drew him to a stand at the corner of a park.

"With mustard and extra onions, please," he said.

The next afternoon James climbed out of a taxi in front of the Manhattan skyscraper that housed the international news network and cable channel where O'Ryan worked. He opened the glass doors and approached the long reception counter with numerous people working at the desk.

"James Waldren here for William O'Ryan. He's expecting me," he told the woman who greeted him. She asked for his identification, which she then scanned on a computer screen. Post-9/11 New York was a different world from his days in the Bureau.

"He'll be right down," the woman said as she hung up a telephone.

James looked out onto busy Sixth Avenue swarming with taxis, vehicles, and people walking quickly beneath the drizzly afternoon.

"Special Agent Waldren. It's been a long time." William O'Ryan strode toward him. The kid journalist was middle-aged now, fit, well groomed, and sharply dressed in a tailored suit. They shook hands heartily.

"I'm retired Special Agent Waldren now," James said with a chuckle.

"You don't act it. Retirement is supposed to be about fishing trips, not digging into an old investigation, am I right?"

"I tried that and some woodworking, but this case wouldn't leave me alone."

O'Ryan motioned for James to follow him. They went through security and up an escalator.

"I can appreciate that. I don't have time for a dozen or more stories that I'm dying to track down. Let's hope you have some progress today. I'm having a hard time leaving you to this. It's one of my unresolved stories as well, you know."

"Yes, I remember that green reporter out to make his mark. Time has been good to you."

O'Ryan laughed as James followed him through a series of elevators and doorways that opened with his security badge.

"We try to fight time, but she never loses. Can I get you anything?" O'Ryan paused at a small kitchen area.

"I'm good, maybe later."

"Help yourself. There's coffee, tea, a vending machine around the corner, and a few sandwiches in the refrigerator left over from lunch. You're going to be here for a while," O'Ryan said, turning down a long hallway.

They stopped at an unmarked door, and James noticed the names across the hall for offices of news personalities he'd watched on television. O'Ryan unlocked the door and flipped on the light.

"Here we are," he said. "I didn't open the boxes yet, but I wiped them down. They've been in the back of my storage since Peter's sister died. By then I'd long since closed that case and moved on. No reason or time for me to go through a dead man's old notes."

"But you couldn't get rid of it?" James said, looking at the white storage boxes neatly stacked on the floor with the name *P. Hughes* written across the front. There were several chairs and a long empty table in the windowless room. Against one wall a large copy machine sat idling beneath a shelf of office supplies.

"Possibilities can't be tossed away. You should see my storage area. Someday I would've opened these up—maybe instead of fishing. I'm glad you can get to it before then. You have me intrigued; it's tough not to stay, but I have quite a bit to wrap up before I leave the office. Remember, if there's a story here, you come to me first."

James was struck by the opportunity standing before him.

"Well, actually, I do have a story for you. One that involves a man about to be executed in Texas."

O'Ryan paused at the door. "You have my attention. What's up?"

"He didn't commit the crime. My daughter serves as a federal prosecutor in Boston; she's helping me with it. I'm hoping the evidence is in here perhaps."

"So you aren't here about Peter—what he was doing behind the scenes, what made Hoover so furious at him."

"Hoover? What are you talking about?" James asked.

O'Ryan glanced at his watch. "Hate to do this, but I need to get downstairs for some quick shots, and I have some calls to make before the end of the day. Then I'll come back, and we'll get this ironed out. For now, see what you can find."

As he heard O'Ryan's footsteps disappear down the hall, James stared at the storage boxes.

In the years after Peter's disgrace from the Bureau and exit from the Waldrens' lives, James entertained all manner of reprehensible thoughts about the man. Maybe he'd been a double agent, working for the Communists. Had he been bought by the Mafia? Or was he a traitor to his country in one way or another? Now O'Ryan mentioned the head of the FBI himself, J. Edgar Hoover, being furious at Peter. Hoover was certainly not an enemy anyone wanted to have. Even US presidents, world leaders, and A-list actors and actresses were terrified of the man.

Perhaps all the answers lay within these boxes.

James found a pair of scissors on a shelf by the copy machine and cut through the tape on each box, freeing the lids.

The first storage box was filled with packets of photographs. The next one was cushioned with foam bubbles and appeared filled with framed images, awards, and degrees.

Another box looked as if Peter's sister had simply dumped the contents of his desk inside. There were notes, writing instruments, paper clips, gambling chips, beer caps, candy bar wrappers, and several yo-yos.

James pulled out a yo-yo, wound it, and flipped it down and back up. He'd forgotten how much his friend liked yo-yos. Peter had tried teaching Lisa once, but she was too young and ended up pulling it around the room by the string. They'd laughed watching her until she swung it around and nearly broke the television.

Beneath the next lid, James found perfectly organized files with marked tabs with Peter's personals: insurance, utility bills, social security benefits, investments, rental agreements . . . Nothing out of the ordinary that James could see.

The fifth box had more files. When James read the tabs, he realized these weren't personal documents but Peter's investigations. The tabs were neatly organized and alphabetized.

One caught his eye: *Gray, B. (1965)*.

James pulled out the file and felt his heart rate increase.

Inside the file folder James found a packet of photographs and moved to the table to set each image out. They were photos from the civil rights rally, but completely out of order.

He stopped when he saw himself and Lisa through the crowd. The image reminded him of his photographs of Lisa and Molly, only these had been taken from farther away. In this picture, he and Lisa had just arrived and were holding hands.

The film negatives fluttered out of the pack and onto the table. They were cut in several pieces but were numbered along the bottom. James rearranged the photos by matching them to the negatives, raising the negative to the light to see the silhouetted image. Picture after picture, he laid them into a timeline that led up to Benjamin Gray's death.

Something was wrong with the numbering. Then James realized that some of the negatives had been removed; that's why they were cut into so many pieces. The matching photographs were missing as well.

James studied the progression and contents of each photograph. In one he saw the entourage of Benjamin Gray moving up the street. But that was the only photo including the man. Most were random shots of the crowd along the sidewalk and marchers with their placards.

On the outside of the photo sleeve, James read his friend's handwriting from when he filled out the information for developing the film. *Single prints, 35mm film, 28 images.*

James counted twenty-two photos on the table. Six images were missing from the negatives, and the printed pictures were gone too. Someone, perhaps Peter, had made sure the photographs would never be seen. Most of the missing photos were at the end of the roll, near the time of Benjamin Gray's death. Two pictures were cut from earlier shots of the rally.

Where were the missing photographs? And what did they show?

James studied the images but finally conceded that he'd hit a dead end. He moved to the rest of the documents in the file.

His impulse was to dig through the file and every storage box to find something, anything, but he knew better. By going through every piece carefully and methodically, he'd have less risk of missing something. He needed to be as thorough and precise as the time allowed.

James found an official FBI report cover as if Peter had filed a report, but the report itself was missing.

The date he'd typed was that of the civil rights rally. The time was late afternoon. The reporting officer was their old superior, Hartgraves. It noted that four pages were included, but the cover was the only page in the folder. James flipped through the rest of the folder but only found newspaper clippings about the shooting.

He closed the folder. But if Peter had filed an official report with the FBI, why wasn't anything done to save Leonard Dubois?

James's eyes moved to the display of photographs lined up across the table.

Why would Peter save the entire roll of film from the day of the parade except for those six photographs? Peter had to know about a cover-up. And from the looks of it, that extended beyond the Fort Worth PD and included James's own Federal Bureau of Investigation.

CHAPTER TWENTY-THREE

I hope you're hungry," Molly said as she drove up to a two-story home overlooking a sparkling lake. The driveway and street in the exclusive subdivision were lined with vehicles.

"Are we intruding on a party?" Lisa asked as she took in the cars. This was supposed to be an intimate meeting with Molly's mother. It looked more like a family reunion.

"That would be my sister's doing," Molly said with a sigh. "I bet she told our cousin Lacy we were coming out and Lacy wanted to say hello, then Lacy told Aunt Miranda, and before long they were talking about food and who else would be hurt if they weren't invited, and here we have it."

Lisa counted more than ten cars.

"I always wanted a big family, but this is a lot," Lisa said as Molly drove past the cars and up to the house. "As a child I begged my mom for a brother or a sister. Unsuccessfully. I swore that when I grew up I'd have six children. Or a dozen."

Molly glanced her way, then sighed dramatically. "I thank the good

Lord for my family, I really do, but they can't leave anything alone. It's bad enough that I'm single, and though I need to lose fifteen pounds, my aunts will say I'm too thin and try stuffing me full of food. They'll be stuffing it into you too when they see that figure."

"So I'll be leaving here with my pants unbuttoned?"

"Maybe unzipped too. We should have worn stretch pants." Molly turned off the engine.

On the drive, Molly had told Lisa stories of her family. The initial discomfort between them had flipped like a light switch since yesterday in Lisa's hotel room. It seemed the attempt on Dubois's life and the intruder in her room had lifted any lasting suspicions Molly had about Lisa and her father, and Lisa's impairing awkwardness had dissipated.

Molly told Lisa that her mother had recently moved from an apartment into the house of Molly's sister and brother-in-law ninety minutes north of Dallas. Lisa wasn't sure why she'd expected a more modest home, and it bothered her that she'd made an assumption. Molly didn't display a sense of prosperity, but her sister was certainly more affluent than the usual minister's lifestyle.

"It's beautiful here," Lisa said as they stepped out of the car. The warm spring day was filled with the scent of rain and sweet flowering jasmine. Children shouted happily as they played down at the sparkling lake that was dressed with tall green trees. Lisa caught the rich smell of food drifting from the house.

Molly reached into the backseat and pulled out a covered pie dish.

"Mom's favorite sweet potato pie, but I think a feast awaits us."

The red front door swung open as they approached, and Lisa and Molly were swept into a ruckus of hugs and greetings. Lisa couldn't remember any of the names; there were too many at once. Molly's family encompassed every age from baby to elderly, and they peppered her with questions about herself until Lisa felt the urge to bolt. She was accustomed to polite social events, not family parties overcome with noise, laughter, and personal questions.

"Did you leave your husband back in Boston?"

"Do you work at that Pentagon? What is a federal prosecutor?"

"I know a lady in Boston. Ellen Robins. She cuts hair, do you know her?"

Molly steered Lisa through her family, apologizing at times for various comments, and around the house, decorated in a Southern style with peach and turquoise accents. Tall windows offered views of the lake at every turn. Lisa kept meeting people until they reached a kitchen laden with dishes of food and more cooking on the stovetop.

"You had to turn this into a family reunion, really, Evelyn?" Molly said after Lisa was introduced to Molly's sister. Evelyn wore an apron and red dress with matching red lipstick and heels. Lisa felt underdressed in her jeans, designer T-shirt, and cardigan sweater.

"I didn't mean for it to happen. Once I told Aunt Miranda you were bringing someone from Boston, she wanted to pop by and meet her, then she told Lacy, Eva May, Jennica, and Auntie Peeps. It moved on from there," Evelyn said with a roll of her eyes that reminded Lisa of Molly. Evelyn grabbed up oven mitts and pulled out a large ham that appeared worthy of Christmas dinner.

"I can't believe all this food," Lisa said. Her family gatherings often centered on food from favorite bistros and bakeries. This was all home cooking, and enough to feed a small homeless shelter.

"This is a normal family get-together. You should see the food at weddings and funerals." Evelyn laughed as she checked the meat thermometer on the ham.

"Where's Mama?" Molly asked.

"Getting some fresh air on the back porch. Go on out and say hello. She's having a good day. She'll be pleased you arrived. That's all she's talked about all morning. But food is served in fifteen minutes."

Lisa followed Molly toward the large glass doors. They stopped to greet a couple with an adorable baby boy in the father's arms, and it took another few minutes to pull away.

Then Molly opened the French doors to a long back porch that overlooked the lake. A petite older woman wrapped in a crocheted blanket sat at the far end with her face upturned toward the bit of sunlight shining through the trees.

"You're going to get a sunburn," Molly chided.

"Oh, girl, don't be silly. Get over here and give your mama a hug and kiss."

Molly bent down and was engulfed in a full embrace and kiss that left a lipstick mark on her cheek.

"It's about time you got here, daughter. I've been enduring all the gossip without you. And where's your guest? I'm excited to meet her." Molly's mother looked around her daughter toward Lisa.

"Mama, this is Lisa Waldren. This is my mother, Bernadette."

"Get over here for your hug and kiss. Molly tells me about a lot of people, but you are more interesting than most."

"Oh really. What did she say about me?" Lisa bent low to receive a hug and kiss from the older woman. She nonchalantly wiped the lipstick from her cheek as Molly had done.

"My Molly said that you're one smart cookie, and if you'd let the Lord get ahold of you, you'd be one fine Christian. She really just wants your tithe and offering every month." Bernadette winked at Lisa.

"Mama, you revealed my secret. You promised not to tell anyone that I became a minister for the wealth it brings me."

Bernadette slapped her leg as she broke into a sweet chiming laugh so infectious that Lisa and Molly couldn't resist joining in.

"Come sit with me, girls. Give us a chance to talk without all that craziness inside the house."

Lisa and Molly carried deck chairs closer to Bernadette's perch on the porch.

"Mama, remember why we came out? We want to talk about that civil rights rally in Fort Worth, back in 1965."

"Yes, you said so. But let's not talk about that nonsense. Let's just enjoy a great day together. It's been raining for the past few days, and now look at this sunshine. Do you two want to stay over? Your sister has more rooms than she knows what to do with now that Jarrod got married."

"We came out so Lisa could hear your story from that day. I told you that she and her father were at the rally too."

"Yes, you did and I remember. But there's nothing new to tell, and you needed to visit me anyway." Bernadette kneaded her hands in her lap.

"I came out last Saturday," Molly said.

"I know it, but I got used to seeing you almost every day when I lived in my little apartment. I'm not sure this big grand house in the country is where I want to live."

"We can talk about that later, when our guest isn't here." A cool breeze rustled the trees, and Molly rose to adjust the blanket around her mother.

A young woman called from the French doors, probably a cousin. "Food is ready. Get in here, Lisa and Molly. Guests go first."

"When did I become a guest?" Molly asked.

"When you brought your friend out. Why don't you ever bring a man? Uncle Louis asked if you were a lesbian."

"Yes, I'm a black, female, lesbian minister in the state of Texas."

The woman laughed. "I gotta tell Uncle Louis that one."

"If you'd have married that Wilcox fella like I told you . . ." Bernadette shook her finger at Molly.

"I think we better get inside for food," Molly said, helping her mother to her feet.

Once inside, Molly's brother-in-law whistled loudly, silencing the room, and asked Molly to say the blessing over the meal. Children ran in, laughing loudly, and were scolded as Molly bent her head and offered a short prayer. The noise erupted with her "Amen."

The table was laden with more dishes than Lisa could remember seeing at any event. As she went down the line with her plate, Molly's relatives kept leaning over her shoulder, nudging her to try this dish or that until her plate couldn't hold anything more. Behind Lisa and Molly were the elderly aunts and uncles.

Evelyn directed them to the dining room where the older relatives soon congregated.

"These are the ones to talk to, and it's best over food. You'll get the most out of them that way," Evelyn said to Lisa as she set a dish of butter on the table.

Lisa was seated between Molly and a woman who looked older than Bernadette. Everyone called her Auntie Peeps. The small talk centered on the food as the sound of laughter and stories drifted in from other rooms.

"I brought Lisa out here to talk to Mama about that civil rights rally and shooting in Fort Worth in 1965," Molly began, and the table quieted, except for Uncle Frank, who mumbled loudly about having too many salads on his plate. The woman at his side elbowed him in the ribs as Molly gave a short background about Lisa and her father, and how they'd found Molly.

"You and your father were at that rally same time as that fella was gunned down?" an elderly aunt asked.

Lisa hadn't seen a smile on the woman's face since their introduction, and her frown only deepened with her question.

"Yes, they were," Molly said.

"Why are folks like you poking into this now?"

"Aunt Lois, this is a friend of mine and she's trying to help." Molly had become a mediator, trying to cut the tension Lisa felt growing in the room. At least Molly now considered Lisa a friend, but that didn't seem to help with her family.

"What's this they're saying? I thought Uncle Louis said Molly and that white lady were lesbians," an elderly man shouted to the woman beside him.

"Uncle Frank, adjust your hearing aid, you're yelling." The woman beside him nudged him in the ribs.

"Well, you don't know about people nowadays, and she's a right pretty lady, just much too thin," Uncle Frank said loudly again with his fingers on his hearing aid.

Molly buried her head into her hands as Lisa fought to keep from laughing. For a moment the tension softened, as though they'd all exhaled after holding their breaths.

"Listen, I know nobody likes talking about these stories, especially with a guest." Molly glanced at Lisa, who knew it was more about her skin color than her being a guest that might clam everyone up when talking about the 1960s. Beyond the dining room, Molly's family chattered loudly, but the mention of the past returned those at the table to eating in rigid silence.

"Lisa and her father are trying to save a man from execution," Molly continued.

"That guy never did it. We all know that," the woman beside Lisa said as she took a bite of food.

"Auntie Peeps, why do you say that?" Molly asked.

"Everybody knew it. People tried to say so at the time, but the police wouldn't listen. Then everybody shut up about it. They had to."

"Molly, you saw the shooting too," Evelyn said from the doorway to the dining room. She leaned in with her arms folded at her waist.

"I only recall some popping sounds and people screaming. Lisa's father thought I may have seen something because of some photographs. It looked like I was facing the shooting, but I don't remember it," Molly said.

"No, you remember," Evelyn said. "At least, you remembered it then. I thought you knew that. You drew it. Over and over again."

Molly gave her sister a quizzical expression.

"I saw you draw the pictures. They showed the shooting. Mom, tell her."

Bernadette sat silently in her chair across from them, staring at her hands clasped together.

"Mama?" Molly asked.

"Why are you digging all this up again?" Bernadette said with frustration. She covered her ears for a moment, shaking her head.

"I told you, the man convicted of the crime is going to be executed soon. Lisa and her father are trying to get evidence that proves he didn't do it." Molly spoke gently to her mother.

"I don't have any evidence other than my own two eyes, and I didn't see exactly what happened."

"All eyewitness accounts can help. This isn't the same age as it was back then. You don't have to be afraid," Molly said.

"You don't know anything about how it was back then," Bernadette said with a note of anger.

Aunt Peeps and Uncle Frank nodded agreement. Auntie Lois only glared at Lisa.

"We raised you in California. You didn't have many problems there."

"There are certainly racial issues in California, Mama," Evelyn said, sitting at the end of the table.

"It's not the same," Bernadette muttered, moving her fork through her plate of food.

Auntie Peeps nudged Lisa. "You have to try those greens," she said, pointing to Lisa's dinner.

"We had to deal with gangs and the tensions of multiracial schools." Molly sighed and looked to Lisa. "We've had long debates about all of this."

"Yes, we have," Bernadette said in a calmer voice. "I'm not taking away what you dealt with, daughter. There were those terrible riots. You had cruel words at school. But for the most part, there was something different in the South."

"We grew up with the law against us," Uncle Frank said, still twenty decibels louder than necessary for the table.

"Yes, that's part of it. The laws weren't made to protect us. Quite the opposite. When a cop pulled us over in our cars, us girls were afraid we'd be raped or our boyfriends or husbands beat, all because we're black . . . but if you don't pull the car over, you're gonna get it worse. There was an underlying terror outside the walls of our own homes. Sometimes it weren't safe even there. Fear was so normal that we didn't know it was fear, until we lived in California for a while."

The table was silent for a moment.

Aunt Lois slammed her fork down with her eyes on Lisa. "That is how it was. Yes, that was it." She took her plate from the table and left the room.

"I loved visiting you out in California," Auntie Peeps said. She took a bite of food. "I loved visiting you out there. Disneyland and Hollywood and the beaches. How'd we get you back to Texas?"

Bernadette sighed. "Oh, there's no place like home. I want to die where I can eat fried okra and smell the wisteria and jasmine outside my window. I want my daughters, sisters, and family close. Home is the South. I couldn't die in California."

"She talks as if she's going to die soon. You've got many more years ahead, Mama," Evelyn said.

"And however many those are, I'll be living 'em out in the South." Bernadette picked up her fork and started eating again.

Auntie Peeps cleared her throat and set her fork down. Most of her plate was already clean. "You young ones don't know how history makes you. It's not just what's a-happenin' now, it's what happened to our family and everyone we heard about for a hundred years before. Such things make up your DNA. You just don't say things have changed and it's all right to be black now and have rights just like everyone else. The fear gets into your bones, and it don't come out so easily."

"It's true what she says," Aunt Miranda said, coming in with a plate in her hand. "You want to know about the 1960s? We had these big-shot leaders coming out of the woodwork, making all kinds of promises and doling out hope like candy for kids. And then they all got killed, both white and black. Even the big and powerful Kennedys. That wasn't imagination, that was real stuff."

Bernadette and Uncle Frank nodded as Aunt Miranda spoke. Lisa felt a sense of shame over the history they spoke of. She knew it wasn't her family or anyone associated with her who had created such an environment, but her skin color brought a guilt she couldn't escape.

"I'll tell you then," Bernadette said suddenly. She studied Lisa from across the table.

Molly glanced at Lisa as if to be sure she was okay.

"We were all excited that day of the parade. Little nervous too. My brother Reggie was marching. Reggie's gone now, from heart disease, but I was always close to Reg. Aunt Hattie and I were watching out for him when this white man and little girl come up by us. Your daddy and you." Bernadette pointed at Lisa and winked.

"I was surprised to see that, but we had them at times—certain white people wanted to be friendly with blacks, usually visitors from the North or people trying to prove that they were different. We always wished them to leave us alone, truth be told.

"But I remember you. Cute little thing. And so nice to Molly, had her sit by you or something, I believe. Then your daddy started taking pictures. We didn't want to be in those, so we turned a bit away. You girls were right at our back. Still safe. Then came the *pop, pop* of gunshots. I knew the sound from my brothers and Daddy shooting. Your daddy was protecting you and Molly, but he had a gun in his hands. He said he was FBI or police or something. It didn't matter, I just wanted my girl. Back beyond us, I saw that Benjamin Gray already on the ground. It all turned crazy then."

"Did you think my father shot Gray?" Lisa asked as the woman paused for a long moment, seeming lost in the memory.

"No, I did not. He was too close and taking those pictures. But it was terrifying anyway, white man with a gun so close to my baby girl. We raced away fast as we could go."

"So, Mama, you didn't see anything?" Molly asked.

"Just that, the man on the ground, and we ran for safety."

"Then how were you convinced that it wasn't Leonard Dubois who killed Benjamin Gray?"

Bernadette stared at Molly. "You convinced me. You had nightmares and drew those pictures of people being shot. But I don't want to talk about that anymore."

Lisa could see Bernadette's hands shaking and feared they'd pushed the woman too far into a past full of unpleasant memories.

"I brought something for you. It's in the car," Lisa said to Bernadette, rising from the table.

"For me?"

Lisa hurried through the house and outside to retrieve the gift from the car. When she returned, she handed Bernadette the gift that Molly had helped her put together the night before.

"I hope you'll like it," Lisa said.

"What is this? I need my glasses." Bernadette pulled her reading glasses up from the chain around her neck. She took the framed snapshot into her hands. "Oh my, my."

It was a copy of one of the photos from the rally.

"I know that day turned out badly, but there's something really sweet about this moment." Lisa glanced at Molly.

"Yes, it is like a picture of what the world should be," Bernadette said as the others leaned over to view it.

"You were a gorgeous woman, Mama," Evelyn said.

"I was gorgeous. Your daddy hated that hat, but I loved it and spent way too much on it. I felt I deserved it."

"Did someone say dessert?" Uncle Frank said loudly, pushing back from the table.

Lisa was pushed toward the dessert line next, though she'd hardly made a dent in her meal. The atmosphere had shifted back to casual family time, though Lisa spotted Aunt Lois eating at another table and eyeing her with continued suspicion. Lisa wanted to ask Bernadette more questions, but she wasn't sure the elderly woman was up for more prodding about the past. There never seemed another appropriate time to bring up the civil rights rally.

As Molly and Lisa made the rounds saying good-bye to the family, they couldn't find Bernadette.

"Where's Mama?" Molly asked her sister.

"She may be taking a nap. Oh, there she is." Evelyn pointed to her mother leaning in from the hallway.

"I'd like to talk to Lisa for a moment." Bernadette motioned for Lisa to follow her down a hallway and into a bedroom. The room was tidy and decorated with porcelain angels.

"I have something for you as well," Bernadette said. She picked up several papers that were sitting on the bed.

Lisa took the thin pages carefully.

"I have more, but they are very similar. I hope this helps to free that man. But keep my daughter safe, you promise?"

Lisa looked up from the images that Molly had drawn as a child. "I will never do anything to endanger your daughter. I promise that."

Bernadette nodded. "Thank you. That's better than empty promises. But now listen to me. You can see how digging up the past brings a lot of bad feelings and memories. It can be dangerous too. There's lots of people who want what's buried to stay there, deep underground and dead. You be careful with all this."

Lisa thanked the older woman and then returned to Molly, who was waiting in the foyer of the house.

"She let you bring the drawings?" Molly said.

"Yes, some of them."

Aunt Miranda came from the kitchen with several plates of desserts covered in plastic wrap.

"I have two more plates of food for you," Aunt Miranda said.

Molly smirked. "What did I tell you?"

On the return drive to Dallas, Molly and Lisa discussed the drawings. During numerous trials, Lisa had worked with child psychologists and underage witnesses. From her experience, Lisa believed Molly's drawings seemed to depict Benjamin Gray being shot by a white man. But that wasn't all. The white shooter was also shot, by another white man. Two shooters and two people injured—they knew that one was a fatality. Who was the other man shot—Benjamin Gray's killer?

"What you saw had to be traumatic," Lisa said.

"I think I was too young to fully understand. But it became an important day for me, and my family. I think my career path was set at that moment. I became a minister, trying to rid evil from people's lives. And it's interesting that you became a federal prosecutor. You try to rid the world of bad guys. Perhaps you remember more from that day than you realize."

Lisa had never considered that her career path in law might have something to do with this childhood event she barely remembered.

She wanted to share what they'd learned with her father, and with Drew. But she knew that while the stories were compelling, they still needed more to stay Leonard's coming execution. They needed facts and concrete evidence.

As the miles moved beneath them, the two women grew silent, lost in their thoughts.

The stories from Molly's family remained with Lisa. She couldn't truly grasp the fear they'd spoken about. As they said, it was ingrained into their history. Yet the closeness, laughter, and bonds of a large family were also things she hadn't experienced.

She stared out the window at the Texas countryside, suddenly melancholy for a home that didn't exist for her. Dad's house was not her own. Her mom and stepdad lived in a seniors-only condo in Orlando. Her house in Boston was the closest thing Lisa had to a home. It was beautiful, cozy, and empty with her son in England for the next year. The rooms were filled with silence now. She didn't even have a dog.

What had she built in her years of striving? An admirable career and an empty house. Perhaps Drew's words were getting to her, because suddenly Lisa wondered, would that be enough?

CHAPTER TWENTY-FOUR

A ny discoveries?" William O'Ryan asked from the doorway.

"A few," James said. He pushed aside the file on the table, frowning at the name on the label. It sounded familiar, but he couldn't place it at the moment. His head was overly filled with names, dates, and information.

He stood and stretched, his back aching after several hours at the table.

"I found these pictures in one of Peter's files." James pointed out the timeline of images with the missing photos and negatives from the civil rights rally.

"These lead up to the time of the shooting?" O'Ryan asked. He grasped the edge of the table and studied the images.

"Yes. They stop immediately before, from what I can tell."

"And some of those photographs are missing. Interesting. Peter may have taken pictures of the shooter."

"Yes. And I think Peter might have shot the killer. My daughter called with further evidence that there were two shooters—both Caucasian—with one person other than Gray injured."

O'Ryan's eyebrows rose. "And the man convicted of this is the one set for execution—oldest man on death row with a death date, right?"

"Yes." James explained what he'd witnessed at the rally in 1965, then how he'd received Leonard Dubois's letter a month earlier and the man's countdown to the needle.

O'Ryan listened, sitting on the edge of the table, deep in thought.

"You've got quite a story going on here. But someone worked hard to keep the truth hidden." O'Ryan leaned over the line of photos.

"I think we have a multiagency cover-up. Fort Worth PD may have been part of putting Leonard Dubois away. Peter and the FBI may have covered up the real killer. But I don't understand why Peter would shoot that killer, then help to hide it."

"Perhaps he wasn't supposed to shoot him."

James frowned, considering this.

"You know, high-level cover-ups make it harder to get your man off death row."

"Yes," James said. The deeper he got into this, the more daunting the task of saving Leonard Dubois—especially with time running out.

"If you want, I'll put some people on researching this. And send me what you have on the inmate. I'll review it while I travel, see what I can do."

James realized that he couldn't have planned a better team than this—his background, his daughter and her contacts, Rosalyn's surprises, and now William O'Ryan's assistance. It gave him some hope despite their challenges.

"What made you contact Peter in the first place?" James asked O'Ryan.

"The JFK assassination. I was a cub reporter for the local Fort Worth news. But what pushed my interest beyond that was Peter himself."

"Peter? Why?"

"I saw him at an event in DC and found out he'd been doing what you did, investigating the Oswalds and contributing to the Warren Commission. He also had that history with the Kennedys."

"What history?" James asked.

"Peter had known the Kennedys since he was a kid."

"The Kennedys as in Robert and Jack and the rest?"

"This guy was your partner?" O'Ryan asked, raising his eyebrows.

"Apparently he kept a lot to himself. He told me he grew up in Massachusetts, but he never talked much about it. He and his sister weren't close when I knew him. His parents were dead."

"His uncle worked with the Kennedys, or there's some connection there. If I remember correctly, Joseph Kennedy pulled strings to get Peter into the FBI. Peter hadn't done well on the written exams, though he excelled at his interview, shooting, and physical tests. He probably had a learning disorder, but people didn't know about those things back then."

It was as if they were talking about a stranger. James had known that Peter couldn't spell or read worth a darn, but his closest friend apparently had a wealth of secrets he'd never revealed.

"But on that last day, the one when Peter died—"

"When Peter killed himself?" O'Ryan said bluntly.

James cringed. "Yes. I can't remember why you were there, at his sister's house."

"I went to ask about a missing key that had belonged to the Kennedys. I'd written to Peter about it, but he wouldn't respond. So I decided to drop in at his sister's in Queens."

James stared at O'Ryan. "You know about the key?"

O'Ryan stared back. "How do you know about it?"

"Peter mentioned it," James replied.

O'Ryan nodded. "I heard about it from former White House staff members and a close family friend. One source swore that Evelyn Lincoln, JFK's longtime assistant, was the keeper of the key after both brothers were assassinated, and she wouldn't give it up. It's common knowledge that she kept many of Kennedy's belongings, even auctioned some off after a number of years."

"Maybe we're talking about different keys?" James said.

"The key I'm talking about is one of many that belong to a historic cabinet located in the White House when JFK was in office. It's a unique piece of furniture gifted to the Kennedys by Queen Elizabeth II. It had been in Windsor Castle for over a century, or was it Buckingham Palace—I'd have to double-check that. I can't remember the craftsman, seems he was French or Italian, but the cabinet had drawers crafted with separate individual keys. One key for each drawer."

O'Ryan tapped on his phone as he talked, then turned the screen around and displayed an image of the Kennedy cabinet. Next he scrolled to a picture of an ornate key, matching the one James displayed in his workshop.

"Yes, that's it. And some of the drawers to the cabinet were missing their keys," James said.

"That's right. When I heard that Evelyn Lincoln regularly hid the tapes of the recordings the Secret Service made for JFK, I went down that trail to see if Evelyn knew anything about the keys to the cabinet or what the drawers contained. She wouldn't talk to me."

James had known about the secret recordings. He'd heard two stories behind the rationale for making them. First, JFK had been infuriated by people changing their stories after top-secret meetings were held, and second, he wanted infallible records about his time in the White House for future biographical purposes.

Whatever his reasons, under the president's direction the Oval Office, Cabinet Room, and telephones in his bedroom were wired with the recording device hidden in the White House basement.

"That must be the key Peter mentioned," James said. His gut had told him to follow this lead, but he'd lost faith in his friend and in turn lost faith in so much that had been connected to Peter in any way.

"What did he say about it? And why do you think he told you about the key when he didn't tell you his other secrets?"

James considered that for a moment. "In the years before he was fired, Peter continually brought up the key. I thought at first it might uncover something new about JFK's assassination. He once said that if I helped him find the key, it would save us both. When I asked what that meant, Peter brought up the Dubois conviction. But he was drinking a lot then, so I disregarded most of what he said.

"I've been wracking my memory for the past few weeks, but all I recall is what you said. The cabinet was moved and one key was missing. Other times he implied that more than one key was missing, but he needed a specific key for what he sought."

O'Ryan crossed his arms at his chest and leaned back in thought.

"Let's talk this through. So after JFK was killed, Bobby went into protection mode. He had locks changed on file cabinets and the Resolute desk—his brother's desk used in the Oval Office—until he could remove all sensitive information before President Johnson, his enemy, could get his hands on it. Bobby also had the Secret Service dismantle the recording devices and move this historic cabinet from the White House. Then less than five years later, when Bobby was assassinated, much of what he had protected became scattered, including keys to various drawers in the historic Kennedy cabinet."

"Yes, but what do you think happened to them?"

"The Kennedys might have them. Or an heir of Evelyn Lincoln's. Back in the day, I'm sure President Johnson wanted them. And of course, so did Hoover. Your old boss wanted every secret he could gather on anyone of any importance. But my hunch? After Robert Kennedy's assassination, Evelyn Lincoln gave one of the keys to Peter Hughes."

"Why would she do that?"

"Evelyn knew what was inside. She knew the secrets. If she gave it to Peter, it was because there was some connection to him."

James pressed his fingers against his temples. "This only gets worse and more complicated."

"Keep looking. I think we're closer than you think. I feel it."

"We?" James said with a smirk.

"You've made this too compelling to walk away from," O'Ryan said, glancing at his watch.

"I could go for some coffee," James said. *So much for green tea*, he thought.

"What about a break for dinner?"

"Even better."

⸻

O'Ryan and James went to a nearby Irish restaurant and found a table in the back. As they enjoyed the best shepherd's pie James had ever eaten, the conversation returned to Peter.

"You do know that Hoover took Peter down," O'Ryan said.

"Peter was caught exposing FBI secrets."

O'Ryan leaned back with a skeptical expression. "Maybe Peter was corrupt. Or maybe he just didn't know where to put his loyalty. He seemed like a pretty good guy from my investigations."

"Yeah. I guess he was," James said.

"But Peter did something that ticked Hoover off. I have numerous off-the-record reports about it. Peter supposedly leaked secrets to the press—but there's no one in the media who confirms this. Peter certainly never tossed me a bone."

James set his fork on his plate. If Peter hadn't leaked secrets, then what had he done? Their waitress stopped by to fill their glasses with iced tea.

O'Ryan asked her for a pen, then pulled a napkin out and started writing down dates. "November 1963, JFK is killed. You were sent to Dallas. When did Peter talk about that key?"

"I think a few years later, '68 maybe. He was a bit obsessed by it, but then I never heard about it again. He was fired in early 1971."

"Which is after Robert Kennedy was assassinated in 1968. So if Evelyn gave Peter the key, it would've been after that. These are a lot of leaps, but let's play them out. If Hoover and the FBI helped to cover up the shooting at your Fort Worth rally in 1965, which included Peter, why didn't Peter get exposed for sharing FBI secrets until 1971? Hoover could have sold him out. There has to be a reason why."

"Maybe Peter wouldn't give Hoover the secrets he wanted."

"Maybe Peter wouldn't give Hoover the key." O'Ryan folded his arms at his chest as he sat back in his chair.

James stared at him. "So Peter's obsessed with finding this key. Then Evelyn Lincoln gave it to him after Robert Kennedy was killed. Hoover either knew or guessed Peter had the key and demanded he turn it over so that he could have the power to use whatever was inside the drawer against even more powerful people. If this is right, what do you think is hidden in that drawer?"

O'Ryan shrugged. "Information that people didn't want revealed. Probably still don't. Look how they won't even release all of the JFK files after all of these years. But everyone was afraid of Hoover, and with good reason. He destroyed people."

James wondered if his former boss really had destroyed Peter or if his partner had done that himself.

Night had fallen over the city as they walked back to the news building.

"Don't you have a flight in the morning?"

"Yes, look what you did to me. I'm not even packed yet, and it's an hour to get home," O'Ryan said without remorse. "You can stay in the office as long as you want. I'll show you how to leave without getting hauled off by security. And make all the copies you want of Peter's files. Really, the boxes should've been sent to you instead of me. I don't know why Peter's sister didn't like you."

"She blamed me for Peter's suicide. I cut him off after the whole scandal. Maybe I was wrong." James felt his stomach tighten at another of his great life regrets. How had striving to do right led him to make so many mistakes, especially with the people he loved most?

"Hey, it's understandable. You were his partner. It would be tough hearing he'd kept all kinds of secrets."

"We weren't good at sharing our feelings," James said with a smile.

"What man is? But especially a suit, and from your era? But you should know, Peter's sister blamed everything and everyone for Peter's suicide. Not just you."

They made the route back to the storage room on the fifteenth floor.

"I'm caught up in this book tour for a few weeks, but if you need something, I'll do what I can." O'Ryan hung at the door a moment longer.

James could tell that he was having a tough time leaving. The two men were similar in that way. For James it was a case, and for O'Ryan it was a story. And once the clues started unraveling, it was hard to turn away.

"There is something," James said, seeing the name on the file he'd been looking through earlier. Now he remembered why the name was familiar. "Peter had this file about a company, the Blackstone Corporation, out of Louisiana and Florida. This is the second time I've come across the name Blackstone. There's a definite tie to the shooting of Benjamin Gray."

"Blackstone? If it's the same name I'm thinking, Stanley Blackstone's daughter is running for Senate in Missouri—Gwendolyn Hubert. Election year, so we're checking the candidates. She changed her name as a child, but I think it was Blackstone. I'll find out."

After O'Ryan left, James stretched in the chair and reopened the box loaded with packages of photographs. For the next hour he sifted through Peter's personal images.

The photos told the story of Peter. They showed his love of the outdoors. Black-and-white rolls of landscapes: a storm moving in across the plains, close-ups of flowers, a series dedicated to trees of all sorts of interesting shapes and sizes.

Some were of events—a party at his sister's, a camping trip, a retirement party.

But most of the packets depicted time spent with the Waldrens. Several rolls of film were dedicated to Lisa's birthday parties and a ballet recital. Others were of holidays and barbecues, and a day out on a lake in a ski boat they'd rented. Some included Peter's short-lived girlfriends that James had forgotten about. Peter never dated anyone for long. The job was hard on Peter's love life . . . or perhaps it was the many secrets the man carried.

Finally, James put the lid back on top and moved the box aside. Its contents had brought his friend back to life for him. This was the Peter Hughes he had known. The one with the quick laughter and sharp wit.

But this was only one side of Peter Hughes. The other boxes told the story of his friend as well, and those revealed a man tangled in secrets and lies that might never be unraveled. At least not in time to save Leonard Dubois.

The reminder of the man on death row sent James through the file boxes one more time. With all of Peter's files, why wasn't there one dedicated to Dubois?

Then James opened a file labeled *A. Snow* and found what he was looking for.

CHAPTER TWENTY-FIVE

The white plantation house rose into view at the end of the tree-lined driveway and up against the brilliant blue sky. Stanley had given only a few hours' notice before arriving at the local airport in his private jet, but the grounds of Red Wolf Manor appeared in perfect order. He made a quick perusal as he pulled the SUV around the circular drive-way. Everything was in bloom, contrasting with the stark appearance of Stanley's last visit in late autumn.

As Stanley walked toward the wide porch steps, the door swung open.

"Mr. Stanley, welcome home. We got the house all prepared for you. How was your flight?" Hollis Jr. wiped his hands on his jeans and took Stanley's travel bag. Stanley kept his black messenger case over his shoulder.

"Relaxing flight. I had a massage," Stanley said.

"I'm sure she was beautiful as well," Hollis said with a grin.

Stanley noticed that the man's blue eyes were bloodshot and his skin had the flushed coloring of someone who drank too much too often. Stanley had liked Hollis Sr. better, but he trusted the son and his wife enough to keep the house and grounds in top shape. By the look of him, Stanley wondered if he was unwise to do so. Stanley didn't tolerate drinkers or drug users—they were too inconsistent.

"Of course she was beautiful. Now, what's all the woodcutting going on up by the front gates?" Stanley paused at the doorstep to scan the lush front grounds. The huge magnolia trees that shaded the front yard had opened their pink-cupped flowers.

Miami smelled of the sea and city, but Red Wolf Manor carried a medley of scents. He could pick out the magnolias, honeysuckle, and jasmine mixed with the smell of fertile soil, the ponds toward the back acreage, and South Fork River. He also caught a hint of coming summer threaded in the air.

Standing there, he was hit by a flood of memories. He remembered shooting bullfrogs with his bow and arrow, swinging from the rope swing into the big pond, building forts in the tall willows. Down near the cemetery he'd dug up square nails, broken pieces of household items, and bits of bone. The old slave barn had been burned to the ground by his great-granddaddy—with many of his slaves locked inside—when the South surrendered at the end of the Civil War.

"We lost those two trees by the gates early winter. I e-mailed you about it in, oh, late January, I believe."

Stanley frowned, barely remembering. Usually he was on top of everything related to his family's land, but the issue with Arroyo had kept him busy until he finally resolved it. Or thought he'd resolved it. That Detective Martin was still digging and prying. Somehow his name had even become associated with the case in one newspaper report.

"Where's Martha?" Stanley asked.

"She's taken sick. Her daughter wouldn't let her leave her bed, she's too bad off. Got the cancer, you know."

"She what?"

"Found out just a month or so ago. Late cancer, I can't remember what stage they said."

"Why didn't someone tell me?" Stanley tried to tally the woman's age. She'd been only sixteen when he was born, and later she cared for Gwen. At least before his divorce.

Stanley loved that woman, even though she was black. And she loved him despite everything. She'd retired decades earlier from her housekeeper duties, but Martha always greeted him on his visits and often barked out orders to the current housecleaning staff when they didn't do things quite right.

Hollis shrugged. "I assumed Martha or her daughter would have told you. She wants you to stop by before you leave."

"Maybe." Stanley turned away from Hollis, no longer wanting to see the man's ruddy face or hear his voice. He stormed into the house, through the entry that danced with light from the glimmering chandelier overhead.

Just like his predecessors, Stanley had changed little about the house except to keep it in top shape and to modernize a few features. The plantation looked as if time had stopped in the 1860s. He'd had numerous requests to display the house as a historic monument, but Stanley would never allow it to become a tourist stop. His family was buried in the small cemetery, and generations of Blackstones had lived within these walls from the time it was built in the early 1800s and grew into a thriving cotton and tobacco plantation.

Stanley heard Hollis's footsteps trudging up the stairway toward the bedrooms where he would deliver Stanley's bag.

There was a fruit and cheese plate prepared by Hollis's wife on the table in the dining room, but Stanley made a clean path toward the library. He unlocked the door as he heard Hollis's footsteps returning from upstairs.

Stanley opened the top drawer of his desk and reviewed the contents. Then he examined the other drawers and took in every inch of the room. He moved to the fireplace and hit the tiny latch hidden under the ornately carved oak mantel.

"Has anyone been in here?" Stanley called to Hollis.

The man came to the doorway. "What, sir?"

"Who's allowed in this room?"

"We have the housecleaning staff come in once a month. But no one else." Hollis shifted nervously from one foot to the other.

"Same staff as always?"

"They have a new girl, but I'm not sure if she cleaned this room or not. I leave them to their work."

"After today, keep the key to this room put away. Only allow them to clean when you or Peg can supervise. It doesn't need cleaning very often anyway."

"All right, sir. You got it." Hollis stood in the doorway as Stanley made his way to the desk. "Supper will be served at six as usual. Are there any other instructions, Mr. Stanley?"

"That's all."

Hollis closed the library door behind him.

———

Stanley walked to the built-in bar along the back wall of the room. He poured himself a small swig of aged Scotch, raised it in a toast to his father, and downed it—a practice from the days when his father was alive and they'd drink a shot of Scotch every morning and right before bed.

He opened the double doors above the bar. The shelf was neatly lined with glasses and bottles. There was no dust on the shelf, he noted. No fingerprints or anything out of place. Stanley took hold of a shelf and carefully slid it to the left, the glasses barely moving as the shelf disappeared into the wall. Behind the shelf, an old safe came into view. Stanley turned the combination and heard the click of the lock, then he opened the door.

Beneath several tight stacks of hundred-dollar bills sat a collection of 8 x 10 photographs. He moved the money aside and took the pile to his desk with the face of Arroyo on top staring at him. From his messenger bag Stanley retrieved a new image, a picture of Arroyo's bloody corpse in the ice cooler.

Stanley had collected the stack of photographs over the decades.

They were reminders of the men he'd faced as opponents, all of whom he'd defeated. The bottom photograph was of Benjamin Gray sprawled out on the pavement.

There was not one image missing. But if the photos were here, how had they gotten onto the Internet from a computer at Blackstone Corp in Miami?

At the very bottom of the safe, Stanley saw the dry, crumbled remains of wildflowers that had once been woven into a crown. Lena. Lena with a crown of wildflowers sitting in the tall green grass and smiling up at him. Until recently she'd nearly disappeared from memory, or so he convinced himself. But Stanley remembered a time when he couldn't go an hour without her filling his head.

He wondered where she was now. Had she ever married? Perhaps she was a grandmother by now. Stanley couldn't picture Lena with a brood of grandchildren climbing all over her, or baking cookies or sewing quilts. The grandmother image didn't work with a woman of such refined sophistication. But she was no longer young, despite the image in his head.

Last he'd heard, Lena had returned to New Orleans and was running the small jazz house her mother had owned. He knew she had never forgiven him. Lena kept such promises.

Stanley returned the images to the safe. He slid back the shelf and clicked the lock under the mantel. Then he walked out to find Hollis.

His caretaker was in the backyard digging a hole beside an automatic sprinkler. He jumped when he saw Stanley.

"Has anyone stayed over or visited the house in the past few months?"

"There was a guy from the Louisiana Historical Society, but I didn't let him through the gate. And, well, Marcus and that woman came up one weekend. He called for me to prep the rooms, but they didn't stay. I think he brought her out to impress her, but she didn't like it."

"Didn't like it? Why?"

"She kept saying how creepy the place was, thought it was full of ghosts and bad karma. Where does he find these women?" Hollis shook his head in disgust.

"When was this?" Stanley asked.

Hollis scrunched his forehead. "Um, guess maybe late autumn. Or no, it was after the holidays."

Stanley knew of several times Marcus had used the private jet. Once he'd taken a short-lived girlfriend to New Orleans for a weekend. But he hadn't mentioned driving her by Red Wolf Manor.

"Did Marcus go into the library?"

"I wouldn't know. They spent the day here, but as I said, she wouldn't stay the night."

"And nobody else?" Stanley said, studying Hollis for any hint of a lie.

"No, nobody."

That evening Stanley sat in a high-back chair beside the huge parlor fireplace, his feet resting on a stool. As he watched the fire crackle, he smoked a cigar and sipped his Scotch, remembering his father in this exact pose. Thoughts of his father never failed to renew Stanley's own strength. The house carried a legacy of ruthless, determined men who cowered to no one and nothing.

His nephew was not made from that stock. And Stanley wouldn't play games with Marcus much longer. He had no patience for mysteries or unanswered questions. The company's computers had been hacked and his private collection of photographs released for the world to see. And Marcus had come by Red Wolf Manor. His nephew hadn't offered that information when they talked on the rooftop. But Marcus would soon come clean about everything, including how he'd found out about the hidden safe.

"Mr. Stanley?"

"What is it?" he growled as Hollis peered into the room.

"You had a visitor at the gate. It's Miss Gwendolyn," Hollis said, sounding pleased.

Stanley dropped his feet to the floor and swung around. "Gwen is here?"

"Yes, sir. I opened the gate, hope that was all right. She'll be driving up now."

Stanley set down his glass and smashed the cigar into an ashtray.

"Should I go wake Peg to cook something? Or I can make some tea or coffee."

"Tea, I think. Yes, make us some tea."

Stanley flipped on lights as he moved to the entry, then swung open the double doors as a car drove into the circle driveway and parked. He glanced down the long driveway for sign of any other vehicles, including Lancaster, the bodyguard he had paid to protect her, but she had apparently come alone.

"Gwendolyn," Stanley said as she got out of the car.

"Daddy," she said with no hint of warmth in her tone. "I called you at your office. They said you were here."

"And you flew down to meet me?" Stanley couldn't believe his daughter was actually standing in front of him. He hadn't spoken with her face-to-face in over a decade.

"I was in Baton Rouge for an event. When I heard you were near, I decided to drive out."

"Come inside. When was the last time you were here, the 1990s?"

"I'm not staying."

"Well, come have a cup of tea. Hollis is making it."

"Hollis is still here?" Gwen asked. She walked up the stairway with hesitant steps, seeming to inspect the house.

"Hollis Jr. took over for his father. But you remember him too. He wasn't that much older than you."

"Creepy guy, as I remember."

"Come inside and let's sit down properly," Stanley said, moving toward her. She pulled away when he reached for her arm.

Gwen walked through the open doors and stopped. She looked up the double stairway to the giant chandelier hanging from the open third story down toward the entry.

"It looked like a castle to me as a child," Gwen said.

He watched her as she looked around. His daughter was dressed casually, yet she always possessed a poise and confidence that made him proud.

"Do you want to walk through? Your room is still there."

"My room?"

"Not much changes here."

Her eyes settled back on Stanley. "I need to talk to you."

"Sure, come to the parlor. I have the fire going, though tonight is hardly cool enough for it. Remember when you'd roast marshmallows in that fireplace?"

Gwen followed as they passed rooms until reaching the grand parlor. Stanley quickly pulled up a chair near the one he'd been sitting in, but Gwen didn't sit down.

"Earlier today I remembered when you and Marcus were playing down at the river. You weren't even ten years old, and you came running home with leeches all over you. Marcus was crying, but you were only furious at the leeches." Stanley laughed loudly at the memory of Gwen's face as she ripped off the leeches that left bloody marks all over her body.

Gwen didn't respond; she just stood there as if weighing his words.

"I've always been proud of you."

She shook her head. "Dad, you never wanted a daughter."

Stanley shook his head and slapped the back of the chair. "Your mother told you that. And sure, before you were born, I wanted a son, because I wanted a child who was strong. But you being a girl and so strong, it made me prouder than if you were a boy."

Gwen stared at him with something he couldn't define in her eyes. Stanley had never had the chance to tell his daughter much of anything. She'd been warped by her mother and stepfather.

"You're here. Sit down and talk to me," he said.

"I'm not here for a visit," Gwen said. She remained standing and crossed her arms. "I know what you've been doing."

"What have I been doing?"

"When the same guy kept hanging out at all of my speeches around Missouri, and then I saw you in Jefferson City, I knew you'd sent him to watch me."

"To protect you. There are a lot of crazy people out there. Look at that woman in Arizona. Shot while she was giving her speech."

"I don't want your help."

"I've kept my distance. Your career wouldn't benefit from my association. I get that."

"You don't listen to me. You've donated to my political fund. How will it look when that comes out?" Gwen said.

"It won't come out. How do you know about it anyway?"

"I have an accountant. We investigate where our donations come from."

"We used a shell company." His daughter was smarter than he thought, or smarter than Marcus, which was no real surprise.

"It wasn't that hard for him to pull up."

"This family has always fought rumors. But I run a clean, legal business. Ask your cousin Marcus."

"Daddy," Gwen said in a tone that reminded him of her mother.

"Listen, darling, I wouldn't lie to you. You're my flesh and blood."

"What about that Arroyo guy who disappeared last month?"

"Arroyo?" Stanley felt a jolt of surprise. How could his daughter possibly know about Arroyo or his connection to the man?

"There's usually some truth in rumors. And you have too many to be completely innocent. Aren't the police investigating you?"

"Gwen, sit down and listen to me." Stanley walked to the doorway. "Hollis, what are you doing in there?"

He heard a dish shatter in the kitchen and Hollis mumble an apology.

"Do you like Scotch?" he asked his daughter, moving toward the bottle on the end table.

"Don't you understand that I don't want to be a part of all this? Our family history disgusts me. I'm trying to dedicate my life to righting those wrongs."

Stanley felt his anger bubble up. Gwen stared at him evenly, and it soothed the anger, making him want to laugh out loud.

"You are my daughter, through and through. Let me tell you a story."

"I don't want a story."

"Back in the early days of Red Wolf—"

"When this place was a slave plantation," she said.

"Yes," Stanley said without shame. "Your great-great-grandfather Crawford Blackstone had a strong-willed daughter named Margaret. She loved reading and studying, and Crawford allowed her to travel extensively. But all those books and experiences put ideas into her head. Then on one of her travels she fell in love with a Northerner, some young man against everything that represented the Southern way of life. Crawford forbade his daughter to see the young man again, so of course she ran away."

Gwen stared at Stanley, looking frustrated. But she was listening.

"Margaret's brothers went up north and brought her home. She swore she'd never forgive her father, and for a long time she didn't. Years later Margaret married a Southerner and moved to a plantation just some miles down the road. On her father's deathbed, Margaret thanked him for what he'd done. She'd come to understand that life isn't as clear as it appears when we're young. And in the end, family is all we really have."

Gwen sighed and shook her head. "You wanted nothing to do with me except for, what, a few weeks during a few summers. Why do you want to know me now? Why protect me and help me, especially when I'm asking you to leave me alone?"

"I always wanted you. Your mother told you lies. She didn't want me around."

"Because she didn't trust you. Because you kill people. Because you beat her."

Stanley stared at his daughter, then spoke slowly. "I had a problem with anger, this is true, and I don't tolerate betrayal. But I'm your father. And I've always loved you. People change."

"Not that much."

"Isn't that what you're all about, helping people change? Improve their lives, rise out of poverty, build solid households and communities? I've listened to your speeches, I read your platform."

He could see Gwen's anger dissipating with his words.

"You are doing good things. You'll make a great senator, or anything you aspire to be. I'll keep my distance, but know that I'm here for you if you need anything, and I mean anything. I swear that to you."

"I may not have a political future, with all of this. Maybe I don't deserve it. The more I find out about my family history, all that this plantation embodies, the more I'm ashamed. Everything has been built by the price of someone else's blood. There comes a reckoning for that."

"This is your heritage, Gwen. Someday you'll see."

Gwen closed her eyes and took a deep breath. "And you will never change."

His daughter left without having tea or Scotch. She walked out just as she'd walked in. Stanley stood at the doorway watching the red tail-lights disappear down the long driveway.

She'd be back; he could feel it in his bones. Gwen would stand in this very place, and at long last she'd thank him for all of it.

CHAPTER TWENTY-SIX

James walked along a meandering pathway in Central Park. The city skyscrapers lined the edges of the more than eight hundred wooded acres, rising above the trees like steel mountain peaks.

James had never explored the park. His few trips to New York were work related, but with several hours until his flight, he'd decided to make his phone calls beneath a blue sky instead of back in the stuffy hotel room.

After checking his phone to be sure the ringer was on, he unfolded a bag of fresh roasted peanuts and put one in his mouth.

Finally, the call from the Texas State Prison came in. While James and his daughter had different investigative methods, they both knew when to use their contacts in a pinch. James had cashed in several favors to get this phone call.

"Hang on the line and we'll connect you once we have him here."

"Thanks."

James saw a bench at the next bend in the near empty path. Several birds took turns singing from different trees. A squirrel raced across a patch of ground, paused to look at James, then scurried away.

In the background James heard the prison sounds: the shrill buzzing before doors opened and slammed shut, the echo reverberating down cold hallways, and finally boots and shuffling footsteps on the tile floor. He sat on the bench as Dubois picked up the phone.

"Hello?"

"Leonard, this is James Waldren."

"Yeah? What is it?" Dubois spoke as if James had interrupted his day.

"They moved you to a safer place."

"They did."

Waldren hesitated. "I called because . . . do you mind answering a few questions?"

"Sure, why not."

James stood. The sound of a police siren cut through the serene setting, reminding him where he was. He didn't like cities, especially this one that was surrounded by water. In Texas, the cities were like sporadic outcroppings popping up from the hundreds of miles of open country where the sky came down to meet the edges.

Again James thought about the man on the phone. The smallness of Dubois's world made his chest tighten.

"In 1962 you were questioned by the county sheriff, then released. What was that about?"

Dubois didn't answer for a long few seconds. "Why?"

James wondered how much to tell the man. How much hope should they toss his way when they were missing too many pieces to offer the promise that he'd still be alive in another month? Peter's file had given him leads, enough to ask Dubois some questions, but not enough to free him.

"Where are you going with this, Waldren?"

"It's related to why you were targeted by the Fort Worth PD. Why they let you take the blame for the Gray shooting."

In the background James heard someone, probably a correctional officer, ask, "You all right?"

"Fine, yes, I'm fine," Dubois said away from the phone.

"Leonard? What happened? This might help."

"There was a shooting. A kid died."

"Go on."

Dubois took a deep breath. "I never told anybody this."

"Maybe it's time you came clean about everything." James realized those words might be for himself as well.

"Maybe."

The voice in the background said, "You got five minutes."

"Leonard," James said. "What happened?"

"I was with my cousin Vic. We were target practicing at this abandoned farm . . . shooting out the windows of the farmhouse and bottles off a fence. Then this kid comes walking out of nowheres with a big smile on his face. My cousin was shooting up a storm like some movie star as the kid comes through the field. He didn't see the kid, and I didn't have time to stop it."

"Then what happened?"

"We ran over. The boy was on the ground, shot through the neck. He was there, spitting up blood, reaching for us."

"He was white?" James said.

"Yeah. We didn't know what to do. If we got help, they'd give us the chair whether the kid died or not. That's what we thought. Vic was nineteen, and I was just eighteen years old. While we were figuring out a plan, the kid died."

"So you ran?" James pinched the skin between his eyes, seeing the scene in his mind. He leaned over the back of the bench.

Leonard's voice lowered to just above a whisper.

"Yeah, we ran. Left that boy in the field. Later heard the kid was some cop's nephew, so we hid out for a long time. Weeks went by, and it seemed to settle down. 'Bout that time, my uncle took us to those meetings that turned into Black Panthers. All the stories of beatings and killing of black folk . . . Heard about a woman raped and shamed in front of her new husband, a college student tortured and lynched. Came to be we didn't care that we accidentally killed one white kid. We kind of figured it was something like justice."

"But the police brought you in and let you go?"

"Out of the blue, a bunch of us got hauled in and questioned. They didn't have no evidence. My cousin was into a lot of bad stuff. So maybe it was the police or maybe someone else, but a few months later Vic was beat to death. Day before Christmas."

"But no one harmed you?"

"Police roughed me up a bit at the questioning."

James expected as much. Dubois was lucky he hadn't ended up like Vic. If they'd known for certain what had happened to the white boy, Dubois would've died all those years ago.

"And they kept watching you?"

"I didn't know it then, but yeah, I suppose so." Dubois paused. "Thing is, that kid died. I didn't shoot him, but he maybe could have lived if we weren't standing around too scared to do anything."

"It was an accident," James said.

"We should've got him help right off."

"Yes. But it was an accident during a very bad time. You would not have lived to see the courtroom."

James wondered what to do now.

"Hey, Waldren?" Dubois said.

"Yes?"

"For a long time, I didn't care about being in here. Once I got death, kind of thought it was God's justice for that little kid, you know? But the truth is, I don't want to die."

A caravan of mothers with strollers appeared along the path, speed walking and chatting amicably. James caught a discussion on baby sleep schedules.

He was silent, waiting for them to pass. He'd gotten off track in his investigation. There were numerous angles to get lost in. The key, Peter, Benjamin Gray . . . but James couldn't lose focus on the goal. Save Dubois's life and get him free for the final years of his life.

"I promise you, we're doing everything we can."

CHAPTER TWENTY-SEVEN

My father talked to Leonard Dubois, and he confessed to a crime before the Gray shooting," Lisa said as Molly followed her into Dad's house.

When Molly had called that morning, Lisa was studying files and reports in her father's dreary workshop. She usually worked best alone, but she accepted Molly's offer to sift through the papers and case files with her.

Lisa updated the other woman as they moved through the house and out to the workshop. They opened the door to the mixed smell of sawdust and musty barn.

"Put me to work. I brought my antiquated laptop," Molly said, lifting up the computer bag on her shoulder.

Lisa cleared off an area along the wooden counter near an outlet and moved a tall bar stool over for Molly. The woman's presence helped clear away the gloominess of the room, and Lisa felt grateful that Molly had volunteered a few hours to help before a church event that evening.

She had enlisted the help of Sweeney and Gertz to get background information on a Caucasian male child found shot in a field on the outskirts of Fort Worth in 1964. From the basement archives Gertz faxed her pieces of an old case file. She wasn't sure why he was helping—complete boredom, she guessed—but she was happy to have him on board. When Lisa updated Sweeney, he laughed about Gertz's assistance.

"He's catching the fever that I got down in that archive basement. Plus, helping a pretty fed prosecutor will liven up his day."

Sweeney went to his journals and found old notes on the case. Between these and Gertz, Lisa put the story together.

Nine-year-old Aaron Snow was found dead in a field on the edge of Fort Worth. His parents were at a neighboring house when the boy disappeared from playing in the yard. They found his body late in the evening. He'd been shot through the neck, just as Leonard told Dad. He was the only child of Charlotte and David Snow, and his uncle was Sergeant Ross of the Fort Worth PD, the same station Lisa had visited. The case was never solved.

Sweeney's notes implied that justice was served outside of the courtroom. Sweeney didn't know the facts, but he'd heard rumors. Sweeney was surprised by Lisa's findings that the boy was Sergeant Ross's nephew. No investigating was done or new leads pursued after late 1964. Leonard's cousin was beaten to death on Christmas Eve 1964.

"If Sergeant Ross believed that Dubois guy was involved in his nephew's killing, then no wonder he helped put the man away," Molly said.

"And that would explain why he'd never cooperate with my father," Lisa said.

In the Aaron Snow case file, Lisa found a list of names. Leonard Dubois was on that list.

Dad's theory appeared correct. With Leonard in police crosshairs after his suspected involvement in the shooting of a young boy, he became the perfect fall guy for the Gray shooting. The boy's death helped eliminate the moral dilemma that hadn't set well with Lisa. Only rarely did cops do something dirty without a reason. But when a child was killed, especially one of their own, ethical lines became easier to cross.

"But no hard facts?" Molly asked.

"I'm afraid we're nearing a dead end. We just don't have enough to move a judge on Leonard's behalf."

Lisa scanned the walls, stopping on the image of Gray.

"I'm putting you on Benjamin Gray. I've done quite a bit of research, but I want you to look at the people closest to him. Many times I get more leads by just putting things out there." Lisa dropped down a stack of papers she'd compiled during her restless nights in Dallas and then printed out at the hotel business center.

"I can do that," Molly said.

"Also, he was dating a woman named Madeline Fitzgerald. Some reports say they were engaged. We've heard rumors that he had a Caucasian girlfriend, but I haven't found more about her. See what you can find about both. And look at Gray's family and background, his friendships as well."

"This sounds intriguing," Molly said, opening her laptop.

Lisa stood in the middle of the workshop and reviewed key points of the case.

The killing of Benjamin Gray.

Leonard Dubois.

The key.

Peter Hughes.

Dad had reminded her—the goal was Leonard Dubois.

Lisa reviewed possibilities, writing down thoughts and scratching them out one by one.

Texas executed the most inmates of any state in the United States. While a governor could pardon a convict, it was an election year, which could help or hinder them. If their discoveries were given to the press along with knowledge of the attempt on Dubois's life, it might create enough controversy to get his execution date extended as the courts reviewed the case. No governor wanted to kill a man who might be innocent. But a Texas politician wouldn't want to appear weak either, so the execution could go through despite the questions.

Lisa sighed. It looked as if the only way to save Dubois was not only to discover the real killer but to get a confession or solid proof.

Her father would be home that evening. And so far Lisa hadn't come up with anything from the information he'd gathered in New York.

"Do you want to talk about it?" Molly had turned in her chair and was studying Lisa.

"What's to talk about? I need to get back to my life and job, and we're not getting far enough here."

"I'm not talking about all of this," Molly said, motioning to the room.

"Then what?"

"Ever since I arrived you've seemed as if something's bothering you."

Lisa frowned. "Do you do this to your parishioners?"

"Some of them, yes. I'm a licensed counselor as well as a minister."

"Are you saying I need counseling?"

Molly laughed. "Don't take it personally. Everybody needs a friend or a psychologist or both."

Usually Lisa wouldn't have liked such prying or teasing, but Molly had a way about her that wasn't off-putting.

"Something keeps nagging at me, and I keep backing off of it."

"What is it?"

"My father was tenacious about his cases. Isn't this a good example?" Lisa said, motioning toward the walls of the workshop.

"I might use another word besides *tenacious*."

"Yes, and this is extreme. But not completely out of character. He was hardly home most of my life because of his career. But what's the real reason he suddenly stopped pursuing the truth in Dubois's case? He's let Leonard rot away in prison all of these years."

"Wasn't he told to back off by his boss? Didn't they demote him or something?"

"Yes, which makes it worse in a way. Dad isn't the type to willingly look away because of his career."

"He may have had other reasons. Have you asked him?"

Lisa leaned back, stretching. She sighed. "My father and I don't talk well, especially when it gets personal."

Molly considered that for a moment. "Asking might give him the chance to explain. He's not ever going to share anything easily. There's a lot locked up. But trying to figure it out without asking, you'll never get the answers you want."

Lisa nodded in thought. She still hadn't asked Dad why he'd brought her to the rally as a child. Obviously he still felt guilt over it. But how could she ask about his seemingly cowardly retreat that kept a man in prison for nearly five decades without it sounding like an accusation?

As Molly returned to her research, Lisa went inside the house to make tea. As she set the kettle on the stove, the past seemed to rise around her. With Dad's long hours, this hadn't been her father's home as much as hers and her mother's. Lisa could almost see her mom in her flowery apron, baking chocolate chip cookies in this small kitchen. Suddenly Lisa missed her mother and wanted to call her in Florida.

Instead, she stepped into the hallway, staring down toward her childhood bedroom. She felt like an intruder, snooping around, but she walked to the room anyway. Since her arrival in Dallas, she hadn't once looked through her old house.

She pushed open the door to what appeared to be a typical spare bedroom with a dresser, full-size bed, nightstand, and lamp. There were a few paintings on the wall that she didn't recognize, but as Lisa stepped into the room she saw remainders of her childhood. A large mirror on the wall had remnants of Scotch tape where Lisa had taped pictures of friends and movie stars.

On bookshelves above a faded collection of *Encyclopaedia Britannica*, many of her old books remained: *Anne of Green Gables*, the Betsy-Tacy series, the entire collection of Nancy Drew books, *A Wrinkle in Time*, the Chronicles of Narnia. There were also some classics mixed with a few romance novels and true crime.

Seeing the books was like discovering old friends she'd nearly forgotten. Many of them she'd bought at a little bookshop that Uncle Peter would take her to for story time. Lisa had consumed books until high school, when she became involved in school activities, soccer, debate team, and her social life.

Lisa felt an ache in her heart that she had worked hard over the years to stuff away, starting with Uncle Peter and continuing through her husband's death.

Most of her childhood mementos had gone with Mom to Florida when she and Dad divorced. At her condo, her mother still displayed Lisa's awards and achievements on what her husband called the Lisa shrine. These books were all Dad had left of her besides his photographs.

Lisa was overwhelmed with just how alone Dad had been, and for the first time she was glad he had Rosalyn. He'd become an old man, retired from the work he loved. He'd lost his family because of his inability to maintain relationships. And like her, he didn't even have a dog.

She heard the back door open and Molly call her name. The teakettle whistled from the stove.

Lisa closed the door to her bedroom and hurried to the kitchen.

"I think I found something," Molly said. She was holding her laptop and set it on the counter.

"Look at this. Madeline Lorraine Fitzgerald. She was born in Alexandria, Louisiana. She's of Creole descent. Her father was French and American, and her mother was black. They moved to New Orleans when she was small, but there is still family in Alexandria."

"Benjamin Gray was from Alexandria," Lisa said.

"Yes, but the other time we've heard of that city was with that Blackstone Corporation. So I looked that up. There's a plantation outside of Alexandria that's been owned by the Blackstone family for generations. Google Maps helped me see that Madeline's family lives in close proximity to the plantation as well."

"So Madeline likely knew the Blackstone family. The photograph of Benjamin Gray's corpse was released from someone at Blackstone Corp. And when I talked to my father, he said that his old partner, Peter, had a file on the Blackstones. I'll run a complete background on the family and the company. I wonder if Madeline Fitzgerald is still alive."

"I think I found her. There's a Madeline Lorraine Fitzgerald in New

Orleans. She's seventy-four years old and still runs a little dinner house in the French Quarter. There are photos, Lisa. She's beautiful and seems to have a mixed-race ethnicity. She might even pass for white."

Lisa felt a quickening of excitement course through her.

"So Gray's white girlfriend and this woman might be the same person." Lisa's mind raced with scenarios.

Molly glanced at the clock on the wall. "I hate to leave, but I have a ministry dinner in a few hours and a short message to polish. But I wish I could stay. We're onto something here."

"This is great, but don't worry. Dad won't be home until late anyway. Send me everything you have, and I'll try to reach Madeline Fitzgerald."

After Molly left, Lisa returned to the workshop to pack up. Her phone rang as she shut the door and punched in a code to the new alarm system Rosalyn had installed.

"Hey, Mom," John said. The background was unusually quiet; he was probably in his dorm, Lisa guessed. Sometimes Lisa hated knowing her son was so far away and on his own without her.

"Let me guess, you have to cancel our video chat tonight?" she said in a teasing tone. She balanced a box of files and her bag and headed toward the house to lock up.

"I forgot that my study group meets today. What about tomorrow?"

"Possibly, but I may be flying. I haven't told you that I'm not in Boston."

"Where are you?" he asked in a worried tone.

"I'm in Dallas. I've been helping my father with an old case of his."

"Really? That's cool. So did he tell you—"

Lisa came through the back door and stopped. "Tell me what?"

Her son hesitated. "About coming to see me."

She dropped the file box onto the counter. "Who? My father? Your granddad came to see you? In England?"

"Uh-oh, yeah. He asked me not to tell you. He wanted to reconnect with you first."

"When was this?"

"Um, February, I think?"

"Why didn't you tell me?" she asked, then regretted the accusation in her voice. She knew why. He wanted to respect his grandfather's request. But Lisa just couldn't believe she'd known nothing about this.

"I wanted to tell you and felt bad keeping it from you, but I didn't know what to do. Grandpa was here for a few days. He said he was sorry for not being part of our lives and that he wanted to change that. All this stuff. He said he'd been a bad father and he wanted to fix that too. It was good, except for the part about not telling you. Sorry, Mom. Really I am."

"It's not your fault. Don't feel bad. It'll all be fine."

"But, Mom. Still help Granddad, okay? I get it if you're mad at him, and at me. But he's old, and this means a lot to him. I've been thinking this over, and I think he really needs to right this wrong as much as possible."

"I'll think about it," Lisa said.

They made plans for their next video chat and hung up. Lisa's hands were shaking as she leaned over the counter. Why hadn't her father told her this? And why had he gone behind her back in the first place to contact John?

If she couldn't trust her father about this, how could she trust him at all?

CHAPTER TWENTY-EIGHT

Before flying back to Florida, Stanley stopped by to see Martha, his old nanny. He couldn't leave without saying good-bye to the one woman who had loved him more than any other, even his own mother.

Her daughter and son-in-law had moved into her small cottage to care for her. Stanley had never liked Martha's daughter, and the son-in-law was worse.

Loretta's cold greeting infuriated him, but she admitted that her mother hoped he'd come by. She pointed to the living room where a hospital bed had replaced the sofa. The curtains rose and fell softly, displaying Martha's flower garden outside.

"Stanley," Martha said, clasping her hands together when she saw him.

The woman in the bed only vaguely resembled the woman he'd known. He felt a shiver run through him at the scent of sickness and imminent death. But it was her deep black eyes that were all Martha.

Stanley went to her bedside and took her hands. They felt like bone covered in tissue paper.

"I'm so grateful you came to see me. I couldn't call and tell you about all this nonsense. Silly cancer."

"You should have. I didn't like learning about it from Hollis."

"Let me look at you." She sighed contentedly. "You were the sweetest baby. Did you know I was only a child myself when your daddy hired me to take care of you? Your mama wasn't too good with children. Just not her gift, I guess."

Stanley had heard these stories a hundred times, but he took in every word as she told the story of first seeing him and how she'd make his bottles and rock him through nights of colic.

"You know, I almost let you die one time."

"No you did not," Stanley said with a laugh. Martha was always full of sass.

"I did, oh yes I did, even though I loved you like my firstborn," she said with a smile that cracked her dry lips.

"How did you almost let me die?"

"You probably don't remember when you fell out of that rowboat in Middle Pond."

Stanley studied Martha, unsure if she was joking. Perhaps her failing health had affected her memory. "Of course I remember. I got tangled up in the weeds at the bottom. I was sure there were dead bodies in there, and I panicked, got tangled worse. You pulled me out."

Martha nodded as if this was an intriguing story. "There were dead bodies in there, that's for sure."

"How do you know?"

"Those ponds have lots of secrets from the past, and much as I love you, your family has evil running right through it. You were only six or seven, but already I saw the evil fighting against the sweetness in you. I thought maybe if you died, the world would be a safer place."

"Lena would say you should have let me die. The world would've been a safer place."

Her eyes perked up. "You haven't spoken my niece's name to me in a very long time."

"When did you last see her?"

"Been awhile. She called when Etta told her about this cancer nonsense. But she don't like coming up here. Too many memories she don't want to remember."

Stanley nodded, but he hid the surprising sting of hurt. Those moments she didn't want to remember had been the happiest of his life.

"It never would've worked with you two," Martha said, squeezing his hands as she'd done a thousand times to console him.

Stanley cringed and pulled away his hands.

"It weren't your fault, not really. Your family raised you in the old ways. But I can't help but love you, no matter what you've done. Maybe God will judge me for it, but that's why I saved you from the pond that day."

Stanley didn't remain with Martha much longer. He kissed her forehead, and she clung to his shoulders with tears in her eyes as he said good-bye.

Loretta and her loser husband were sitting on the front porch smoking cigarettes.

"I'll pay for a nurse to check on her every day," Stanley told Loretta as he walked toward the stairs.

"That would be great. Her retirement doesn't cover a lot."

Stanley turned and faced the woman's snide expression. "You don't seem to have a problem living off it," he said.

"Now wait a minute." Her husband stood up.

Stanley smirked at the man lumbering toward him, acting like some big tough guy. In a surprisingly simple move, Stanley grabbed the man's shoulders and shoved his face down onto the wooden railing. Loretta screamed as her husband rose up with his nose already squirting blood down his face and all over his shirt. Stanley hammered a hard uppercut to the man's throat and a left to his stomach. The man folded in half, groaning in pain as Loretta tried to help him while crying and shouting at Stanley.

Stanley pulled out five hundred-dollar bills from his money clip and set them on the porch railing. He clenched his throbbing fist. He wasn't as strong or as vicious as he'd once been, but Loretta's husband didn't know he should be grateful for that.

"I want updates on her," Stanley said to Loretta, who was helping her husband to a chair.

Loretta stared at the money. She glared at Stanley, then picked it up.

As he drove away, heading for the private airport in Alexandria, he knew he'd never see Martha alive again.

Late that afternoon Stanley sat outside his Florida mansion smoking a cigar and watching the steady roll of ocean waves. Marcus came up the back walk carrying his briefcase.

"Hello, Uncle. I hope your flight was good." Two sweat marks circled his underarms, and he carried his sport coat in one hand.

"Yes. Clear skies. What do you have for me?" Stanley said. The evening was warm with a light breeze off the water, cooling Stanley's face.

"Some developments," Marcus said, wiping a line of sweat from his brow. "That Detective Martin came by again about Arroyo's disappearance. Mentioned an ATM camera at the corner by the marina where the boat is docked. He's coming back in the morning."

Stanley nodded and stared at the end of his cigar. He was getting quite tired of Detective Martin.

"Also, Waldren flew to New York and met with a TV news guy, William O'Ryan. I can show you everything on the computer. Waldren's daughter is still in Dallas. She's been digging up old police files. Gaining a lot of information."

A melancholy had attached itself to Stanley since he'd left Louisiana that morning. Perhaps it was seeing Martha or thinking about Lena after so many years, but he didn't want to deal with his nephew right now. He didn't want to do what needed to be done.

"Let's get this over with," Stanley said, putting out his cigar.

Marcus followed him into the home office. He stopped suddenly when he saw two other men waiting there.

"Hey there, Frank and Billy. What are you guys doing here?" Marcus looked like a caged rabbit, his eyes darting for an exit as Stanley closed the patio door.

"Frank and Billy are sitting in on this conversation. I've had some developments as well, but go on with what you were telling me. Have a seat."

Marcus sat on the edge of a chair. "Uncle, what's going on? I don't know what you think, but you have it wrong. You're my uncle, my only flesh and blood."

"You were at Red Wolf a few months ago." Stanley sat on the edge of the desk in front of Marcus.

Marcus nodded. "Yes, I was. I didn't tell you because we didn't stay overnight. Leslie didn't like the plantation. I didn't want to tell you that."

"How could documents that I store at the plantation become available on the Internet? It seems that someone wants to get attention pointed our way."

"What would I have to gain? This company and family are my life. And I don't even know the combination to the vault."

"These documents weren't in the plantation vault. They were in another location," Stanley said, inspecting every twitch and shift in Marcus's reactions. Either his nephew was smarter than he appeared or he was telling the truth. Stanley knew a few fingernails would get to the bottom of this once and for all.

He rubbed his eyes, weary of all of this. "I get very impatient about these things. My time can't be spent figuring out who is loyal and who isn't. There's enough to worry about without questioning my own people."

"I know that, Uncle Stanley. I've always been loyal." Marcus turned to where Billy and Frank sat like bored statues.

The phone on Stanley's desk rang. He looked at it, trying to keep his anger at bay. He hit the speaker and heard his assistant's voice.

"Jill, I told you to hold every interruption for the evening."

"Yes, sir, but I wanted to be sure this wasn't important. I took a message from a man who says he's retired from the FBI."

Stanley picked up the phone. "What's the message?"

"His name is James Waldren. He said he's a retired special agent, and he wanted to ask you about some old events in Texas, back in the sixties. I have his phone number."

Stanley thanked Jill and hung up the phone. There were too many pieces closing in: Gwen's political run, the upcoming Dubois execution, the past coming back to haunt him, Arroyo's death disrupting his progress.

The three men in the room watched him, waiting for his next move. Stanley never worked long in the defense; he'd always been an offensive player.

"No more observing. It's time to turn the tables."

CHAPTER TWENTY-NINE

James moved along the airport security line, hoping he wasn't leaving New York too soon. He'd gone through Peter's belongings, but he'd had little time to fully dissect everything. Messing with his usual meticulous process left him uneasy, but he was torn, ready to get back home.

His phone rang, and as he pulled it from his jacket pocket, he saw Lisa's name. Every time she called, a sense of panic assaulted him. He forced out a calm, "Hi."

"I just got off the phone with John," Lisa said.

"John?" His mind raced through the names in this multilayered case as he stepped a few feet forward in line.

"My son, John? Your grandson?" Lisa's voice was laced in anger.

"Oh," James muttered, instantly aware of where this was going.

"Oh? That's it?"

James turned around, pushing and bumping through the people behind him, wheeling his carry-on bag back toward the entrance of security.

"I'm at the airport," James said as if that might calm his daughter.

They didn't need this right now. They were making real progress. He should have told Lisa about John before she'd come to Dallas. But those were mistakes he couldn't change.

"You went to England and visited him? Months ago?"

"Yes. I wanted to tell you."

"When? And you put John in a terrible position, asking him to keep it from me. How could you do that?"

"Because I wanted to tell you myself . . ." James knew it sounded like a lame excuse, but initially he had planned to talk to her before contacting John. Then he was going to do it before he went to England. He kept putting it off. He wasn't afraid of bullets or criminals, but his daughter's anger reduced him to a dog retreating with its tail between its legs.

"So you only contacted me when you wanted help on a case."

"No. It's not that." James lowered his tone as other travelers glanced his way.

"And I should have asked this in the beginning, Dad. Why did you let Leonard Dubois sit in prison for almost five decades when you knew he hadn't committed the crime?"

James wasn't prepared for that one. He stumbled to find words, but none sounded right at the moment.

"Can we talk when I'm back? You can stay at the house, or I'll come to the hotel tonight or in the morning. My flight gets in at ten."

"I'm going back to Boston. Everything I'm doing now I can do from home."

"Wait until I'm home."

"I don't know. This is a tough one, Dad."

"Please. One more day."

James sat at his gate, rehearsing conversations he might have with his daughter. None of them sounded right. He'd already made enough mistakes with her. The past few weeks working together, spending time

and becoming acquainted, were more than he'd hoped for. But being together had made it harder to tell her about John.

James didn't regret the e-mails and days in England with his grandson. John was a great young man, someone to be proud of. Lisa had done an excellent job raising him. He couldn't wish for a better grandson, and James wanted to tell Lisa those things, but where did he start? He considered writing it out in a letter, but he'd never been good at that either. Yet James knew he'd lost his wife over good intentions that never became real actions.

His flight was called over the speaker, and people began to gather for boarding. His phone rang again, and he was beginning to lament the thing. What happened to the days without constant connection? Then he saw the name on caller ID.

"O'Ryan, aren't you on a book tour?" James asked, gathering his belongings.

"Arrived in LA a few hours ago. But I have two things for you."

"That was fast. I just saw you yesterday." James tugged out a notebook and pen from the front zipper of his carry-on bag.

"News moves fast. I've learned to keep up. Anyway, my assistant sent me pages of information on the Blackstone Corporation and the owner, Stanley Blackstone. I'll forward them to you. Just as I thought, his daughter is Gwendolyn Hubert."

"The politician?" James asked, writing down her name.

"Yes. She's an independent, and people thought she had no chance of winning, but she's holding her own. Doesn't seem to have any connection with her father. Grew up with her mother and stepfather. Lower-middle-class family as a child, then her stepfather opened a small business that did well. I think he has fifteen stores across Missouri and Illinois now."

James scribbled notes as O'Ryan spoke, while keeping an eye on the boarding process.

"She's into small business, working middle class, but numerous social programs are important to her as well. We haven't found anything controversial about her, except her father. I'm telling you that because Stanley Blackstone is on the other end of the spectrum. He's big business, old money, and he's developed Blackstone Corp into a huge company with international assets and construction projects all over. Over the decades the company and the family have been investigated numerous times by the FBI and local police, but they can never prove anything.

"There seems to be criminal history in the bloodline. Blackstone's father had ties to the Chicago Mafia and was a member of the KKK, as was his grandfather. Stanley Blackstone's father was very powerful for a time in the fifties and sixties. He bought support in Washington, had many political puppets, and used any means of blackmail to get what he wanted. It looked like he was going to make a run for office himself, then suddenly in the midsixties the family sort of went underground. Did I say that the Blackstones own a plantation outside of Alexandria, Louisiana?"

"No, and that's interesting," James said. "Benjamin Gray is from Louisiana. And the sudden disappearance—right around the time of Gray's killing."

"In addition to that, Stanley Blackstone went to college in Dallas from 1963 to 1965. He dropped out a month before graduation."

"That would have been April 1965?"

"It doesn't specify the exact month, but spring semester. That puts him in the Fort Worth area when Benjamin Gray was killed."

"This could be our killer," James said with a surge of excitement in his gut.

"Now all you have to do is prove it," O'Ryan said.

"This helps a lot." James rose from the chair and tucked the paper into his jacket pocket. "Did you say there's something else?"

"Yes, I called Cole Elliot, nephew of our buddy Peter Hughes. He didn't know his uncle well and was estranged from his mother, Peter's sister. But as the only heir, he obtained Ann's house and everything in it when she died. I asked if he'd ever found anything that belonged to his uncle."

"What made you think of that?" James asked.

"Old habit, I guess. It started nagging me that maybe Peter's sister didn't send me everything. There had to be mementos and personal items that she would've kept, most women would. Anyway, there was a package addressed to you from Peter. His sister never sent it."

James stopped gathering his belongings, and for a moment the airport disappeared around him. For years James had gravitated between sorrow and anger toward his former friend. Peter wasn't the type to take his own life, and then he did and without final words to any of them.

"Peter left something for me before he died?"

"Yes. I gave Cole your address in Dallas. He's sending it."

"He didn't say what it was?" James asked.

"Well, he said that he didn't open it, but you never know. He's sending it, that's what matters."

James realized that the crowd at the gate had disappeared. "This is . . . more than I could've hoped for, but I need to board my flight now."

"The package should arrive in the next few days. And I want to know what's inside. You're making it hard for me to concentrate on this book tour," O'Ryan said.

"You sound like the William O'Ryan I met back in the sixties." James chuckled.

"Yeah, I still can't turn my back on a story. Talk soon."

James hurried toward his gate, his head spinning with thoughts of Lisa and with O'Ryan's discoveries.

Stanley Blackstone might just be the real killer of Benjamin Gray. But why had he shot him, and in such a public and foolish way?

But more than that, James would finally get the message his former best friend had sent from the grave.

CHAPTER THIRTY

Lisa hit the top of the clock, then realized she was still in the hotel in Dallas and it was knocking that had awakened her, not the alarm.

It wasn't even seven o'clock.

The knocking didn't let up.

Lisa dragged herself from the bed. She'd been up till two, talking to Drew and diving into some preliminary work on a federal murder case that was coming up.

Through the peephole, she saw Rosalyn's coiffed hair rise into a beehive, then shrink back onto her head as the woman leaned forward, peering into the hole as she knocked, then stepped back.

Lisa glanced at herself in the mirror, then just opened the door. What did she care what she looked like?

"Morning. Oh, did I wake you? You said you were a morning person," Rosalyn said much too cheerily for so early. She carried two steaming cups in her hands and a large bag on her shoulder.

"This couldn't wait? Maybe after a phone call?" Lisa grumbled.

"Sorry. I brought green tea. Your father said you don't drink coffee. And he also said that you're leaving for Boston."

"I don't know what I'm doing," Lisa said, rubbing her eyes and sitting back on the bed.

"Well, I got really excited about something I found last night, but I waited till this morning to show you."

"What did you find?" Lisa said, trying to sound more civil. But what kind of a person just showed up at someone's hotel room at 7:00 a.m.?

Rosalyn set one cup on the nightstand beside Lisa and dropped her bag onto the floor at the end of the bed, hitting the end of Lisa's toe. She cringed and moved her feet as Rosalyn unpacked her computer.

"So you know how I found that one photograph on that website? Well, I kept searching for more photographs of Benjamin Gray, but then I tried a different direction. Instead of looking for more about Gray, I searched for other images that came from that IP address. What I found was interesting. Whoever it is, they're releasing other incriminating evidence, though I don't know who they're trying to incriminate, because it seems like it's themselves."

"What kind of incriminating evidence?"

"Numerous photographs of dead people, but they aren't crime scene photographs. I brought copies for you to look at and maybe send to your friend who helped with your dad's snapshots. I think they show bodies *before* they were found by police. So how does this person have pictures of their corpses?" Rosalyn's eyes gleamed with excitement. "And did your father tell you that he believes Stanley Blackstone is the one who killed Benjamin Gray?"

"No, what? When did he put that together?"

"On his trip. He can tell you about it. But it seems we may have someone helping us or just trying to release information to cause trouble for the Blackstones. Stanley Blackstone is currently being investigated in Florida for the disappearance of a local businessman." Rosalyn looked at Lisa hopefully and said, "Maybe you can come to the house this morning?"

So she was mainly here as an intermediary.

"I just woke up, but I'm tired of being away from home."

Rosalyn nodded and pulled up a chair. "I get sick of hotels too, though you could stay at your father's. He'd love to have you. You know, your father is upset."

"My *father* is upset?" Lisa stared at the woman.

"I promised myself that I wouldn't stick my nose into this, but . . . well, I'm breaking that promise."

"No offense, but this has nothing to do with you."

"It has to do with someone I really care about. And something I've seen in my cases again and again is that people who love each other are often their worst enemies. I'm not talking about when the divorce proceedings begin and war is declared. I'm talking before that."

Lisa decided it would be easier not to argue but to endure the woman's little life lesson. That would get rid of her faster.

"In trying to protect each other, people can create huge messes. This entire case is like that. It has people trying to protect others, and mess after mess results."

"Dad didn't tell me about John because he was protecting himself."

"Yes, I'm sure he was. It wouldn't be easy to face you after all of these years, especially not for your father, who can't string together his feelings to save his life. And he didn't walk away from the Dubois case without reason."

"He told you I asked about that?" Lisa didn't want to talk about this with Rosalyn. She rose from the bed. "Listen, I'll go talk to my dad before I leave. I'm not abandoning this, it's just time for me to go home."

She pulled her suitcase from the closet, hoping Rosalyn would get the hint.

"During Leonard Dubois's trial, your father was still trying to find answers even after he was demoted, which was a huge blow to him. But he kept digging. You know how he is. But only one thing would make him stop."

"And what was that?" Lisa asked, no longer trying to sound civil.

"You were the reason. You and your mother."

"What are you talking about?"

"He received a threat. It had detailed information about your school, your routine, your dance teacher's name, your bus route. The threat was clear. If he didn't back off, something would happen to you."

Lisa considered her words. They made sense.

"Your father wouldn't turn his back on a case for any other reason than to protect the ones he loved. And then he lost you and your mother anyway."

Rosalyn's words stung. They also resonated and amplified as she realized their meaning.

"So one reason Leonard Dubois has been in prison all of these years is because someone threatened me?"

"I suppose. All I know is that your father was trying to protect you."

Lisa sat back on the bed.

"Your father should have contacted you before contacting your son. He should have told you about it right away. Maybe all those years ago, he should have gone to a higher authority when he received the threat. But I don't know who he could have gone to . . . his own superiors were against him."

A sudden weariness came over Lisa. She wanted to pull the covers over her head and go back to sleep. She'd been furious at her father, questioning his integrity, suspicious of his motives. Since childhood, she'd felt abandoned by him. How did so much pain result from love?

"See what I mean—all this trying to protect each other, and it ends up causing more hurt."

Rosalyn hopped up from the chair as Lisa remained on the bed. "Please come talk to your father," Rosalyn said. Then she packed up and left almost as quickly as she'd come.

Lisa sat in the empty room, bruised by Rosalyn's words. The truth rolled over her. Lisa was making many of the same mistakes as her father.

<hr />

Lisa sat in bed after Rosalyn's departure and called the person who never failed to make life better.

"Hi, Mom," she said.

"Sweetie, I'm sorry, but I'm heading out the door in about fifteen minutes. Are you okay? I can see if Norris can change our tee time."

"No, it's all right. We can talk later," Lisa said. Just hearing her mother's voice improved her mood.

In the fifteen years since their divorce, Mom's life had flourished. She'd gone on cruises, taken up golf, traveled, and fallen in love again. Mom and Norris had gone on a leisure cycling and wine-tasting trip in Italy the year before, even though both were well into their seventies.

"Tell me what's going on. How are you surviving Dallas?"

"I don't know." Lisa rubbed between her eyes. Though she hadn't spoken to her mother since her trip to Texas, they updated each other through e-mail on a regular basis. Her mother had been concerned but hopeful about this trip to see her father.

"What's bothering you specifically?" Mom said, and Lisa could picture the countless times she'd used that same tone as she'd sat on the edge of Lisa's bed or brought her into the living room with cups of homemade hot cocoa. Mom was always there. She'd spent several weeks with Lisa after John's birth and again after Thomas's death. At every important event—good or bad—her mother could be counted on—the exact opposite of her father.

"Too much for one phone call," Lisa said with a laugh. "But there is one thing I've been wanting to know."

"What is it?"

"Why did Dad take me to that civil rights rally in the first place?"

Lisa heard Norris laughing and talking to someone in the background, then it sounded as if Mom had moved to a quieter room.

"It was the job. He convinced himself that it would be safe. I was shopping that day with my mother, who was in town visiting. Your father said he was taking you to the park. I was furious when I found out what happened. Well, more terrified at what might have happened, but furious at your dad. But he was upset enough that I didn't say a lot to him about it."

"What do you mean?" Lisa pulled a blanket over her legs.

"That day was the beginning of a change in him. First, he became obsessed with finding the killer of that civil rights man. He was sure it wasn't the guy they arrested. I knew a lot of this obsession was because he couldn't get over putting you in danger.

"Your father was always dedicated to his job. I understood that, and growing up in a military family, I was prepared for it as much as I could be. Wives had their duties and sacrifices. We took care of the home and the children while our men saved the world. That's how I was raised. But your father pulled away from us after that day even more. I assumed it was guilt. But I didn't know how to help him."

"So he took me there for no other reason than the job?"

"Yes, he was a 'kill two birds with one stone' kind of guy. He probably thought he'd go take photos and observe the rally while spending time with you. He probably even told himself it was a learning experience for you, even if you were four."

"But you'd think having such a scare would make him see what was important. He was such a workaholic as far back as I can remember."

"He tried making up for it, in his way. He kept pushing for answers about that shooting. He made someone at the Bureau angry, and he got demoted. The next few years only made him worse in trying to regain respect at the Bureau. If not for Peter, we might have lost your father to his job completely."

"What do you mean?" Lisa said, kicking off the blankets and moving to her desk.

"You remember Peter, right?"

"Of course, but he disappeared from our lives so fast." Lisa had never talked to Mom about how deeply she'd felt the loss of Uncle Peter. She remembered the last time she'd seen him, when she was nine or ten years old. He'd hugged her till it almost hurt, and his tears struck fear through her. Uncle Peter was the one who took her to baseball games, taught her to ride a bicycle, and showed her numerous yo-yo tricks that she performed at a talent show in second grade. Dad had come with them at times, but usually he was consumed with whatever case was currently on his plate. Peter was the constant she could depend on, like Mom. She didn't doubt his love . . . until he was gone.

Lisa had never seen him after that good-bye, and she'd tried to bury the sense of abandonment she'd felt then and even more when she later learned of his suicide.

"Peter helped your father with perspective. He pulled him away from the job over and over for family barbecues and outings. But just when I hoped that your dad was getting better, Peter was fired. Your dad felt lied to. And not long after, Peter killed himself. That was a blow to all of us. But your dad never recovered from it."

Lisa heard Mom's name being called in the background.

"You need to go, Mom. Enjoy your game of golf."

"No, I can talk more. I'm worried about you."

Lisa smiled. It was probably driving her mother crazy that they had this space between them. She'd probably mail a box of homemade cookies after today's conversation.

"You already helped me. Thanks, Mom."

Lisa hung up the phone and headed for the shower. She was still angry with her father over the John incident, but this wasn't the time for a division in their ranks.

Despite his faults, Dad needed her. Perhaps in forgiving him, she'd find what she was longing for from him as well.

CHAPTER THIRTY-ONE

Stanley stared at the expanse of blue gulf water stretching beyond view from the tiny window of his private jet. Being in the sky always gave him time to think, and today he needed precise planning.

At the back of the plane, Billy and Frank played poker. A few rows ahead, Marcus sat in his seat, supposedly going over financial reports. His nephew usually slept or worked when they flew, but he was doing neither today. He winced when Frank shouted his frustration at losing a hand.

Stanley studied the back of Marcus's head, the swirl of a cowlick that reminded him of his nephew as a pale, skinny boy who seemed to jump at his own shadow. He'd always needed someone stronger than himself, like one of those pilot fish that followed a shark, eating the parasites and leftovers but never venturing out on its own.

But once a pilot fish had a host, it rarely left. Stanley had heard stories of the fish following a boat for weeks that had snagged its shark.

Marcus had fed off Stanley for decades. It was a mutually beneficial relationship. Though he'd never abide disloyalty, Stanley almost hoped that at last Marcus had done something brave on his own. But it didn't fit with his nature.

Stanley stretched out the kinks in his back and took a long drink of the lemon water in the seat's cup holder. There was a more pressing matter. The Waldrens had pushed too far and dug too deep.

Stanley thought of his father. What would he do in this situation? When would he be decisive, and when would he sit by with complete confidence that nothing could harm him?

Stanley's youth was plagued with hard lessons as he'd fought to rein in his temper. He bore the scar of a gunshot wound and the memory of a terrifying escape through panicked crowds until he somehow reached his car and found a pay phone before passing out. He'd made decisions as a young man that cost the family dearly, forcing them to live a more obscure existence. His father's political aspirations were stopped by Stanley's actions, and he knew his father had never fully forgiven him for it.

Now Gwen followed the same path. She believed this was motivated by her ideologies and the drive to right her family's wrongs. But his daughter was naive in many ways. Her blood was Blackstone. At some point she'd stop denying that and even embrace it. He had no doubt about that. Until then Stanley wouldn't give her reasons to blame him for her failed dreams.

"Marcus," Stanley called. His nephew jumped, dropped something, and then hurried from his seat.

"Yes, Uncle, can I get you something?"

Sometimes Stanley wanted to slap some sense into the man. "You aren't a flight attendant, you're the VP of a multibillion-dollar company."

"Yes, I know. Just thought I'd get you something, you know?" Marcus sat in the seat beside Stanley.

"When we land, I need you to send an e-mail or get a message to Gwendolyn. And it has got to be on a secure line or e-mail account or something."

"Of course."

"Of course? With all this hacking and police interest, I need to know you can do that."

"Yes, I can. What do you want to say?"

"I'm working on that. It shouldn't be direct or incriminating. I mainly want her to know how much I enjoyed seeing her, and that she doesn't need to worry about anything. I'm taking care of everything."

Stanley thought of his quick encounter with his daughter at the plantation. He needed more time with her; then slowly, little by little, she'd soften toward him and her family's past.

"Are we headed to Dallas, then?" Marcus asked.

Stanley studied his nephew, and Marcus squirmed beneath the stare.

"It'll be a surprise," Stanley said. "But stay here. I'll tell you a story. First, do you remember what I told you about loose ends?"

"You always say to wrap them up, even if something doesn't appear important. And that a man has to clean up his messes by himself."

Stanley slapped Marcus on the back and laughed. "That's right, you are listening. No matter how much time passes, at some point, loose ends must be wrapped up."

"If I can do anything to help?" Marcus asked with an expression that made Stanley sick to his stomach—the weakling trying to please his master.

"You can. But we'll get to that very soon."

Sometimes his old nanny's sayings and examples still came in useful. Stanley was always leaving food in his bedroom as a child, and he'd wake up to ants in his bed or covering the plate of food on the floor.

Instead of stomping on the insects, as Stanley liked to do, Martha showed him a better method. First, she'd clean up the food, then she'd leave a trail of crumbs back out the door.

"Sometimes the easiest way to clean up a mess is to let the mess do the cleaning," she'd say. "We've got to lure them out. That way they'll go wherever we want."

CHAPTER THIRTY-TWO

Let's not talk about John right now," Lisa said when she arrived at her father's house.

"Are you sure?" Dad asked, clearly on edge.

"We'll take it up later, as well as why you stopped investigating the Gray case years ago. Rosalyn told me about the threats when I was a child."

"She wasn't supposed to do that," Dad said, clenching his jaw and looking to where Rosalyn sat with her laptop at the dining room table. She wore earphones and bobbed her head to an unheard beat. Other than waving at Lisa when she'd arrived, Rosalyn seemed to be in her own little world.

"I'm glad she did. You should have told me. I'm a mother, don't you think I'd understand? I'd do most anything to protect my son."

Dad opened his mouth as if to explain, then stopped.

"Let's save this, really, Dad. We need to focus. I talked to Leonard's attorney. They won't delay his execution date. We're running out of time. The court system is slow. Even if we finally get what we need, the court could still take a bit of time."

"Yes, okay," Dad said. "Should we go out to the workshop, then?"

"Sure. I want to go over everything you learned in New York. And Molly and I uncovered a few things as well. We can put that together with what Rosalyn found."

Lisa caught Rosalyn's smile, though the woman kept her eyes on the computer.

"Then we should get started," Dad said, looking as if a weight had lifted.

Lisa noticed the freshly cut lawn in the backyard as they moved between the house and the workshop. It reminded her of how Dad had resorted to yard work when he and Mom had conflicts. Lisa found it somewhat humorous, but she didn't remark.

Dad unlocked the workshop door.

"The other thing is, I'm going home tomorrow. I already told the hotel, and I booked an afternoon flight."

"What?" Dad turned from the door. "Why?"

"You know how it feels to be gone from home too long. Let's do what we can today. Then we can work just as effectively with me in Boston. And I have a great security system there as well."

"Okay," Dad said, sounding resigned.

Lisa couldn't keep a slight grin from the edges of her lips. He'd only be happy if she moved back into her old bedroom, at least until this case was completed. But she was more than ready to get back to Boston. She wanted her own house, her own stuff, and her own bed.

And she felt ready to see Drew. There was much to say to him, and it couldn't be spoken over the phone.

The harsh fluorescent lights flickered on inside the workshop. Lisa wished they could stay beneath the sunshine instead of spending the day in the Bat Cave.

"And one more thing." Lisa put a hand on his shoulder before they stepped inside.

Dad raised an eyebrow.

"When this is all over, you need to get rid of all of this and get a new hobby."

"What's wrong with this hobby?" Dad said, motioning to the walls of crime scene photos with an exaggerated look of confusion.

"Uh-huh," Lisa said.

"Okay, let's go through it all." He moved inside and flipped on the extra lights over the workbenches. "I'm pretty certain we know the killer."

"Stanley Blackstone." Lisa pulled up her usual stool and let her eyes pan over the walls.

"Yes."

"But what's the motive?" Lisa asked, thinking of a judge cutting through their theories. "We need to answer every question before facing the courts."

"We don't have motive. Most likely Blackstone and Gray knew one another in Alexandria. They were in segregated schools, but there are too many connections to be a coincidence. They graduated high school only a few years apart. Benjamin Gray was three years older. Alexandria isn't a big city, especially back in the 1960s. Stanley attended college in Dallas and dropped out at the time of Gray's shooting."

"Still no motive," Lisa said. She had her theory but wanted to hear what her father had discovered.

"Perhaps Stanley killed him because of their history. He saw this black man becoming someone of importance, fighting for everything he and his family stood against, so he went to the rally and killed him." Dad leafed through papers he'd compiled on Stanley Blackstone.

"But it was a foolish way to kill him. Why so public? It speaks of passion."

"Passion?"

"The motive may be simple," Lisa said.

"What?" Dad stopped looking through the papers.

"A woman."

Lisa explained how they'd discovered that Gray's fiancée was prob- ably Madeline Fitzgerald and that her family had ties to the plantation owned by the Blackstone family.

"So all three of them knew each other back in Alexandria," Dad said. He moved to one of his boards and wrote down some notes on a 3 x 5 card.

"Yes. If we have the right Madeline, her father was white and her mother was black. She's been the proprietor of a dinner house in New Orleans for decades, and she was a gorgeous woman in her youth. She's still beautiful, from the website photos, and she must be in her seven- ties. Another point, she could almost pass for white."

"You think Stanley Blackstone was in love with her?" Dad said doubtfully.

"It happened, even in situations like this. And Stanley might have felt entitled to Madeline. Her aunt was his nanny. Maybe he even felt as if he owned her. Then later she gets engaged to a black man he knows from his hometown. That's a recipe for a crime of passion. The shooting at the rally wasn't thought out or methodical."

"And Blackstone is usually careful," Dad said. He explained that he'd talked to a detective in Florida earlier that morning. The man believed Stanley Blackstone was involved in the killing of a wealthy local businessman, Blackstone's rival, and the man's mistress.

"They think he dumped the bodies in the Atlantic, but there's no evidence. And according to Detective Martin, this is far from the only crime they suspect him of, but they never have enough evidence for an indictment."

"The rally shooting was extremely sloppy," Lisa said, "but Blackstone was young then—early twenties. He could have easily been caught that day. There had to be a powerful reason."

Dad didn't look convinced. He leaned his elbows onto the workbench and studied some black-and-white photographs on the wall. "Even if he loved her, Blackstone knew he couldn't be with that woman. Mixed-race marriage was against the law in the South until maybe the late sixties or early seventies. And his family would've certainly disowned him."

Lisa thought of Drew and the reasons she'd told herself that a relationship beyond friendship shouldn't occur. But she couldn't imagine one of those reasons being the law. "How would that apply to someone who was half black?"

"She still would've been considered black. But if she looked white, it would've been hard for her to be with either of the men during that time. Neither community would have accepted her. I can see how New Orleans was the right place for her."

"There may be an easy way to answer this," Lisa said, digging into her bag.

"How?" Dad asked.

"I'm going to ask her."

Lisa studied the website for Fitz House. The images displayed a small dinner house tucked into a courtyard in the French Quarter. Wrought-iron gates opened into a cobblestone patio with hanging baskets that overflowed with flowers. The inside shots displayed tables with red velvet chairs and couches, a black marble fireplace, and gold-colored lighting hanging from the ceiling. There was also a small dance floor and stage.

In one picture Madeline Fitzgerald stood at the side of an ornately carved wooden bar. She wore a floor-length dress from an era gone by.

Lisa leaned close to the screen to study the woman. Her black hair was pinned up in an elaborate twist. She didn't smile but stood regally with one hand resting on the bar. Lisa couldn't imagine what this woman had experienced, growing up half white and half black in a small Louisiana town during the turbulent fifties and sixties.

"I'm trying to reach Madeline Lorraine Fitzgerald," she said after calling the restaurant. Dad pulled up a chair beside her.

"I am Madeline Fitzgerald," a woman said in a smooth Southern accent.

Lisa explained who she was and asked if she had an aunt in Alexandria who had worked at the Red Wolf Plantation.

"It seems you already know that answer," Madeline said, her voice suddenly sounding strained and suspicious.

"My father and I are looking into the death of Benjamin Gray."

Silence.

"You were in a relationship with Benjamin Gray at the time of his death, is that correct? You were engaged?"

"I would rather not answer these questions. You are a prosecutor, you said. Is this a formal query? Should I contact my attorney?"

"Please, Ms. Fitzgerald, I'm not doing this in any official capacity. Leonard Dubois has spent his entire life in prison over this. We know he isn't the killer. And I believe you know that as well."

"I cannot help you."

Dad sighed and stood from the chair. He started pacing around the small room.

"Don't you want justice for your fiancé?" Lisa said in a gentle tone.

"I wanted my fiancé to live a long life with me. Then I wanted my own long life. Justice doesn't always come until we pass over."

"I know Leonard Dubois is hoping for some justice. His execution date is only weeks away."

"I didn't know that, and I'm sorry," Madeline said.

"Did you know Stanley Blackstone and Benjamin Gray when you were young?"

She started to speak, paused, and then said, "I did. We knew one another at that time. But that is all I'm going to say. Please, I have put that behind me, long ago. There is nothing I can do to help that man in prison."

"Will you answer me one more question?" Lisa hoped the woman wouldn't hang up. Dad stopped his pacing and sat near her again.

Madeline didn't respond.

"Did you have a relationship with Stanley Blackstone?"

Lisa caught the woman's sigh over the line.

"Yes. Stanley wanted to marry me. When we were younger. But other times he wanted nothing to do with me."

"What happened?" Lisa clenched her fist in excitement. Finally, they were getting a solid motive.

"His father forbade it, of course. And Stanley was a conflicted man. He didn't want me, but he didn't want anyone else to have me. That is all I will say. Please, leave me alone."

Lisa heard the line go dead as she opened her mouth for another question. She set down the phone, both excited and frustrated with the many answers she still sought.

"Perhaps I should talk to her in person."

"In New Orleans?" Dad said with a frown. Lisa knew the break-in at her home and hotel room continued to haunt him.

"People can't hang up or easily dodge questions when face-to-face. I could make an overnight stop there on my way home." Lisa had always loved New Orleans. She had been there right after Katrina and mourned the devastation. But the city was resilient, and she'd longed to return as it continued its restoration. For a moment she thought of Drew meeting her down there.

"You could show up and she might not open the door for you," Dad said.

"She owns a business. She can't slam the door on a customer," Lisa said, getting more excited about the idea as she spoke.

If Madeline had lost her fiancé because of Stanley, she might be the right person to finally bring Stanley down.

CHAPTER THIRTY-THREE

Stanley savored the look of confusion on Marcus's face when they exited the plane at a private airport in New Orleans. He was keeping the kid on his toes, that was certain. Marcus did not appear to enjoy it.

When they reached their hotel, Stanley made sure to be noticed, talking to the woman at the registration counter and tipping the door-man and valet exceedingly well.

Once in their three-bedroom suite, he reviewed the latest report from Dallas that tracked the father's and daughter's movements. Pieces of it didn't make sense. A local woman minister had become attached to them for some reason. Lisa Waldren had visited the minister's family.

However, it was James Waldren's trip to New York that concerned him most. What had he learned there that made him call Stanley at his corporate office? The more he knew, the better Stanley could manage the fallout or any surprises that might come with the disappearance or accidental deaths of the Waldrens.

He reviewed his targets once again. What were their weaknesses? That's how it always worked best. Find where they'd hurt, where they'd crumble. Even the hardest man had a breaking point.

"Why are we in New Orleans?" Marcus asked after knocking on the sliding door to Stanley's room.

"Business and pleasure," Stanley said cryptically.

"But I thought we were taking care of . . . a problem. And I'm needed at corporate."

"Have Roberts step in for a few more days."

Marcus stared at him, looking pathetic. Stanley knew his nephew's mind was bouncing all over the place with dreaded possibilities. The boy needed some reassurance, even if Stanley hadn't decided his nephew's fate quite yet.

"Other VPs step in when they're needed, that's what they're for. I'm not firing you, don't worry so much. You'll be back behind the helm in a few days."

Marcus calmed considerably. After he left the bedroom, Stanley reviewed his options again. Bodies could be difficult to hide. No suspicion could fall on him this time; his future with Gwen might depend on that.

In the early evening, he announced that he was going for a walk. He motioned to Billy to keep an eye on Marcus before he left the suite.

Downstairs, he tossed back just one shot of whiskey before walking into the French Quarter at dusk.

He adjusted his tie and smoothed his tailored suit. In the window of an antique store he looked himself over. The dinner house was two blocks away.

Stanley had never felt comfortable in New Orleans. There were too many conflicting elements there. Everything was acceptable. There were no lines of race, culture, or even class. Miami was bad enough, overrun by Latinos, but New Orleans was another story. There was something unsettling in the people and the streets. But he understood why she'd come here. It was a perfect place to lose the past and become whoever a person wanted to be.

The dinner house was nearly empty at that hour. A pretty hostess came toward him.

"Table for one?" she said in a coy Southern drawl.

"I'm looking for the owner," Stanley said.

"I believe she's in her office upstairs. I'll call up."

"No, please don't. I want to surprise her. We are old, old friends," Stanley said with a smile.

The girl's smile widened as if he'd let her in on a secret.

"Well, I'm not supposed to let anyone up without calling first," she said apologetically. She picked up a phone at the wooden podium. "How long has it been since you've seen her?"

Stanley put his hand over the girl's, holding down the phone. "Please. It's been a very long time. I want to surprise her. You see, she was my first love," he said, lowering his voice.

The girl's eyes widened and she set the phone down. "The stairway by the kitchen. Her office is at the end of the hallway."

As Stanley walked through the small restaurant, he took in the scents coming from the kitchen, mixed with flowering potted plants. A French singer played over hidden speakers as a band set up on a small stage. Everything in the place reminded Stanley of her, making his head light with both memory and anticipation.

He moved up the stairs with a growing mix of anticipation and anxiety. He'd imagined this moment over the many decades, and now he was knocking on a door with her name written on it.

"Come in," she said.

Stanley couldn't believe how his heart raced. It was hard to catch his breath as he turned the doorknob.

She sat at a desk and then rose when she didn't recognize him.

"Lena," he said.

She stopped just as she'd taken a step from behind her desk. Only one person on earth called her by that name.

"Stanley."

He walked inside, closing the door behind him. She flinched as the door clicked shut. She'd aged, of course she had aged. But she was still beautiful, still radiant.

"I didn't say anything." She remained at her desk. The light came in from the window, surrounding her thin frame.

"You didn't say anything?"

"To that woman, the prosecutor."

Stanley stopped short. "Lisa Waldren contacted you?"

"This morning."

Stanley's feet moved toward her.

"That's not why I'm here." He came around the desk.

"Please," she whispered. Even terrified, she looked regal.

Her black eyes were like a well he couldn't climb out of. He wished he could hear her laugh again as she had when they were young. When they escaped into the woods away from everything and everyone. When they were together for the first time, and then every time they had a chance to be alone.

"I've been thinking about you and the past. What went wrong . . ." Stanley felt intoxicated by her.

"Everything went wrong," she said. "But remember, you left me."

"I had to. You were . . ."

"Black?" she said.

That's when he saw the hatred in her eyes.

Stanley cringed. "We live in a different time now," he said, though he wasn't sure what that meant to him, or to her.

He moved closer, even as her body tensed.

"Don't you understand what you did? You stole everything from me."

She flinched as he reached for the ivory comb, pulling it from her hair. Strands of salt-and-pepper hair tumbled down her back and over his hand.

He reached to touch her face when he heard the click of a gun's hammer. It rested on the desk beneath her left hand. The barrel was pointed at him.

"Leave now, please."

Even after all this time, he knew her expressions.

"You wouldn't," he said, but her face said she was stronger now. It made him want her more while knowing he would never have her.

"Go now. I've kept your secrets, but they are looking for you." She kept her hand on the gun. "And, Stanley, don't ever come back."

CHAPTER THIRTY-FOUR

For Lisa's last night in Dallas, Rosalyn cooked a Tex-Mex feast and insisted they all gather at Dad's house.

"It'll be fun," Molly said as if to convince Lisa when picking her up. The scent of a pineapple upside-down cake filled Molly's car. They stopped by a wine shop, and Lisa found a favorite Sonoma Valley Cabernet. At least the wine would be good, she mused.

Dad's house was filled with mouth-watering scents, and the table seemed weighted with food. To Lisa's surprise, it tasted even better than it smelled and looked—Rosalyn was an excellent cook. Score another point for the quirky woman in the Mexican dress with a large plastic flower behind her ear.

"Can I help with anything?" Lisa asked Rosalyn.

"I got it. Relax. Enjoy time with your father."

Lisa watched Rosalyn flutter around the tiny kitchen where her mother once stood, surprised at her own lack of animosity. Her father's girlfriend was growing on her. And Lisa knew it would be easier for her to leave knowing her father wasn't alone.

I don't want to be alone either. The realization surprised Lisa, and she thought of Drew back in Boston.

Over dinner Molly asked Dad about his years in the FBI, especially the investigation of the JFK assassination. They sat at the table for hours, eating, drinking, and listening to her father's stories, many of which Lisa had never heard before. Even with Rosalyn chattering over Dad, sometimes telling his stories for him, Lisa savored the time together.

Much later, as she packed her luggage and talked to Drew in her hotel room, Lisa realized how much the night meant to her.

"It was the best night I can remember with my father."

Drew didn't respond.

Lisa sat on the bed, pulling her legs up close.

"Go ahead and say I told you so. If you hadn't pushed me into this, I doubt I would've come."

"Me, push you? Never." Drew's tone had *I told you so* all over it. "But you should trust me. I might know more about making you happy than you realize."

Lisa stared at her bare toes. "That's another thing to discuss when I get back. It's harder to leave after tonight, but I'm ready to be back in Boston."

"I'm looking forward to it myself," Drew said.

"Tomorrow night in New Orleans, and then I'm home."

She heard his groan and the sound of his desk chair creak. "If only I didn't have that meeting with corporate, we could've made it several nights in New Orleans," Drew said in a gravelly tone that made her wish it as well.

But Lisa needed to remain focused. As she gained the courage to step forward into unchartered possibilities with Drew, she was determined to get the final answers to free Leonard Dubois, and hopefully bring Stanley Blackstone to justice. She needed to rein in the tumult of emotions for just a while longer.

Before saying good night, Drew added with a hint of residual worry, "Promise me you'll be careful. No risks, just get yourself home."

Lisa crawled into bed with *Casablanca* playing over the television, then reached for her cell phone for a quick glance at her e-mail. A name in the in-box brought her sitting straight up in bed. *Gwendolyn Hubert.*

Lisa opened the e-mail that Stanley Blackstone's daughter had written her.

Ms. Waldren,

I believe you are already aware of who I am, and who my father is. I would like to talk to you privately and off the record as soon as possible. I'm willing to fly to wherever you are. Please be careful and contact me soon.

Sincerely,
Gwen

Lisa studied the e-mail, reading it numerous times, wondering if it was really from Gwendolyn Hubert.

The aspiring politician had an auto-signature at the bottom of her e-mail. When Lisa clicked the link, the *Hope in Action! Hubert for Senate* campaign website opened. The contact numbers in the e-mail had area codes from Missouri, and one matched the number on her website. It appeared the e-mail might be authentic.

But why would the woman contact her? And what exactly did she want to discuss?

Lisa spent the next few hours reviewing her information on Gwendolyn Hubert and her estranged father, Stanley Blackstone, until she fell asleep in the earliest hours of the morning.

When she woke, Lisa forwarded the e-mail from Gwendolyn to Dad and Drew. She'd be seeing her father later in the day. She didn't enjoy good-byes and had attempted to be done with them after last night's dinner. They'd made plans to get together soon either in Dallas or Boston before the days of Leonard's life clicked away. Then, as she was leaving his house, Dad insisted that he drive her to the airport today, even after she explained how easily she could drop off the rental car before her flight.

"Can you pick me up at three?"

"Three it is," Dad had said.

Lisa decided to e-mail Gwendolyn from the airport after she'd had more time to discern why the woman had reached out to her. She took the last hours to prepare for her meeting with Madeline Fitzgerald and to organize the pile of papers, police files, and photographs she had accumulated since her arrival. She'd bought an additional piece of luggage in a hotel shop to lug it all home. Tonight she would approach Madeline and try to obtain the truth.

From Lisa's research she'd found conflicting reports about Madeline Fitzgerald's presence at the civil rights rally. But what caught Lisa's attention were two reports of a disturbance the night before, never explored by law enforcement. The altercation was between Benjamin Gray and an unknown man. One report mentioned Madeline's presence at the hotel where the men were staying.

If Madeline hadn't attended the rally, she could at least explain about this incident the night before. Lisa suspected it was between Benjamin Gray and Stanley Blackstone. And if the woman had attended the rally, she likely witnessed the shooting.

As Lisa read and jotted down notes, a text from Molly popped up on her phone.

Can you meet me at the church?

Lisa and Molly had said good-bye the night before. She typed back, Is everything okay?

I need to show you something.

Lisa dialed Molly's number, but it only rang and went to voice mail.

What is it? Lisa typed.

No answer. Lisa stared at her phone, then hopped up from the desk. She sent a quick text to Dad, knowing he might not see it anyway. Then she wrote Molly.

I'm on my way.

Lisa had only a few hours until her father picked her up at the hotel. Molly's church was a half hour away. She left her luggage in the room and grabbed her bag. The hotel had been more than accommodating to Lisa's requests after the room break-in. The housekeeper personally apologized and relayed her story that matched their assumptions about the man convincing her that it was his room and Lisa's, but Lisa was glad the woman hadn't been fired. The manager provided Lisa with complimentary room service and knocked off several nights from her bill. Today they gave her a late checkout with no fuss at all.

She hurried downstairs. Molly wasn't an overly dramatic person, and she wasn't one to impose upon a friend who had a flight to catch unless it was important.

A late spring storm had rolled in overnight with gusts of wind sending flower blossoms tumbling along the ground and rain pelting the earth. The cool temperature felt more like a Boston spring than Dallas, and Lisa wished she'd brought her jacket.

She drove faster than usual, checking her phone at stoplights with hopes that Molly would call or text her again. Perhaps the battery had gone dead or she had it on silent. Lisa tried to come up with logical reasons for Molly's cryptic text. Perhaps she'd uncovered something that couldn't be conveyed over the phone.

Molly's car was in the parking lot. One of the front doors to the church was open a crack.

Lisa entered the foyer and called her friend's name. She strode down to Molly's office, but it was empty. She glanced at open classrooms on the way back to the sanctuary, calling her name again.

Dialing her number, Lisa heard the ringtone of Molly's phone coming from a distant room. She followed it back to the main sanctuary. The phone silenced as she entered. Lisa strained to see as the stained-glass windows cast a soft light down upon the sanctuary.

"Molly, are you in here?" she called softly.

"Lisa, run! Get out of here."

Before Lisa could react, she saw a man at the front and heard someone behind her. Then Lisa saw Molly on the side steps to the altar. Lisa hurried toward her.

"I'm sorry. They took my phone," Molly said, wrapping her arms around Lisa.

"It'll be okay," Lisa said, assessing the situation. The man standing nearest made no move or threat, but his presence and hands in his jacket spoke volumes. Molly appeared unhurt but certainly rattled.

Lisa heard a door open, and she turned toward the sanctuary entrance. A stocky older man walked down the center aisle. There were men on each side of the sanctuary and one sitting on a pew in front, making a total of four.

Her attention returned to the older man walking toward them. From his demeanor, Lisa knew he was the one in control.

"Hello, Lisa Waldren. I'm Stanley Blackstone. I believe you've been looking for me."

usted their
remember.
dn't tried.
wished he

he found
m Peter's
that he'd
ings after

the thin
rds writ-
request:
seal and

er object
out, and
eeling its

ject he'd
oric cabi-
s opened

ne for
ow it
close
best.
has

think

t the

THIRTY-FIVE

parture on his mind, James forgot that a
ve until he heard the knock on the door.
a deliveryman scurry through the heavy
uck.
rstep. The return address was from Cole
. Peter's nephew.
ge inside, shutting out the gusty wind that
atterns.
old mantel clock ticking from the wall, and
rom the kitchen were the only noises around
x. His mind reeled through memories of his
d spent countless hours at this very house,
aying with Lisa in the backyard, or tinkering
ebird in the garage because his condo didn't

Peter had been the brother James didn't have. They'd t[...]
lives in each other's hands more times than James could[...]
Then suddenly, they never spoke again . . . not that Peter h[...]
Now he'd finally hear Peter's final words to him. How Jame[...]
could say a million words back.

James opened the box on the dining room table. Insid[...]
a worn and crinkled manila envelope as well as a note f[...]
nephew apologizing for not sending it along sooner. He wro[...]
only discovered it after looking through his mother's belon[...]
O'Ryan called him.

James recognized Peter's handwriting on the outside o[...]
envelope. The seal hadn't been broken. Perhaps Peter's w[...]
ten across the front had scared his nephew into abiding by h[...]
For FBI Special Agent James Waldren ONLY. James broke th[...]
looked inside.

There was a note folded in thirds. James stared at the o[...]
sitting at the bottom of the envelope. He poured both item[...]
an antique brass key clattered onto the table. He picked it up,[...]
weight. He knew exactly what he was holding.

O'Ryan was right. Somehow Peter had obtained the o[...]
been looking for—one of the keys to President Kennedy's his[...]
net. Had he used it to find the secrets he was looking for? Jam[...]
the letter.

Jimmy,

My mistakes are big and vast, ol' buddy. I hope you can forgive
them. There's much I wanted to tell you. It was best not to, despite
seemed. But in protecting you and your family, the only family I've bee[...]
to, I lost all of you. Know that my intentions have always been for t[...]
Loyalty and truth can become complicated in our field. But my loya[...]
always been with you, despite how it seemed.

Someday please explain it all to Lisa-belle. I wouldn't want her t[...]
Uncle Peter didn't love her. She meant the world to me.

I hope the key helps to right the wrongs. Be careful with it. Don't tr[...]

Bureau with it, or anyone else. Get to the source and unlock it yourself. That's the only way to be sure. The answers should be there.

You were the brother I never had.

Peter

James read the letter three times, wanting more, much more. He wanted explanations and more clarity in his friend's last words.

He sat down in a chair. Peter had died in 1971. He'd wanted James to get this back then, not all these decades later. James looked inside the envelope once more and saw an address written inside. Peter knew the address—it was in Washington, DC, and most likely where the Kennedy cabinet was stored.

James found his phone and called Lisa. She didn't answer, and he didn't leave a voice mail. But his mind raced with ideas. They could go together to DC and get to the bottom of this once and for all.

Glancing at the clock, he realized it was nearly time to pick Lisa up at her hotel. He wondered what to do with the key and letter. For too long it had been floating out in the world. He stuffed it into a small safe in his bedroom and tried calling Lisa again. Again, no answer.

James drove to her hotel more excited to see her by the minute. He had the key. The fact was settling in slowly; James could barely believe it. For decades he'd wondered if it even existed, and now it had arrived on his doorstep. His gut said that this was more than just a key to a cabinet—it was the key to saving Leonard Dubois.

Lisa wasn't in the lobby yet. He was twenty minutes early. He called her again, then called her room from a hotel phone. No answer either time.

He wandered by a large fountain to one of the attached restaurants, peering in at the mostly empty tables. Then he walked back and sat beside a marble statue. He glanced up at the statue, shaking his head. He'd never feel comfortable in a place like this.

"Has Lisa Waldren checked out yet?" James asked the woman at the front desk.

She studied him and said, "Uh, I'm not able to give out guest information."

"Never mind, I'll go up to her room."

"Is she expecting you?" the woman asked, standing from the stool.

"Yes. I'm her father."

"I was told to get my manager if anyone asked for Ms. Waldren. One moment, please."

James waited, drumming his fingers on the polished wood and scanning the lobby for his daughter. He dialed Rosalyn's number while he waited.

"Didn't Lisa say for me to get her at three?" he asked.

"Um, I think so," Rosalyn said, and James wondered why he was asking the woman who was notoriously late.

He hung up with Rosalyn as the hotel manager arrived.

"If I can't go up to her room, will you send someone? I'm getting concerned." James showed the manager his retired FBI credentials.

"Oh, sorry, sir. Please come with me, and we'll see if she's there."

The hotel manager unlocked the door to Lisa's room. As they walked inside, James was struck by that old instinct that something was terribly wrong.

Lisa's suitcase was still open. Several of her belongings were on the desk and her toiletry bag hung in the bathroom. He found the car rental agency papers on her bedside table. But no one was there.

CHAPTER THIRTY-SIX

U ncle Stanley, we can't do this. We can't . . . you know . . ."

The man on the front pew appeared nervous. Lisa sat with Molly on the steps to the altar assessing each person and trying to formulate a plan.

"We can't do what?" Blackstone asked pointedly.

"They're . . . women. That one's a minister."

Blackstone burst into a loud laugh. "Marcus, my boy, I never suspected you for such a superstitious old lady. We are in a church, she's a minister. What does any of that matter?"

"It matters," Molly said without a trace of fear in her voice. "Not the part about me, but you're in God's house."

"God's house?" Blackstone scoffed.

"It also matters that I'm a federal prosecutor," Lisa said, more to rattle the man named Marcus and perhaps Blackstone's men on the sidelines. "You'll all get the needle, every one of you, if something happens to us. You are already holding us here against our will. That is aggravated kidnapping."

Lisa had prosecuted men like Stanley Blackstone in federal court. They sat confidently in the defendant chair, and even with the evidence piled against them, they were stunned to be found guilty. Blackstone's charm, arrogance, and pride were a dangerous combination when matched with power and a twisted morality. He'd gotten away with so much for so long that he had a subconscious belief in his own invincibility. While this made him deadly, it also made him prone to mistakes.

Lisa knew it was essential to create value for her and Molly, or they wouldn't be alive for long. Next she needed either instability in his core group or a way for Blackstone to exit this situation gracefully. Other than Marcus, Blackstone's men acted unwaveringly loyal.

"Let us calm down with all this and have a conversation," Blackstone said in a light tone. He sat beside his nephew and slapped him hard on the back, making Marcus wince and sit stiffly beside the older man.

Lisa kept aware of the other men as well. One stood at the side, watching every move. The other moved around the church, out the doors of the sanctuary, and eventually back inside.

Molly reached for Lisa's hand, but Lisa didn't sense fear in the woman. When she glanced at her, Molly gave a slight nod as if to say she was with her, no matter what.

"It's come to my attention that you've been gathering information about me. Why is that?"

"Why would I answer you?" Lisa asked. She wasn't going to make this easy for him. And if he wanted answers, he needed to keep them alive.

"There's one particularly good reason. Please give me your telephone," Blackstone said, holding out his hand.

Lisa rose from the step, dropped her phone, and stomped on the screen.

"Now why would you do that?" Blackstone said, shaking his head.

"You aren't calling my father from my phone."

Blackstone smiled. "Even though you've hardly seen him in years, you're a protective daughter. That's nice to see."

The man actually sounded genuine when he said this.

"You have a daughter as well. Gwendolyn Hubert, isn't that right?"

Blackstone's back straightened at the mention of his daughter's name.

"Do you know why she e-mailed me last night?" Lisa asked, studying every nuance and intake of air. She also saw Marcus react to this news, glancing at his uncle, then back to his hands.

"Gwen e-mailed *you?*" Blackstone said, and Lisa could almost see his mind clicking through reasons why. She assumed from his reaction that while Gwendolyn had distanced herself from him, he didn't expect betrayal from his daughter.

"She doesn't use your last name. You're estranged, correct?"

"I'm her father." His tone had turned deadly.

Marcus chewed on the corner of his thumbnail.

"I don't believe that she e-mailed you," Blackstone said, now studying Lisa.

But Lisa knew he didn't have the experience of dissecting people, not the way she did. That was her life. He wouldn't be able to guess her methods or motives. He obviously wasn't in tune with his nephew or daughter, though his narcissism probably made him oblivious to this fact.

"I can show you the e-mail, but not from my phone." Lisa looked down at the screen, shattered in a spiderweb pattern. She might regret that, but she wasn't going to risk Blackstone luring Dad here as he'd done to her through Molly's phone.

Blackstone's demeanor had changed completely. This was getting to him. The pieces weren't as clear, and Lisa knew that made him more unstable than usual. She needed to be very careful.

"Mr. Blackstone, we have a lot of information on you. And it's spread around now. You can't contain this." She tried to sound compassionate. She sat beside Molly again and realized the woman was silently praying.

"This all began with your father trying to help some black man in prison? A man like that, he was on the fast track to the pen anyway," Blackstone said in disgust.

"He didn't kill Benjamin Gray."

Blackstone didn't react.

"What did your father find in New York?" Blackstone asked, leaning forward with his elbows on his knees.

"He was investigating some items that belonged to his old FBI partner, Peter Hughes."

"I'm unfamiliar with Peter Hughes."

"He's the one who shot you at the rally in Fort Worth," Lisa said, as if everyone knew the fact.

"Interesting," Blackstone said, but still he had not confessed.

"Was Madeline Fitzgerald a witness of the shooting as well?" Lisa saw the man's immediate irritation at her name. Another weakness.

"We know that she was engaged to Benjamin Gray," Lisa said.

Marcus looked at his uncle from the corner of his eye. So the nephew didn't know this story.

"She would not have married him," Blackstone said.

"You were friends with her when she was young. Lovers perhaps?"

Blackstone stared at her, and Lisa continued, "But she was half black."

Marcus's eyes widened, and the crony on their left reacted ever so slightly as well.

"Do not talk about her again," Blackstone said through clenched teeth.

Lisa decided to pull back. "When my father was in New York, he met with a newsman he's known since the late sixties or early seventies. William O'Ryan. He's quite well known now."

"William O'Ryan, the news guy?"

Lisa nodded and spoke as if concerned about Blackstone. "O'Ryan has gathered quite an extensive background on you and your company. And also on your daughter, Gwendolyn, especially since she's running for Senate."

Again Blackstone appeared upset. His daughter was certainly his greatest weakness.

"Mr. Blackstone, we've sent out information all over the place. But we hadn't found enough to prove Leonard was unfairly convicted or any evidence that a DA could use to prosecute you. At least, there wasn't enough before today."

Marcus dropped his face into his hands, and Blackstone glanced at him with disgust. Lisa's heart kept making odd leaps, but she couldn't give way to the fear. She took a few deep breaths and then pushed forward, hoping she was saying the right things.

"We have dozens of paper trails, and they all lead straight to you. My father talked to that Detective Martin in Florida. He's convinced you murdered a local businessman and his girlfriend. He's piecing together evidence.

"Then in my hotel room, my house in Boston, my father's house, a major news agency in New York, colleagues of mine . . . we've enlisted a large network to help us free Leonard Dubois before his execution. Are you going to track down all of that and make it disappear? How will you cover this up, Mr. Blackstone?"

Blackstone leaned back and crossed his arms at his wide chest. He stared at Lisa, seeming to weigh her words. Marcus looked crushed.

Blackstone cleared his throat. "What you don't understand is that we are not in Dallas. You are, but our plane is in New Orleans. Right now we are in our suite, sleeping off a late night on Bourbon Street. We have witnesses who saw us. We'll have witnesses who are seeing us today as well."

"That is good but not foolproof. It's, what, seven or eight hours between the two cities? Did you go through any toll roads, bridges, or pass under any surveillance cameras at traffic lights? And how will you dispose of all the . . . evidence?"

"I like you," Blackstone said, chuckling as he regained his sense of power. "And as for evidence, there are always options. In fact, there's a cemetery in back of this church. There's a fresh grave already there. More than one body can fit in a grave."

Lisa squelched the shiver that ran through her spine, and she realized her hands were shaking. She'd forgotten to eat, what with getting ready to leave. If this lasted too long, her strength might fail her.

She thought of John, of Drew, of Dad, suddenly fearing she'd never see them again. Her calm exterior was a sham, and it wouldn't take much for Blackstone to realize it.

"We have my old family plantation on the drive back to New Orleans, or my private plane. An uncharted stop at a private airport in Mexico wouldn't be difficult. And your father's house and all of the papers and information inside are quite flammable. You see, my dear, there are plenty of possibilities. And you said yourself there is no evidence against me. With all of these paper trails, as you called them, nothing is conclusive. Remember, that is essential."

"Essential for a conviction, yes. But if a pastor and a federal prosecutor disappear—the daughter of a retired FBI agent—you'll have more than one agency after you. The Justice Department, FBI, the IRS. Every inch of your business, your plantation, your homes, your plane . . . every part of your life will be torn apart. Some won't follow the law, like my father. They won't stop with you either. Your daughter's life and campaign will be exposed and scandalized. Whether she's innocent or not, she'll be linked to you and crucified in the press. You didn't think this one through. Just like the first one back in 1965."

Blackstone's features had turned to stone.

"But I do have a solution," Lisa said.

Marcus looked up from staring at his hands, while Blackstone sat with an unwavering glare since she'd mentioned Gwen again.

"You can get on your private jet and be in South America or a Caribbean island before anyone tracks you down. I'm sure you have money in offshore accounts. You can live in luxury in a dozen different countries."

Lisa could see Blackstone waver. She'd struck a nerve, brought some hard truths that showed the cracks in his plan, but going on the run would be hard for him to accept.

"You wouldn't get caught, and you wouldn't be a hunted man, because other than this short episode, there are still no real crimes against you."

Marcus turned to his uncle with a look of expectation.

"You think I'd give up everything?" Blackstone asked.

"Uncle Stanley, this makes sense. If they go through the company, you'll lose everything. Not just the plantation. They'll turn over every rock, and they will find enough then."

"It's a sacrifice. But one to save your daughter," Lisa said.

Stanley Blackstone's eyes jumped to hers, holding her for a long moment. He rose from the front bench and walked up the stairs of the altar. He stood at the pulpit, grasping its sides and gazing across the empty sanctuary. No one spoke for what felt like a long stretch of minutes.

There was a silence to the church that Lisa found to be beautiful. It surprised her, especially given the circumstances. Perhaps it was Molly's praying, but she doubted that Blackstone could feel it as well.

"You made good points, Ms. Waldren, however—" Blackstone was interrupted by a loud noise outside, disrupting the quiet.

The double doors to the sanctuary burst open, and her father ran inside. "Lisa?" he called.

No, Dad, Lisa wanted to cry out as she and Molly stood.

Dad raced to her, grasping her arms.

"Are you all right? Let me see you." Dad looked her over as if afraid she'd break into pieces.

"What are you doing here?" Lisa asked quietly.

"I was looking everywhere for you. I was at your hotel when a man approached me and told me where to come, but that I was not to tell anyone."

Blackstone watched them from the pulpit with interest.

"You didn't need to break your fancy phone after all," Stanley said, raising his eyebrows. "But the sentiment was nice. Special Agent Waldren, your daughter was trying to protect you. After all of your failings as a father, isn't it comforting to know your daughter would do that?"

Dad ignored Blackstone. He reached for Molly's arms and seemed to assess her for injuries as well.

Blackstone walked away from the pulpit and down the stairs. His jacket opened as he walked, and Lisa realized he carried a gun at his waist.

"Dad," Lisa said, but her father had bent down and grabbed a pistol from his ankle holster.

Dad turned, keeping himself between Lisa and Blackstone. He pointed his pistol at Blackstone before anyone could react.

"You didn't check for a gun?" Blackstone said to the man coming from the back of the sanctuary. The man on the side wall hurried forward, drawing his gun as well.

"I did take his gun, I thought," the man said.

Blackstone laughed. "We have you slightly outgunned here, Special Agent Waldren. Frank, let's start by killing the black minister, unless Waldren puts the gun down so we can resume our discussion."

There was a moment of indecision. Dad kept his gun trained on Blackstone. Blackstone's men had guns pointed in their direction. But if Dad relented, they'd all be dead. Dad knew this as well.

"I'm not giving up the gun. We can talk, but this isn't going anywhere," Dad said. He motioned for Molly and Lisa to sit down behind him. Lisa took Molly's arm as they sat on the edge of the altar, somewhat shielded behind her father.

"Not an ideal arrangement for a discussion," Blackstone said with an edge in his tone.

Then from outside, a loud commotion of cars and sirens burst the quiet, growing louder until they seemed to overrun the church. Red and blue lights flashed through the stained-glass windows.

"We were so close to resolving this peaceably. Your daughter is an excellent negotiator. But you had to call the police?" Blackstone pulled out his own gun, looking at Dad as if he were incredibly stupid.

"It wasn't me," Dad said. He remained stationed in front of Lisa and Molly with his gun trained on Blackstone. Lisa wanted to pull him behind or beside her, but Dad firmly pushed back.

"It was Gwen," Marcus said, jumping to his feet and wringing his hands.

"Gwen?" Blackstone turned to Marcus in disbelief.

"It had to be her. She's been following you for a while now. She's determined to take you down. She told me."

"When did you speak to Gwen?" Blackstone asked.

"She planned on leaking the photographs from the plantation. She flooded the Internet with them, knowing someone would eventually find them. That's not all she's done."

"And how did she do that?"

Marcus took a step back. "With my help." He blinked his eyes. "I made copies when I took Leslie there."

"How did you know where I kept them?"

Lisa wondered if this was their moment to escape. Blackstone appeared distracted; however, his other two men were not.

"Gwen told me. When she was a little girl, you showed her the safe and the photos because she needed to know what was required of a Blackstone. She said your father had done the same with you. You told her the combination was the address to the plantation."

Blackstone frowned in thought.

"You never showed me the safe. You never showed me anything like that because you never trusted me," Marcus said, almost whining.

"You're such a parasite, Marcus."

"Gwen was taking you down. She didn't want to, but you have to be stopped."

"Did you ever think that you'd be going down with me?"

"She said she'd try getting me immunity or something. This wasn't all Gwen. I planned the poisoning at the prison—she wasn't happy about that, but if the prison had done a better job, that would've led to you. How's that for initiative?" Marcus spoke as if trying to be brave, but he was moving closer to Dad as he spoke, as if her father would protect him.

Suddenly the doors at the side of the sanctuary burst open and police officers raced in.

"Put the guns down and get on the ground!" an officer shouted.

"Get down," Dad shouted to Lisa and Molly. He pushed his gun out a few feet in front of him and called out, "I'm FBI."

Blackstone kept his gun trained in their direction. Lisa could see the barrel focused specifically on Dad. Blackstone's man on the side had put out his hands and was already being cuffed.

"Slow down now and just back off," Blackstone said over his shoulder to the approaching officers.

"Put the gun down," the lead officer said.

Blackstone glanced at the cop and laughed. "You've got to be kidding me."

"Put the gun down!"

"I'm not backing down to you," Blackstone said.

Then Lisa saw that the officer was black. She knew Blackstone wouldn't give himself up now.

Shots erupted from close by, followed by several from around the church.

"Hold your fire," the officer in front shouted.

Lisa opened her eyes, fearful of what she might see. Her father and Molly were sprawled out near her.

Lisa saw Blackstone staggering backward, the gun dropping from his hands. His chest was pocked with bullet holes, and blood spewed down his shirt.

From the floor a few feet away, Lisa saw Marcus holding Dad's gun.

"You?" Blackstone muttered, staring at his nephew with surprise.

Marcus's face reflected terror, his hands were shaking, but he fired again, then dropped the gun to the floor.

Blackstone collapsed backward, crumpling against the rise of the altar.

Marcus dropped to the ground and covered his face as he broke into sobs.

"It's over," Dad said as his hand grasped Lisa's, squeezing it tightly.

The police interviewed them, then the FBI arrived and the questions started over again. Someone brought them coffee, and Lisa didn't refuse it, but she quickly ate a granola bar from her purse to avoid waking up on the ground.

An EMT checked their vitals despite Dad gruffly trying to refuse. Crime scene investigators came in, and the coroner arrived. Marcus and Blackstone's two men were arrested and led away.

Finally, they were allowed to leave the church sanctuary. Night had fallen and the church grounds buzzed with activity. Police vehicles, the SWAT van, and several ambulances surrounded the parking lot,

blocking in their cars. Crime scene tape kept out some curious onlookers and several media trucks. Camera crews were taping every piece of
the scene and turned immediately upon them.

"Jimmy!" Rosalyn pushed around numerous police officers and
raced toward her father, nearly tackling him as she burst into tears. "If
something had happened to you . . . ," she cried.

"I'm all right." Dad grinned as he patted her back.

She pulled back. "I arrived right after the police, but they wouldn't
let me in. I used that locator app I put on your phone when I heard over
my scanner that the police were coming here."

"So who called the police?"

Rosalyn motioned toward Gwen. "She did."

"That's Gwendolyn Hubert, Stanley Blackstone's daughter," Lisa
said, motioning to the woman talking to an FBI agent with her arms
wrapped protectively around her chest.

"Yes, she's been tracking her father since before she started running for office. Her cousin called about Blackstone's intentions, and she
informed the police."

Gwendolyn met Lisa's eyes. Lisa walked toward the woman, who
stepped away from the agent to meet her.

"You're Lisa Waldren?" she asked.

"Yes. And you are Gwendolyn Hubert."

The woman nodded.

"They said he's dead." She stared toward the entrance of the church.

"Yes, he is."

"I didn't want that," Gwendolyn whispered.

Lisa wasn't sure how to respond.

"He's done so many bad things. I've known that since I was a little
girl. But he loved me in his own way."

"And he was your father," Lisa said softly, turning to look at Dad.
Molly had been engulfed in a group of people Lisa assumed were church
members, and Dad was shaking hands with several FBI agents.

"I want to go see him. They said that I can, after they're finished
gathering evidence." Gwendolyn stared at the church.

"You might not want to do that," Lisa said.

"I have to," Gwendolyn said with a shrug.

"I probably would as well," Lisa admitted, placing her hand on the woman's arm for a moment.

A single line of tears rolled down Gwendolyn's cheek, but she quickly brushed it away.

"Since I was young, I wanted to make the world a better place. My father and his father and those before, they'd done so many terrible things. I wanted to right our wrongs, I guess. That's why I went into politics. A ridiculous idealist."

"You'd make a great senator," Lisa said, wishing for better words to say. "We need more people like you."

"More people who betray their families? My father's last thoughts were that his only child betrayed him. I doubt that I'll continue the campaign," she muttered.

"You saved our lives today," Lisa said.

Gwendolyn met Lisa's eyes and gave a wan smile. "I'm just glad you're all okay. If he had hurt any of you . . ."

An officer approached them. "Ms. Hubert, we're ready for you now."

"Do you want me to go with you?" Lisa asked.

Gwendolyn gave her a grateful look. "Thank you, but I need to do this alone. It's sad to say, but today I did make the world a better place."

CHAPTER THIRTY-SEVEN

Washington, DC

The Capitol Mall

The early morning had dawned fresh and blue. The Washington, DC, Mall never ceased to amaze Lisa when she visited. Most of her trips to the nation's capital were work related, large federal cases, with little time to explore the many museums, memorials, and monuments. Later in the day the walkways and streets would be packed with visitors, but at this hour the area was sparsely populated, dotted with runners and cyclists.

"Are we ready for this?" she asked Dad and Molly as they walked up a sidewalk toward an unimpressive gray building. Its modern façade appeared plain compared to the castle-like buildings of the Smithsonian that rose grandly up against the early morning sky a hundred yards away.

"It's been a long time coming." Dad paused for a moment.

The three of them had been together at the civil rights parade, and now they were together for what Lisa hoped was the final answer to the questions that had begun that day.

"It's pretty unassuming," Lisa said, staring at the edifice before them.

"I guess that's the point. But somewhere inside are hidden chambers holding untold numbers of US secrets. Few have ever entered where we are going," Dad said.

"But hopefully all have exited." Molly gave them a half grin.

Even with the key, it had taken days and lots of paperwork and leg-work to gain access to the obscure vault that stored national artifacts. Leonard's execution date weighed heavy on all of their minds. But the key had to be authenticated, and even with their pushing and calling in favors, Lisa wasn't sure how many departments they contacted before permission was granted.

Lisa wished Drew had come with them this morning. He'd been such a part of this, and since her return to Boston, they'd been mostly inseparable. A strange and intoxicating change for both of them. Now he waited for the news, and hopefully they'd celebrate the revealing in just a few hours.

The trio had been told to come early, hours before the museum complex and Capitol opened for the day. Around the side of the building, they found the plain entrance that said Employees Only on the door.

"Let's go on in," Dad said.

Before he tried the handle, a security guard opened the door. Inside, they showed their IDs and were directed down a hallway where they met with two other guards. They went through X-ray and put their thumbs onto a screen that scanned their fingerprints. Lisa and Molly turned over their purses for inspection.

"This is more extensive than the Texas State Penitentiary," Molly whispered to Lisa.

After security, a tall man wearing a navy blue suit that contrasted with his pale skin and pale eyes met the trio and welcomed them formally.

"My name is Horace Kratz, and I am the curator of the archival vaults. I will escort you to your specific location, and you will be given as much time as necessary to examine the contents. Beforehand, we will review the instructions. This way, please."

The curator escorted them to a small chamber that reminded Lisa of an interrogation room, where they were given a fifteen-minute instruction of rules and regulations.

"No photography of any kind. Your activity will be closely recorded, so photography is unnecessary. If you'd like a copy of the recording or individual frames printed out, we can provide that service as long as permission is granted by my supervisors upstairs."

Horace pressed the fingers of one hand against his other fingers as he spoke in a deeply serious tone.

"Do not touch anything other than what is in your designated object. Do not explore or examine any other artifact besides the one you've been granted access to. I have set up a worktable near your artifact for your use, as well as a ladder. There is a box of gloves that you are required to wear if touching the object or anything within its contents. Anything you wish to remove must be cataloged before your departure from the facility today and again be met with supervisory approval. They will be loaned to Ms. Lisa Waldren as a representative of the United States government and must be returned to the archive within thirty days. Any questions so far?"

Molly's mischievous expression nearly made Lisa laugh, but she bit her lip as the man continued in his dry monotone.

"There are personal facilities near the entrance if needed, and emergency exits with lighted paths will guide you to a secure location should there be an emergency."

Horace pulled on a pair of rubber gloves and retrieved a box from another room. "Here is the key. We have verified its authenticity."

"Thank you," Dad said. Lisa knew it had been hard for her father to release the key into the care of the archive, but it was required to grant their entrance. Dad feared it would become "lost" like so many other national secrets.

"Gloves, please," Horace said, pulling the box away from Dad's reach.

"It's been in an attic for the past forty years," Dad grumbled as he pulled on a pair of plastic gloves and then picked up the box with the key.

"The key opens one drawer and one drawer only. Do you know which one?" Horace studied Dad.

Lisa glanced at her father as he shrugged.

"No. How would I know that?"

This seemed to satisfy the curator. "This way, please."

They went to an obscure service elevator after passing a more public-looking one. This elevator opened on both sides and was triple the size of a usual one.

The curator pushed the button for B5, and the elevator descended five stories. Lisa knew Washington had a secret underground, but this was a surprising depth.

"Be careful in your attempts to open the lock. Each key was especially designed for the individual drawers, as I believe you understand. We know of only one other similar cabinet made by this builder and with the same design. It was located in England; now we believe it is somewhere in India or the Middle East."

The elevator doors opened, and they followed Horace into an empty hallway lit by fluorescent lights. The curator went forward and unlocked two double doors. He pushed a button on a remote he carried, and a small row of lights illuminated a path straight ahead. Though Lisa couldn't see far, the room felt vast, with a sense that the walls were far beyond view. Lisa could tell it was climate controlled. It reminded her of a crypt with its cool temperature and cement-like smell.

They followed Horace down the lighted center, passing rows and rows of tall shelves that disappeared into the darkness. Several rows were stacked with sealed boxes with numbers written across the front. Another row had sculptures from what Lisa guessed was the Roman era.

Down one aisle Lisa saw numerous vehicles, including a Model T Ford riddled with bullet holes, a sleek sports car that reminded her of something 007 would have driven, and something tractor-like but with pontoons.

Horace looked back at them, and Lisa felt caught doing something wrong, but every row held something of intrigue she wished to explore.

Finally, the curator turned down a row. He touched a remote in his hand, and a single spotlight down the aisle lit up, revealing an enormous rectangular cabinet the size of several wooden wardrobes.

"There is your artifact," Horace said. "The worktable is there, and the hanging ladder. Be sure the ladder does not touch the object. It is attached above and can be moved by the rollers as instructed earlier."

"Thank you," Lisa said.

Dad was already moving toward it.

"When you are ready to leave the facility, return to the elevator and I will meet you there. Now I will leave you," Horace said, turning and walking silently away.

The antique cabinet was not what Lisa expected. She had pictured a chest of drawers the size of her bedroom dresser. This cabinet was about ten feet tall and fifteen feet long. There were three sets of double doors on hinges closing off the inner sections of the cabinet. Each door was carved in an intricate design.

"I wonder who the cabinetmaker was. This is amazing," Molly said, looking at the carvings closely. Each panel had a unique design of animals, trees, or mountains with border designs cut in a unique pattern that Lisa had never seen before.

Lisa was anxious to open the drawer and discover its contents, but she knew this was their one chance to really see the Kennedy cabinet.

Dad set the box with the key on the worktable, pulled up his gloves, and investigated the cabinet closely. He pulled the handles on one set of doors and swung them open, revealing two lines of drawers. He opened each of the three sets of hinged doors to find matching rows of drawers.

"This might take awhile," Molly said, gazing up at the cabinet.

"I guess we just try each one," Dad said, retrieving the brass key from the box. "Who would like to start?"

"You do it," Lisa said.

"Are you sure? One of you could—"

Molly shook her head. "This one belongs to you."

Dad began at the bottom right drawer.

Lisa held her breath as he placed the key in the first lock. It didn't seem to connect with anything at all. Her father moved up to the next drawer. That lock didn't allow the key inside. He continued up the first row, using the ladder that was suspended a few feet out from the cabinet, until he reached the top and worked his way down the next row of drawers.

About ten minutes into it, they heard a discernible click. The drawer was toward the bottom of one of the middle rows. Dad turned to look at them.

"This is it," he said.

Lisa felt her heart racing as she and Molly moved closer.

He turned the key further, and the drawer popped open a few inches.

"It's heavy," Dad said as he pulled the drawer and it slowly opened.

They looked inside and saw a folded newspaper.

"So the last person to open this drawer was Robert Kennedy?" Molly asked in awe.

"That's right. The cabinet was stored down here soon after his death."

"Don't forget the gloves," Dad said.

"Yes, Mr. Igor might be watching," Molly said, looking around for the unseen camera. Lisa and Molly pulled out gloves from a box on the table and returned to the drawer.

"Let's be sure that our actions are recorded so that we have proof that each item we bring out with us was actually retrieved from this drawer."

Her father nodded and kept some distance as he pulled out the newspaper from the top of the drawer and carefully set it on the table. As he unwrapped the paper, a packet was revealed.

"Look at the date," Lisa said, pointing to the headline of the Fort Worth, Texas, newspaper. April 14, 1965.

Lisa saw her father's hands tremble as he opened the package.

"These are the missing pictures and negatives from Peter's roll of film," he said. He lined them up along the table.

"Look at that," Lisa said, pointing to one of the photographs. It clearly showed a man in his twenties who looked like a young Stanley Blackstone with a gun pointed at Benjamin Gray. The others showed Stanley in the crowd but from a distance.

"That's Leonard's ticket to freedom, right? I've been praying we'd get something definitive for him."

Lisa leaned in closely, picking up the photograph. Benjamin Gray's face had a shocked expression, and Lisa knew that was the last moment of his life. Peter must have taken this last picture, then he'd pulled his gun. Dad now believed his old friend had shot Stanley Blackstone immediately after taking the photos, either as a way to protect Lisa and her father or to stop Blackstone from escaping, or both. They'd never know for sure.

"I don't think we'd find a court who would refute this, especially with the newspaper dating it and the fact that it's been locked in here all of these years."

"They can also match the type of gun shown in Blackstone's hand to the bullets found at the scene," Dad said.

"What else is in the drawer?" Molly asked.

Dad brought out a thick document of several hundred pages fastened together. The outside read *Top Secret* and had the presidential seal marking the cover. The date was 1962.

"This was compiled before JFK was killed," her father said.

"So it's one of the documents that President Kennedy's brother didn't want found when Kennedy was assassinated."

"It could be," Dad said.

He turned the covered page and read the subject of the secret file.

The Blackstone File
Red Wolf Plantation

Lisa pulled up chairs as they flipped through the pages.

Some of the first pages showed copies of photographs. It was easy to identify John F. Kennedy in several of them. The caption at the bottom gave dates and names, including Redmond Blackstone, Stanley's father. In another that appeared to be a private dinner, the caption read, *Redmond Blackstone, Stanley Blackstone, John Kennedy, Robert Kennedy, Lyndon Johnson*, and other names Lisa didn't recognize.

"It looks like they were all friends," Molly said with a tone of disgust.

"That's why this report was compiled," Dad said. "Once we read through this, I think we'll have the full facts. But it appears to me as if the Blackstones were strong Southern supporters of JFK at first—the dates show 1959 and 1960. However, then Bobby or someone started putting together this report and found out who the Blackstones really were."

Dad flipped through the pages, skimming them as he spoke.

"Look, here are reports of KKK activity by Redmond Blackstone, and here, suspected of being part of the lynching of two black men in Alexandria as well as the disappearance of several others back in 1956."

Lisa and Molly leaned in closer as they pored over different elements of the file. There were financial reports and also a report on campaign funding.

"This looks like the Kennedys returned the Blackstones' campaign money and supported a civil rights law that the Blackstones were furious about," Lisa said.

"So John Kennedy turned his back on the Blackstones before he was even elected president?" Molly asked, studying a page of threatening letters sent to Senator John Kennedy by Redmond Blackstone.

Dad leaned away from the file, nodding in thought.

"Yes, but even still, the early campaign support, photos, and appearance that they were friends would've provided a Kennedy rival, or someone like my old boss Hoover, a huge advantage. It could've turned the election. This appears to connect the Kennedys and Lyndon Johnson to a KKK family, giving the appearance that JFK supported the anti–civil rights movement and a Southern racist mentality. It would've been explosive to the campaign. It could have been used against Robert Kennedy's campaigns for Senate and the presidency, as well as Lyndon Johnson's."

"So that's why Hoover wanted this file."

"Yes. O'Ryan believes that Evelyn Lincoln, JFK's longtime assistant, gave Peter the key after Robert Kennedy was assassinated in 1968," Dad added.

"But when Peter wouldn't help Hoover, he exposed Peter as a disloyal agent." Lisa explained to Molly how the former head of the FBI compiled scandalous information to blackmail and threaten politicians, world leaders, wealthy Americans, and even US presidents, among them President Kennedy and his successor, Lyndon B. Johnson.

"Bobby Kennedy probably put all of this evidence in here to keep it from Hoover and any of their other enemies."

"But it also was part of convicting Leonard Dubois instead of Stanley Blackstone. Robert Kennedy had to know that," Molly said.

"We don't know for sure, never will," Dad said gravely. "Maybe Bobby would've released this and gotten Leonard free. He was killed in 1968, not long after Leonard's conviction and just as he was running for president. It was expected that he'd win. Perhaps he was waiting until the election was over."

They continued to read through the file. It provided a long history of atrocities committed by the Blackstone family and Red Wolf Plantation. Finally, they reached the last page, and Dad closed the document.

They stood from the table, and Dad returned to the drawer to be sure nothing else had been left inside. As he pushed it closed, Lisa stopped him.

"Do we need to bring the Blackstone file with us?" she asked, glancing back to the thick stack of top-secret documents.

Dad studied her face. "Do you mean, put it back in the drawer?"

"What's the benefit of us taking it? Maybe it's better kept right here."

Dad considered this for a moment. "What do you think?" he asked Molly.

"If the crimes that the Blackstones committed were unsolved, I'd want us to bring it out and give those families or at least history some peace. But from what I read, everything is already historic and public knowledge, even if no one was prosecuted. It was included in the report to give background on who the Blackstones were, right?"

"Yes," Lisa said.

"Then let's put it back," Molly said. "It's about the Kennedys; why open this up after all this time?"

"We'll bring the newspaper and Peter's photos, but that's all, then?" Dad asked as if to give them one last chance. "I have to give the key to Horace after we leave here today. It'll be part of the archival system."

"I think that's how it should be," Lisa said.

Dad put the top-secret document back into the drawer and pushed it closed. He turned the key and checked to be sure it was locked.

"I guess we're done then," Dad said as the three of them stood looking at the drawers of the cabinet.

"I wonder what's inside all of the other drawers," Molly said.

"They may be empty. But this one will save a man's life." Dad closed the doors and picked up the newspaper wrapped around Peter's photographs.

"Uncle Peter wanted you to do this a long time ago," Lisa said.

"I thought he betrayed us, but he was more of a friend than I ever knew," Dad said.

"He trusted you. That's why he tried sending you the key when he died."

Dad nodded. "I couldn't have found any of this out without you. Without either of you."

They walked in silence along the lighted aisles until they reached the vault door leading to the elevator.

Lisa turned back. In a moment they'd leave the enormous vault and never return.

"If the Kennedy cabinet is full of secrets, just imagine all the other ones locked away down here," Lisa said.

Her voice seemed to disappear across the vast room. The three of them stood in silence, as if the hundreds of artifacts and sealed boxes might reveal their mysteries if they listened hard enough.

Then the lights shut off section by section along the path they'd taken, hiding the secrets away.

They emerged from the basement archive into a morning bustling with the ordinary activity of a weekday on the Capitol Mall. Lisa walked with her father on one side and Molly on the other. She took out her phone from her purse and stopped a couple carrying a map.

"Excuse me," she said. "Will you take our picture?"

READING GROUP GUIDE

1. The snapshot at the core of this book (and on the cover) is an actual photo of Lis Wiehl that her FBI agent father snapped at a civil rights rally in 1965. What stands out to you as you look at the photograph? How might your impression be different depending on where you live in the US and what decade you were born in?

2. Drew prods Lisa to help her father with his old case, reminding her of his own regrets when his father was dying. What are your thoughts about such parent and adult child relationships, especially when the parent seems to not fully realize the hurt he or she has caused in the past?

3. Though fictional, *Snapshot* is based on many true events and real people. Can you identify some of the historically true elements of the story?

4. When Lisa joins her father in investigating the killing of Benjamin

Gray, she puts her skills as a federal prosecutor to work. However, her father follows his old-school FBI methods. How did the blending of old and new help uncover answers and clues? Do you think one method could have solved the mystery without the other?

5. As a single mother with a professional career, Lisa struggles with mom-guilt and the question of how she might have been a better mother to her son. James Waldren has his own regrets as a father. In what areas of your life do you struggle with guilt and regret?

6. Many of the relationships throughout the book are tainted with past pain, unanswered questions, questions never asked, as well as lies and good intentions that went bad. Can you identify some of these? What discoveries can be found through such mistakes that relate to your life?

7. What personal experiences have helped you understand your parents in a new way? Did you judge them more harshly as a child or young adult?

8. Though there are many conspiracy theories, what historical events do you believe are truly "covered up"?

9. The missing key to the Kennedy cabinet was finally recovered and revealed its secrets. Do you think there are similar mysterious historical objects that are hidden from the public?

10. Our nation has become quite divided. How might Americans from all walks of life find ways to understand one another better? How might our country improve through such understanding, or do you think it would improve?

11. Lisa Waldren is an intelligent, career-driven woman with a solid understanding of the world around her—she thinks. She is surprised when Drew reveals the racial prejudices he regularly encounters. Then as her friendship develops with Molly, Lisa's discoveries of Molly's and her family's experiences bring new understanding to the issue of race, the civil rights movement, the struggle between races today, and the differences in what diverse Americans experience. How have you found surprising

revelations about the perspective of people from other ethnic, racial, and/or economic levels? Did this discovery shape the way you view life and other Americans on the whole?

12. What were your favorite parts of *Snapshot*?

A NOTE FROM THE AUTHOR

I found these old snapshots. Do you want them?"

My father handed me the two black-and-white photos with little ceremony. He'd been going through old family and FBI memorabilia.

The moment I saw the pictures, I was riveted. Transported back in time.

When I was a young child, my family moved to Fort Worth, Texas, in late 1963 just after the assassination of President John F. Kennedy. My father, a special agent with the FBI, helped in the investigation, mainly gathering information about the killer, Lee Harvey Oswald, and interviewing Oswald's widow, Marina. His work became part of the famous Warren Commission that reported to the president and the world what had happened that tragic November day.

So now that Dad had begun consulting on the book *Killing Kennedy* by Bill O'Reilly and Martin Dugard, he started opening old boxes. He found notebooks full of his interviews, leads, and findings. He also found two photographs he'd taken at a 1965 civil rights rally in Fort Worth. The focus of the photos was a little African American girl and me sitting together, oblivious to skin color, the marchers going by, or the tumultuous world around us.

As I stared at these snapshots in the days and weeks to come, my mind began to weave stories from the images. What had happened at this rally? Who was the other little girl? What had become of the people at the parade, and what were their lives like in Fort Worth in 1965?

Ruminating on these questions, and drawing on my own history as a federal prosecutor and daughter of an FBI agent, this novel came to life. As I lived out the imaginary exploits of the characters, I found myself haunted by a past not as far removed from today as we'd like to believe.

THE MYSTERIES OF OUR NATION

We all love a good mystery. I especially enjoy historical intrigues wrapped around our nation's past. In *Snapshot*, the key and the contents of the cabinet are entirely fictitious; however, these elements were inspired by many real unsolved mysteries in our nation's history. For example, we know that Bobby Kennedy changed the locks on the cabinets in the White House immediately after hearing of his brother's death. What was he hiding from the newly-sworn-in Lyndon B. Johnson? My father's old boss, J. Edgar Hoover, was known to keep secret files on politicians, diplomats, the CIA, and even US presidents. There are missing files, innumerable rumors, and no doubt real places where the answers to our historical mysteries are locked away. These what-ifs were fun to explore in this novel, and even more intriguing to consider in real life. And that was just one aspect of this book.

THE STRUGGLES OF 1965

All through the writing of *Snapshot*, I continued to return to those photos. They became much more than family keepsakes and inspiration for a novel. Looking at those two little girls—one being myself—I couldn't stop thinking about how innocent they were of the volatile world around them. It reminded me of just how tumultuous this time was. And how close it is to us today.

Our country may be fragmented in its politics, but rarely are Americans in danger of brutality and murder by other Americans for our beliefs. That wasn't true in 1965, the year my father took those snapshots.

That year there were marches throughout the South to protest acts against voting rights and to push for basic civil freedoms for African Americans. Leaders were brutalized and peaceful demonstrations often turned tragic.

One such peaceful rally for voting rights was held at Zion's Chapel Methodist Church. Four hundred participants prayed, sang, and shared stories. None were armed.

Twenty-six-year-old army veteran Jimmie Lee Jackson was in attendance. For years Jackson and his grandfather had tried to register to vote, but they were consistently turned away at the registrar's office on one excuse after another. Though the rally had pledged nonviolence, the police arrived in full riot gear. Streetlights were knocked out, and the brutality began.

Marchers of all ages and even numerous photographers and newsmen were injured. Jimmie Lee Jackson was shot by a police officer as he tried protecting his mother and elderly grandfather as they were being clubbed. Jimmie Lee Jackson's mother and eighty-two-year-old grandfather received head wounds and were taken to the hospital. But Jimmie Lee Jackson had been shot twice at point-blank range in the stomach. He died eight days later. The state trooper who shot him wasn't prosecuted until forty-two years later.

The death of Jimmie Lee Jackson strengthened the resolve that change must occur in the South and inspired the famous Selma to Montgomery marches. The first march on March 7 brought six hundred people along the route between the town of Selma and the state capital of Montgomery. As they walked, once again unarmed men and women were attacked by state and local law enforcement wielding tear gas and weapons. This day became known as "Bloody Sunday."

Two days later 2,500 protesters set out again from Selma but were forced to turn around when a federal district court judge issued a restraining order against the march.

The third attempt began on March 17 when the restraining order was lifted due to the First Amendment's right to protest. With FBI and National Guard keeping a watchful eye, the marchers walked the fifty-four miles from Selma to Montgomery over a course of eight days.

On March 25, 1965, more than 25,000 people climbed the final steps to the state capital. Such sacrifice and dedication changed the course of American history. Later that same year President Johnson signed the Voting Acts Right of 1965, giving African Americans the right to vote by mandate of federal law.

Of course this was just one of many key turning points in 1965. It was the year Malcolm X was killed and of the American Football League's boycott of New Orleans after numerous acts of discrimination against its black players. That football game was moved to Houston.

In the surrounding years, the nation endured the assassinations of JFK, his brother Robert Kennedy, and Martin Luther King Jr. The Vietnam War was taking lives and dividing a nation, the Cold War had people digging out bomb shelters and schoolchildren doing drills in the event of nuclear war, and the hippie generation created a counter-culture movement in this post–World War II era.

This was the age in which two little girls, one black and one white, sat together with all the promise of friendship.

THEN AND NOW

We live in a different America today. Yet 1965 was not so long ago, and it should not be forgotten. We have not eradicated hatred over skin color, over birthplace, or over differences in beliefs, race, and culture. Some Americans will never know such prejudice, while other Americans live with it on a constant basis, even today.

These snapshots remind me of that.

Today my life revolves around my family, friends, the law, the news, and writing. Perhaps it's because this novel involves all those aspects from my present but is also built on our shared and complicated past that *Snapshot* is my most personal novel to date. My hope is that it will entertain and inspire you, dear reader.

Lis Wiehl
New York, 2014

CHILDHOOD PHOTOS OF LIS WIEHL

285

LIS WIEHL INTERVIEWS HER FATHER, RICHARD L. WIEHL

Richard L. Wiehl served as an FBI agent, federal prosecutor, and lawyer from 1960 to 2003. He's also father to Lis Wiehl and her brother, Christopher Wiehl. The following is an interview Lis did with Mr. Wiehl in the spring of 2013.

LIS WIEHL: Dad, you took your four-year-old daughter to a civil rights march in the 1960s. As a parent myself, I have to wonder, what were you thinking?

RICHARD WIEHL: It was a pleasant spring Sunday as I recall. There had been a series of speeches by civil rights leaders in Fort Worth—all very peaceful. I knew it was history in the making, so without any further concern, we jumped in our little red car and went to the square in downtown. All of us enjoyed the occasion. The speaker that day was one of the top national leaders.

LW: And why did you take those snapshots?

RW: I took a few photos, as did others, and have long since thrown the rest out. I thought these were unusual—and really what the rally was all about—played out by you two little girls. I would note that there were several children at the rally.

LW: And what did Mom think?

RW: Your mother was quite interested in the whole scene. As I recall, she found people to talk with.

LW: I'm a third-generation federal prosecutor, after you and Granddad. What brought you to and kept you in law enforcement?

RW: I always wanted to be an FBI agent. But in those days you had to be a lawyer first, so I went off to law school at the University of Washington in Seattle. At the Bureau I worked with federal attorneys. Later I had an offer to be a federal attorney in my hometown. For me that was a no-brainer.

LW: As an FBI agent, you were assigned to debrief Marina Oswald in Texas after the assassination of JFK. How did that come about? What were your impressions of her?

RW: The decision was made by my Special Agent in Charge, probably at the recommendation of my former Special Agent in Charge. I considered it quite a promotion as it brought me into the security field. Marina was at first afraid. Over time and after hundreds of interviews, that changed. She was intelligent, a good mother to her two children. And she wanted to stay in the USA.

LW: Dad, as you uncovered information about the life of Marina and Lee Harvey, and ultimately of JFK, what did you think about the racial and political climate at the time? Were there any black agents in the FBI working with you?

RW: There were no black agents involved in the investigation. I think one of the first black agents was the younger brother of a close companion of mine on the track team at the University of Washington. That took place several years later. Times were changing rapidly—and if the law could help, within the law, so much the better.

LW: You worked on the President's Commission on the Assassination of President Kennedy, also known as the Warren Report. Do you think there was a conspiracy to kill JFK?

RW: Conspiracy? No. We were looking for that from the beginning. There were hundreds of theories. None held water upon investigation. The simple truth? Only one man was involved. If more had been involved, I believe we would have known about it. A conspiracy would have made our job much easier in that information might have been had from several people. In this case the only man who had the information was Lee Harvey Oswald.

LW: Dad, you've taken a lot of snapshots of me. Why did you give me this particular snapshot?

RW: Last year I was going through old albums—throwing things out, mainly—and I spotted several photos of you that I thought were "keepers." Frankly, these were special, but my real favorite is you as Superwoman.

ESSAY FROM JUAN WILLIAMS

JUAN WILLIAMS IS AN AWARD-WINNING JOURNALIST, NEWS ANALYST, AND BEST-SELLING AUTHOR OF *EYES ON THE PRIZE: AMERICA'S CIVIL RIGHTS YEARS, 1954–1965*

The best description of what it was like to be a black child in the 1960s, the time of Lis Wiehl's new novel *Snapshot*, comes from Dr. Martin Luther King Jr.

In 1963 King led a march of hundreds of children in Birmingham, Alabama, to confront city officials about segregation at stores and restaurants. The young people, with a clear sense of right and wrong and no adult worries about losing their jobs or being arrested, defied a ban on protests and followed Dr. King into the streets.

When he was jailed for leading the march, King wrote a letter explaining why he urged young people to march despite calls for him to wait for a political settlement. In his April 16, 1963, letter, Dr. King wrote it was important that people understand why he could "wait" no longer for racial justice.

"This 'Wait' has almost always meant 'Never,'" he wrote.

King then offered an example of how racial segregation was impacting his own children, specifically his daughter.

When you suddenly find your tongue twisted and your speech stammering as you seek to explain to your six-year-old daughter why she can't go to the public amusement park that has just been advertised on television, and see tears welling up in her eyes when she is told that Funtown is closed to colored children, and see ominous clouds of inferiority beginning to form in her little mental sky, and see her beginning to distort her personality by developing an unconscious bitterness toward white people; when you have to concoct an answer for a five-year-old son who is asking: "Daddy, why do white people treat colored people so mean?" . . . then you will understand why we find it difficult to wait.

Lis Wiehl's story of a fateful street-corner meeting between two girls, one white and one black, reads as an extension of King's "Letter from a Birmingham Jail." It is in line with Huck Finn, a white boy, finding a friend in an escaped black slave. Childhood friendships across racial lines have been a tradition, a constant in America. Those pure hearts and innocent relationships often fade as they are complicated by the rules of race among adults. But as children, those young minds have no investment in the adult world's racial hang-ups.

Lisa and Molly, the girls in Wiehl's book, find themselves caught in the web of history. At age four they have no idea about the larger historical picture. They know nothing about the nation's two hundred years of struggle with the original sin of slavery; a Civil War in which six hundred thousand died and the Supreme Court's approval of legal racial segregation—"separate but equal"—despite America's founding declaration that "all men are created equal."

The girls also had no clue about the violence that so often surrounds race in America, including the history of lynchings, bombings, and assassinations. And as we see in Wiehl's book, that violence includes making scapegoats out of black people when a bad guy is needed to satisfy the public's outrage.

The arrest of a black man for a crime he did not commit is reminiscent of Harper Lee's book *To Kill a Mockingbird*. In Lee's novel, a white Southern lawyer named Atticus Finch defends a black man who allegedly raped a white woman. As he grapples with the prejudice of the Alabama town, he offers his two small children the example of an adult who holds on to values of tolerance and acceptance of all people.

That lesson often involves getting children to open their eyes to the unpleasant reality of racial prejudice.

Two years before Lisa and Molly arrived at the parade, four little girls about their age made real-world headlines. Racists with bombs blew a hole in the side of the 16th Street Baptist Church, killing the four black girls who were attending Sunday Bible school. Their tragic deaths became a story told in books and movies. It is also brought to life in a far more racially diverse America by the poignant personal recollection of former Secretary of State Condoleezza Rice. She was a young playmate of one of the girls. Rice would rise from the segregated streets of 'Bombingham' to become the first African American woman to be the US Secretary of State. Imagine the loss if America never knew Ms. Rice because she was killed by the bombs.

In *Snapshot*, the two girls, who wear their pretty dresses for the big day, have no idea of the larger evils surrounding their simple pleasure of being at a parade. They can't see the hidden hatred, the violent racial agendas about to unfold in the form of assassination, convenient lies, and corruption.

The joyful innocence represented by the two girls watching the parade also extends to their nascent womanhood. They are two girls who look on with marvel in their eyes, with no predisposition about society's color line cutting sharply between black and white female beauty. A white man's sexual attraction to a pretty mulatto woman would not have puzzled the four-year-olds. The stunner for them would be the white man's conflict between his love for this woman and his racist beliefs.

What comes next reveals so much about what happens in America as young people grow up and get caught up in the racist stereotypes, the racial suspicions, and the social norms of racial separation that come to dominate our everyday adult experiences.

In so many ways, that is the genius of Lis Wiehl's fictional construct for *Snapshot*. The girls become the personification of the innocence lost during this 1960s period of shifting racial rules. Just as they watched the parade, they also watch as the adults in their world kill, lie, riot, and generally turn on each other even as Congress passes a civil rights law, a voting rights law to advance racial equality in the United States.

Lisa and Molly then come to learn how difficult it can be to communicate honestly across racial lines as they see the complexities of the long history of racial distrust in the United States. The fact that the white girl's father, an FBI agent, is asked by a black man to help him find the truth, offers hope. It is an example of pursuing truth across racial lines and shows there are adults who grew up in the midst of racial division but never lost their capacity to see truth across the color line. More importantly, they can pass these values on to their children and grandchildren.

Even today, in the early twenty-first century, with America more racially diverse that ever, the heartbreaking divide between children of different races and classes continues to complicate simple friendships.

The complicating factors begin at birth. They range from the higher infant mortality rates for black children to the high rate of out-of-wedlock birth rates that leave black children in poorer, single-parent families and goes on to the disproportionate rate of black high school dropouts. Segregated neighborhoods remain commonplace in America in the twenty-first century. And so do differences between blacks and whites in levels of education, economic class, and attitudes toward gun ownership rights, sentencing for drug crimes, and even how much racism remains in American society.

And when it comes to crime, the instinct to retreat into old racial tribes quickly becomes apparent. Today about half the population in prison is made up of people of color, largely black men like the suspect in *Snapshot*. This connects directly to the frequency of violent crime committed by poorly educated, unemployed, and often impoverished young black men. This remains a disturbing fact of modern American life. It is still a taboo topic for most discussions in proper, polite society—be it black or white.

Instead the conversation about race and crime moves to small-minded arguments, bickering over the discrepancies in sentencing for crack cocaine versus powder cocaine or the higher incidence of the police stopping blacks on the street as suspects, such as with the New York Police Department's use of a controversial "Stop and Frisk" program that disproportionately targets black men.

In 1960s America, there was no need to call such a policy "Stop and Frisk" as the two little girls observe in the streets of their town. The reality of a prejudiced, all-white police force was true to the time and harassment of black suspects was commonplace as we see in the novel. That's no fiction.

And it is no fiction that in 1989 a white man, Charles Stuart, said a black man had murdered his pregnant wife. Later Boston police found out he had done it. In 1994 Susan Smith, a white woman, said a black man hijacked her car and put it in a lake, killing her children. Police discovered she did it so she could marry a man who did not want children.

The challenge that comes from reading *Snapshot* is in understanding that it is truly a snapshot of our lives and our times. It is a snapshot of racial fear mongering and blame games that still blind us to the possibility of seeing the best in each other or just seeing people doing their jobs. The distortions caused by race become obvious when Stanley Blackstone, the white racist in *Snapshot*, does not lower his gun because the policeman approaching is black.

The story may be fictional, but its power comes from those two little girls and their very real moment of trust that is ultimately much larger than the adult corruption swirling around them. The final mystery would be whether they could find that same kind of friendship as adults.

To quote Dr King at the 1963 March on Washington:

I have a dream that one day . . . the sons of former slaves and the sons of former slave owners will be able to sit together at the table of brotherhood . . . I have a dream that little children will one day live in a nation where they will not be judged by the color of their skin but by the content of their character . . . I have a dream that one day . . . little black boys and black girls will be able to join hands with little white boys and white girls as sisters and brothers.

Snapshot is fiction. But it takes us along the twisted path of race in America in a way that is closer to the human experience than most history books.

ESSAY FROM BILL O'REILLY

BILL O'REILLY, TELEVISION HOST AND BEST-SELLING AUTHOR, WRITES ABOUT HIS OWN EXPERIENCES REPORTING IN THE YEARS FOLLOWING THE ASSASSINATION OF JOHN F. KENNEDY.

Thirteen years after John F. Kennedy was murdered in Dallas, Texas, I arrived in that dusty town from the Northeast. I had been hired as a reporter for WFAA-TV, the ABC affiliate in Dallas.

The station was just a few blocks away from that historic West End district of downtown Dallas where JFK was shot, Dealey Plaza. I found myself wandering over there from time to time, looking up at the window where Lee Harvey Oswald fired the shots that ended the President's life. What struck me about Dealey is how compact it is. An elevated marksman would have little trouble hitting a target in that zone.

Dallas in 1963 was a far different place than it is today. Provincial and suspicious of outsiders, most folks wanted no part of any discussion about the assassination. Truth be told, they were ashamed. For many Dallasites, the story was over. My initial attempts to seek new leads with these folks didn't get very far.

But after a short time on the job, I began hearing rumors about a man named George de Mohrenschildt, a Russian immigrant who taught at Bishop College, a black school in town. The story was that de Mohrenschildt knew Marina and Lee Harvey very well. Also, that the Russian had CIA connections.

Intriguing? You bet.

I began investigating the teacher, but did not come up with much. Then I found out that investigators from the House of Representatives were also looking at de Morenschildt and that they'd called him to testify before a congressional committee concerning events from that November day in 1963. I convinced the news director at WFAA-TV that the man needed to be confronted by me and a camera crew.

As detailed in my book *Killing Kennedy*, this led to an intense chase across state lines which finally ended in tragedy. As the camera crew and I approached the house of de Mohernschidt's adult daughter, a shot rang out. He'd killed himself.

For me after all these years, the Oswald-de Morenschildt connection remains a frustrating piece of mystery that remains largely incomprehensible.

Though I know Oswald was the assassin, there are many questions I still want answered. During the writing of *Killing Kennedy*, I interviewed retired FBI Special Agent Richard Wiehl who had never spoken on the record about his involvement in investigating the Kennedy assassination and in debriefing Oswald's widow, Marina. When I heard that he'd found some old snapshots from that time in Texas of his daughter, Lis Wiehl, I was intrigued. I had to read the manuscript for *Snapshot*. I found myself particularly intrigued by the character of William O'Ryan. He was clearly modeled after me.

Like me, O'Ryan built a successful career and moved from college newspapers and small local news to a major network. But catching the scent of a good story still gets his blood pumping. He's tempted to toss his responsibilities and join retired FBI Special Agent James Waldren to find answers.

Though fictional, the ties to the real stories such as mine are woven throughout the book. Bobby Kennedy did change the locks on cabinets in the White House immediately after his brother JFK was assassinated. He instructed listening devices throughout the White House to be removed and the tapes hidden. Even while devastated by the loss, the younger Kennedy knew what needed to be done to protect his and the President's secrets from people they didn't trust, including FBI head Hoover and the newly-sworn-in President Lyndon B. Johnson. Many of these secrets have yet to be revealed today.

These many decades later, the mysteries surrounding the 1960s are great fodder for new stories, like the one found in the pages of this book. And you can bet that, like my doppelganger, O'Ryan, I'd jump at the chance to follow new leads on de Mohenschildt or any connection to the Kennedy secrets.

I might have to beat out Lis Wiehl for that story.

Bill O'Reilly
New York City
September, 2013

ACKNOWLEDGMENTS

Cindy Coloma, my collaborative editor, who brought her vision, smarts, and humor to make writing this book a labor of love. Cindy and I share a passion for telling a story, and she jumped into this project with all of her amazing heart and soul. I am so grateful.

Inga Wiehl, my mom. Thank you does not even begin to express how I feel. You knew those snapshots were meant to frame a story. Without your unwavering encouragement, I would not have had the courage to tell it.

Let me tell you a bit about this publishing team. I arrived in Nashville two years ago to meet with them. I had two snapshots in hand. And an idea in my head. We sat around what I've affectionately dubbed the "King Arthur's Roundtable" and brainstormed for hours. Daisy Hutton (Vice President and Publisher), Ami McConnell (Senior Acquisitions Editor), Amanda Bostic (Editorial Director), Becky Monds (Editor), Kristen Vasgaard (Manager of Packaging), Ruthie Dean (Marketing and Publicity Specialist), Jodi Hughes (Associate Editor), Kerri Potts (Marketing and Publicity Coordinator), Katie Bond (Director of Marketing and Publishing), and Allen Arnold (former Vice President and Publisher). We explored many questions. Why did an FBI agent take his little girl to a civil rights march in Texas, what did the girls see that day, how can the girls be reunited to save a wrongfully convicted man, and what is the connection to President Kennedy? And on and on. That meeting inspired me to craft this story. Thank you.

And thank you to LB Norton, line editor with a keen eye, quick pen, and great sense of humor.

Thank you to Bill O'Reilly (aka William O'Ryan in the book), who said about *Snapshot*, "You've got it."

And to Juan Williams, my colleague and friend. Thank you, too, to Deirdre and Don Imus. I showed them the snapshots early on in the process, and, for once, the I-Man had nothing negative to say. Thank you to Roger Ailes and Dianne Brandi.

My book agent, Todd Shuster, of the Zachary, Shuster, and Harmsworth Literary Agency. My friend, you changed my life all those years ago when you said I had a book in me. Many books later, I am beginning to believe you. Thank you.

Last but never ever least, *Snapshot* is for my children, Dani and Jacob. I hope you enjoy the story that your grandfather started all those years ago when he took the snapshots. To you I give my unconditional love. Always.

All the mistakes are mine. All the credit is theirs. Thank you!

AN EXCERPT FROM *A MATTER OF TRUST*

If life was like a play, then the director had the ultimate power. The power to blight men's lives, or to give them what they most longed for. Even the power to utter the ultimate yes or no.

Tonight was a special engagement. One night only. Never to be repeated. The stage was a hundred-year-old two-story house, lit from top to bottom as if electricity cost nothing. The director watched from the quiet residential lane. At the director's side was the killer. It was a walk-on role with no dialogue.

Now for the lead actress to make her entrance.

Anticipation grew, thrumming like a bow string.

But where was she? Ah, there. In the basement by the window, phone clamped between ear and shoulder, pulling a box from a shelf.

The director nodded, and the killer raised the gun.

The lead bent over and set the box on the floor. Then she knelt beside it, dropping from view before the killer could take aim.

The director motioned for the killer to wait. Exhaling slowly, the killer lowered the gun.

———————————

"It was all right there on Facebook," Mia Quinn said into the phone as she tugged at the lid on the blue plastic eighteen-gallon storage tub. "Darin's dad made screen captures in case anyone tries to take anything down. He showed me a few of them."

"Facebook is God's gift to prosecutors," Colleen Miller said. "A couple of months ago I had this defendant on the stand. He swore on his mama's grave that he didn't sell drugs and that he'd never even held a gun. Then I asked him to explain why, if that were true, he had a Facebook status update showing himself holding a Glock, smoking a blunt, and flashing a sheaf of hundreds." Colleen laughed. "It was all over right there."

"It's hard to argue with proof that we can put right up on the screen in front of the jury." Mia finally managed to pry off the lid, revealing fishing supplies: a tan canvas vest, a tackle box, and a reel.

There, that wasn't so hard, she told herself. *This stuff can go in the garage sale, no problem.* The cold from the basement's cement floor seeped through her old jeans, worn soft as flannel. Outside, the dark pressed up against the windows, half set in the ground. Summer had passed in a blur, and now winter was coming.

Colleen said, "I love how defendants can't help but post incriminating pictures of themselves flashing gang signs and all the stuff they're not supposed to have. Now if only we could get our witnesses to stop using it. You know the other side is checking it as much as we are."

As prosecutors for Washington's King County District Attorney's Office, Mia and Colleen didn't get to choose their clientele. The hard truth was that sometimes the victims and the witnesses they built a case around were only a little bit better than the bad guys they were trying to put away. This was blue-collar law, not white-shoe. It was down and dirty, blood and guts, real people as opposed to companies squabbling genteelly over money.

But being a prosecutor also meant you made a real difference. Which was why Mia had been glad to go back to work at the same office she had left nearly five years earlier, even if the reason she needed to return was terrible.

"When I left, I don't think we were checking the Internet nearly as much." Still on her knees, the phone pressed up against her ear, Mia dragged over another box from the nearest shelf. No matter how much she didn't want to face this, it had to be done. "Now everyone Tweets or has a blog or at least a Facebook page. Even my dad is on Facebook, although his picture is still that generic blue silhouette."

Mia pulled the lid from the second box. It held the vintage black pin-striped suit Scott wore when they got married. In the wedding photos he had looked all ears and teeth and Adam's apple—too young to be getting married. Over the years he had fleshed out to the point he complained about love handles.

Underneath the suit was a cardigan his mother had knit him in college, cream colored with two stags rearing on the back. He had never worn it. The sweater and the suit were like so much else down here, stuff Scott had never quite parted with.

"A lot changed while you were gone," Colleen said. "Frank's the district attorney, the murder rate is lower than it's been since 1955, even though the economy is in the toilet, and now a killer is likely to be some crazy guy with a grudge and a bunch of guns and a plan to take out a whole restaurant full of people. And of course everyone's on the Internet now, even bad guys. Right before you came back I prosecuted a guy who claimed he didn't even know the victim. Only I found photos of them together on his friend's Flickr account." Colleen's low laugh was tinged with sadness. "If there's one thing this job has taught me, it's to turn over rocks—but sometimes you don't like what you find underneath. Lately I've been thinking how flat-out ugly it can get when you start looking."

Mia nodded, forgetting for a moment that Colleen couldn't see her. A familiar smell teased her. And suddenly it was like Scott was right there in the room with her. She closed her eyes and imagined him pulling her to her feet, slipping behind her to lift her hair and kiss the back of her neck.

How long had it been since he had done that?

"Still there, Mia?" Colleen asked.

She shook herself. "Sorry. It's like every box I open is a surprise package. How about you? Have you found anything you want to add to my garage sale?"

"I'm rooting around in my basement, but all I've found so far are some old albums. I'm talking vinyl. Do you think anyone would want Fleetwood Mac's *Rumor and Sigh*?"

"You never know. I wish Gabe would start playing that instead of whatever it is he does listen to." Even from the basement Mia could hear her fourteen-year-old's music two floors above. Discordant, angry. It wasn't singing so much as yelling set to a thrumming bass line and pounding drums.

Colleen said, "You know, you could probably get more if you put your stuff on Craigslist."

Mia had thought about this when she sat up late at night with her computer and her calculator and her file full of bills. "Yeah, but then I'd have to set up meetings with every potential buyer. That takes too much time and just lets a lot of people know too much about me. A garage sale will get it all over with at once."

"Still, before you go pricing everything at a quarter, let me come over and look through it with you," Colleen insisted. "Some stuff might do great on eBay."

"Sure." Mia lifted her head and scanned the basement. It was over-whelming. Boxes and boxes and boxes, some filled with Scott's old files. A bench and a rack of weights. Gray Rubbermaid cabinets, some of them filled with pantry items, others with cans of paint, plastic bottles of automotive additives, baby food jars full of screws. And what about Scott's power tools? In the corner was an electric saw. That should defi-nitely go before Gabe decided to make something one afternoon and sawed his fingers off.

Colleen cleared her throat. "And, Mia, I know things have been hard, so if you're tight for money, I could maybe—"

Mia cut her off. "We're fine," she lied. The hole was so big that no matter what she threw in, it would never be filled up. Just like the hole in her heart. She returned to her original question, the one that had prompted her to call Colleen on a Sunday night. "I want to file against those kids," she said. "I know you didn't get a chance to look at them, but their posts were like weapons. It hurt *me* to read them. I can't imagine what it was like for Darin Dane."

Mia was still trying to figure out exactly how the politics of her job had changed, and it was easier to ask Colleen off-line without worrying if she was stepping on toes. "Darin's dad has more than enough proof that these kids hounded his son to death. We can charge them with cyberstalking, harassment, violation of civil rights . . ."

"I don't know . . ." Colleen's voice trailed off. She had been the first to talk to Darin's father but had ended up asking Mia to step in because her caseload was too heavy. "I just keep imagining what Frank will say." Frank was Frank D'Amato, once just Colleen and Mia's co-worker, now the King County prosecutor. He prided himself on the office's winning record. But key to that record was taking on cases you couldn't lose. "This kid was fragile to begin with. He's been in counseling since, what—since he was eleven or twelve? Frank will say his demons were all in his head, not at the school."

"But those messages they posted about him were vicious. They said he was ugly, deformed, stupid, crazy. They urged him to kill himself." Mia regarded the shop vac. If she kept it, what would she use it for? If she tried to sell it at the garage sale, would anyone buy it? Or should she just give up and haul it to Goodwill? And then there were the leaf blower, lawn mower, and extension ladder. She had never used any of them. Even before Brooke was born, Scott had taken care of the outside part of their lives. Now she would have to get over her fear of heights if she wanted to make sure the gutters didn't overflow during Seattle's rainy season. Which was pretty much November through May.

"Some of the posts said the world would be better if he were dead," she continued. "It's a hate crime. Darin was gay, or at least everyone thought he was."

Her eyes suddenly filled with tears at the thought of Darin, the same age as Gabe, although the two boys could not be more different. And while she had no worries that Gabe was being bullied, Mia had made it clear to him that he had to show her his computer screen or share his passwords anytime she asked.

"Frank will say it's normal for teens to have spats, to have hierarchies, even to ostracize one kid," Colleen said. "And school's only been in session for, what—two weeks? Frank will say that short of a time period isn't enough to prove causality."

Mia took a deep breath. "Yes, but these kids had been targeting him for months. And it didn't let up just because school was out for summer. They were relentless, and the Internet made it easy to harass him around the clock. The only thing school being back in session gave them was easy access to his physical person. The autopsy found bruises consistent with his having been hit, kicked, and punched."

The silence spun out so long Mia thought their connection had been dropped. Then Colleen said carefully, "You might need to be realistic, Mia. Frank's up for reelection this fall. To win he needs a big war chest. And the kids you're talking about, the ones who went to school with Darin Dane, also happen to be the sons and daughters of some of Seattle's richest parents. People who are software engineers, doctors, lawyers. They're not going to let someone smear their kids, especially not right when they're trying to get them into good colleges. And they're not going to support a DA who lets one of his attorneys do that."

"Doesn't Frank want to do what's right more than he wants to win?"

"Nothing is black-and-white," Colleen said simply. "Nothing."

Mia lifted the top from the next box. It was filled with Scott's ski clothes. Just another hobby they hadn't had time for since Brooke was born.

Mia lifted a pair of black ski pants and blinked in surprise at what she found underneath. It couldn't be—could it? She pushed herself to her feet.

Mia must have made a little noise, because Colleen said, "Mia? Is something wrong?"

A head bobbed at the bottom of the window. There. Finally. She was getting to her feet.

At a motion from the director, the killer stepped out of the shadows, lifted the gun, and carefully lined the sights up on the white column of her throat. The director watched dispassionately. The lead wasn't a person anymore, but she hadn't really been one for a while, had she? She was a problem.

A problem that could be solved with a single twitch of the finger.

The director nodded, and the killer pulled the trigger.

The story continues in *A Matter of Trust* by Lis Wiehl.

When life is **MURDER**,
who can you trust?

A Matter of Trust

A MIA QUINN MYSTERY

LIS WIEHL

WITH APRIL HENRY

NEW YORK TIMES BEST-SELLING AUTHOR

Available in print and e-book

A Deadly Business

A MIA QUINN MYSTERY

LIS WIEHL

WITH APRIL HENRY

NEW YORK TIMES BEST-SELLING AUTHOR

Available June 2014